THE
USES OF ARGUMENT

THE
USES OF ARGUMENT

BY

STEPHEN EDELSTON TOULMIN

CAMBRIDGE
UNIVERSITY PRESS

PUBLISHED BY THE PRESS SYNDICATE OF THE UNIVERSITY OF CAMBRIDGE
The Pitt Building, Trumpington Street, Cambridge, United Kingdom

CAMBRIDGE UNIVERSITY PRESS
The Edinburgh Building, Cambridge CB2 2RU, UK   www.cup.cam.ac.uk
40 West 20th Street, New York, NY 10011-4211, USA   www.cup.org
10 Stamford Road, Oakleigh, Melbourne 3166, Australia
Ruiz de Alarcón 13, 28014 Madrid, Spain

First published 1958
First paperback edition 1964
Reprinted 1969, 1974, 1976, 1980, 1983, 1986, 1988, 1990,
1991, 1993, 1994, 1995, 1997, 1999

Printed in the United States of America

Typeset in Garamond

A catalog record for this book is available from the British Library

Library of Congress Cataloging in Publication Data is available

ISBN 0 521 09230 2 paperback

CONTENTS

PREFACE

THE intentions of this book are radical, but the arguments in it are largely unoriginal. I have borrowed many lines of thought from colleagues and adapted them to my own purposes: just how many will be apparent from the references given at the end. Yet I think that hitherto the point on which these lines of argument converge has not been properly recognised or stated; for by following them out consistently one is led (if I am not mistaken) to reject as confused a conception of 'deductive inference' which many recent philosophers have accepted without hesitation as impeccable. The only originality in the book lies in my attempt to show how one is led to that conclusion. If the attack on 'deductive inference' fails, what remains is a miscellany of applications of other people's ideas to logical topics and concepts.

Apart from the references to published work given in passing or listed at the end of the book, I am conscious of a general debt to Professor John Wisdom: his lectures at Cambridge in 1946-7 first drew my attention to the problem of 'trans-type inference', and the central thesis of my fifth essay was argued in far greater detail in his Gifford Lectures at Aberdeen, which were delivered some seven years ago but are still, to our loss, unpublished. I am aware also of particular help, derived mainly through conversations, from Mr P. Alexander, Professor K. E. M. Baier, Mr D. G. Brown, Dr W. D. Falk, Associate Professor D. A. T. Gasking, Mr P. Herbst, Professor Gilbert Ryle and Professor D. Taylor. In some cases they have expostulated with me in vain, and I alone am answerable for the results, but they deserve the credit for any good ideas which I have here appropriated and used.

Some of the material worked into these essays has been published already in other forms, in *Mind* and in the *Proceedings* and *Supplementary Volumes* of the Aristotelian Society. Much of Essay II has already been reprinted in A. G. N. Flew, *Essays in Conceptual Analysis* (London, 1956).

STEPHEN TOULMIN

LEEDS
June 1957

PREFACE TO THE PAPERBACK EDITION

No alterations have been made in the text of the original edition for the purposes of the present printing; but I am glad of the opportunity to say that, five years after the original publication, I still feel that the questions raised in the present book are as relevant to the main themes of current British philosophy as they were when the book was first written. The reception which the argument of the book met with from the critics in fact served only to sharpen for me the point of my central thesis—namely, the contrast between the standards and values of practical reasoning (developed with an eye to what I called 'substantial' considerations) and the abstract and formal criteria relied on in mathematical logic and much of twentieth-century epistemology. The book has in fact been most warmly welcomed by those whose interest in reasoning and argumentation has had some specific practical starting-point: students of jurisprudence, the physical sciences and psychology, among others. Whether the implications of my argument for logical theory and philosophical analysis will become any more acceptable with the passage of time remains to be seen.

S. T.

October 1963

INTRODUCTION

Πρῶτον εἰπεῖν περὶ τί καὶ τίνος ἐστὶν ἡ σκέψις, ὅτι περὶ
ἀπόδειξιν καὶ ἐπιστήμης ἀποδεικτικῆς.

ARISTOTLE, *Prior Analytics*, 24a10

THE PURPOSE of these studies is to raise problems, not to solve
them; to draw attention to a field of inquiry, rather than to survey
it fully; and to provoke discussion rather than to serve as a systematic
treatise. They are in three senses 'essays', being at the same time
experimental incursions into the field with which they deal; assays
or examinations of specimen concepts drawn rather arbitrarily from
a larger class; and finally *ballons d'essai*, trial balloons designed to
draw the fire of others. This being so, they may seem a little incon-
sequent. Some of the themes discussed will recur, certain central
distinctions will be insisted on throughout, and for literary reasons
I have avoided too many expressions of hesitancy and uncertainty,
but nothing in what follows pretends to be final, and I shall have
fulfilled my purpose if my results are found suggestive. If they are
also found provoking, so much the better; in that case there is some
hope that, out of the ensuing clash of opinions, the proper solutions
of the problems here raised will become apparent.

What is the nature of these problems? In a sense they are *logical*
problems. Yet it would perhaps be misleading to say that they were
problems *in* logic, for the whole tradition of the subject would lead
a reader to expect much that he will not find in these pages. Perhaps
they had better be described as problems *about* logic; they are
problems which arise with special force not within the science of
logic, but only when one withdraws oneself for a moment from the
technical refinements of the subject, and inquires what bearing the
science and its discoveries have on anything outside itself—how
they apply in practice, and what connections they have with the
canons and methods we use when, in everyday life, we actually
assess the soundness, strength and conclusiveness of arguments.

Must there be any such connections? Certainly the man-in-the-
street (or the man-out-of-the-study) expects the conclusions of
logicians to have some application to his practice; and the first words
of the first systematic treatise on the subject seem to justify his

expectation. 'As a start', says Aristotle, 'we must say what this inquiry is about and to what subject it belongs; namely, that it is concerned with *apodeixis* [i.e. the way in which conclusions are to be established] and belongs to the science (*episteme*) of their establishment.' By the twentieth century A.D. it may have become possible to question the connection, and some would perhaps want to say that 'logical demonstration' was one thing, and the establishment of conclusions in the normal run of life something different. But when Aristotle uttered the words I have quoted, their attitude was not yet possible. For him, questions about 'apodeixis' just were questions about the proving, making good or justification—in an everyday sense—of claims and conclusions of a kind that anyone might have occasion to make; and even today, if we stand back for once from the engrossing problems of technical logic, it may still be important to raise general, philosophical questions about the practical assessment of arguments. This is the class of questions with which the present essays are concerned; and it may be surprising to find how little progress has been made in our understanding of the answers in all the centuries since the birth, with Aristotle, of the science of logic.

Yet surely, one may ask, these problems are just the problems with which logic ought to be concerned? Are these not the central issues from which the logician starts, and to which he ought continually to be returning? About the duties of logicians, what they *ought* to do or to have been doing, I have neither the wish nor the right to speak. In fact, as we shall discover, the science of logic has throughout its history tended to develop in a direction leading it away from these issues, away from practical questions about the manner in which we have occasion to handle and criticise arguments in different fields, and towards a condition of complete autonomy, in which logic becomes a theoretical study on its own, as free from all immediate practical concerns as is some branch of pure mathematics; and even though at all stages in its history there have been people who were prepared to raise again questions about the application of logic, some of the questions vital for an understanding of this application have scarcely been raised.

If things have worked out this way, I shall argue, this has been at least partly because of an ambition implicit in Aristotle's opening words: namely, that logic should become a formal science—an *episteme*. The propriety of this ambition Aristotle's successors have rarely questioned, but we can afford to do so here; how far logic *can* hope to be a formal science, and yet retain the possibility of being applied in the critical assessment of actual arguments, will be a central question for us. In this introduction I want to remark only on two effects which this programme for logic has had; first, of distracting attention from the problem of logic's application; secondly, of substituting for the questions to which that problem would give rise an alternative set of questions, which are probably insoluble, and which have certainly proved inconclusive.

How has this come about? If we take it for granted that logic can hope to be a science, then the only question left for us to settle is, what sort of science it can hope to be. About this we find at all times a variety of opinions. There are those writers for whom the implicit model seems to be psychology: logic is concerned with the laws of thought—not perhaps with straightforward generalisations about the ways in which people are as a matter of fact found to think, since these are very varied and not all of them are entitled equally to the logician's attention and respect. But just as, for the purpose of some of his inquiries, a physiologist is entitled to put on one side abnormal, deviant bodily processes of an exceptional character, and to label them as 'pathological', so (it may be suggested) the logician is concerned with the study of proper, rational, normal thinking processes, with the working of the intellect in health, as it were, rather than disease, and is accordingly entitled to set aside as irrelevant any aberrant, pathological arguments.

For others, logic is a development of sociology rather than psychology: it is not the phenomena of the individual human mind with which the logician is concerned, but rather the habits and practices developed in the course of social evolution and passed on by parents and teachers from one generation to another. Dewey, for instance, in his book *Logic: the Theory of Enquiry*, explains the character of our logical principles in the following manner:

Any habit is a way or manner of action, not a particular act or deed. When it is formulated it becomes, as far as it is accepted, a rule, or more generally, a principle or 'law' of action. It can hardly be denied that there are habits of inference and that they may be formulated as rules or principles.

Habits of inference, in other words, begin by being merely customary, but in due course become mandatory or obligatory. Once more the distinction between pathological and normal habits and practices may need to be invoked. It is conceivable that unsound methods of argument could retain their hold in a society, and be passed on down the generations, just as much as a constitutional bodily deficiency or a defect in individual psychology; so it may be suggested in this case also that the logician is justified in being selective in his studies. He is not simply a sociologist of thought; he is rather a student of *proper* inferring-habits and of *rational* canons of inference.

The, need to qualify each of these theories by adding words like 'proper' or 'rational' has led some philosophers to adopt a rather different view. Perhaps, they suggest, the aim of the logician should be to formulate not generalisations about thinkers thinking, but rather maxims reminding thinkers how they should think. Logic, they argue, is like medicine—not a science alone, but in addition an art. Its business is not to discover laws of thought, in any scientific sense of the term 'law', but rather laws or rules of argument, in the sense of tips for those who wish to argue soundly: it is the *art de penser*, the *ars conjectandi*, not the *science de la pensée* or *scientia conjectionis*. From this point of view the implicit model for logic becomes not an explanatory science but a technology, and a textbook of logic becomes as it were a craft manual. 'If you want to be rational, here are the recipes to follow.'

At this stage many have rebelled. 'If we regard logic as being concerned with the nature of thinking, this is where we end up—either by making the laws of logic into something psychological and subjective, or by debasing them into rules of thumb. Rather than accept either of these conclusions, we had better be prepared to abandon the initial assumption.' Logic, they insist, is a science, and an objective science at that. Its laws are neither tips nor tentative generalisations but established truths, and its subject matter is not 'thinking' but something else. The proper ambition for logic becomes in their eyes the understanding of a special class of objects called 'logical relations', and its business is to formulate the system of truths governing relations of this kind. References to 'thinking' must be sternly put on one side as leading only to sophistry and illusion: the implicit model for logic is now to be neither an explanatory science nor a technology, but rather pure mathematics. This view has been both the explicit doctrine of philosophers such as Carnap and the practice of many contemporary symbolic logicians, and it leads naturally enough to a conception of the nature, scope and method of logic quite different from those implied by the other views.

The dispute between these theories has many features of a classic philosophical dispute, and all the resultant interminability. For each of the theories has clear attractions, and equally undeniable defects. In the first place, there is the initial presumption, acknowledged by Aristotle, that logic is somehow concerned with the ways in which men think, argue and infer. Yet to turn logic into a branch of psychology, even into the psychopathology of cognition, certainly makes it too subjective and ties it too closely to questions about people's actual *habits* of inference. (There is, after all, no reason why mental words should figure at all prominently in books on logic, and one can discuss arguments and inferences in terms of propositions asserted and facts adduced in their support, without having to refer in any way to the particular men doing the asserting and adducing.) In the second place, the sociological approach has its merits: the logic of such a science as physics, for instance, can hardly be discussed without paying some attention to the structure of the arguments employed by current practitioners of the science, i.e. physicists' customary argument-forms, and this gives some plausibility to Dewey's remarks about the way in which customary inferences can become mandatory. Yet again, it cannot be custom alone which gives validity and authority to a form of argument, or the logician would have to wait upon the results of the anthropologist's researches.

The counter-view of logic as a technology, and its principles as the rules of a craft, has its own attractions. The methods of computation we learn at school serve us well as inferring-devices, and calculations can certainly be subjected to logical study and criticism. Again, if one is asked why it is that the principles of logic apply to reality, it is a help to be reminded that 'it is not so much the world which is logical or illogical as *men*. Conformity to logic is a merit in argumentative performances and performers, not a sign of any radical docility in the things argued about, so the question why logic applies to the world does not, as such, arise.' Yet the idea that inferring is a kind of performance to be executed in accordance with rules, and that the principles of logic play the part of these rules, leads in turn to its own paradoxes. Often enough we draw our conclusions in an instant, without any of the intermediate stages essential to a rule-governed performance—no taking of the plunge, no keeping of the rules in mind or scrupulous following of them, no triumphant reaching of the end of the road or completion of the inferring performance. Inferring, in a phrase, does not always involve calculating, and the canons of sound argument can be applied alike whether we have reached our conclusions by way of a computation or by a simple leap. For logic is concerned not with the *manner* of our inferring, or with questions of *technique*: its primary business is a retrospective, justificatory one—with the arguments we can put forward afterwards to make good our claim that the conclusions arrived at are acceptable, because justifiable, conclusions.

This is where the mathematical logician comes on the scene. For, he can claim, an argument is made up of propositions, and the logician's objects of study are the formal relations between propositions; to ask whether an argument is valid is to ask whether it is of the right form, and the study of form is best undertaken in a self-consciously mathematical manner; so we must sweep away all references to thinking and rationality and the rest, and bring on the true objects of logical study, the formal relations between different sorts of propositions....But this is where we came in, and the ensuing paradox is already in sight. We can hardly sweep away *all* references to thinking without logic losing its original practical application: if this is the price of making logic mathematical, we shall be forced to pose the Kantian-sounding problem, 'Is mathematical logic at all *possible*?'

The question, 'What sort of a science is logic?', leads us into an impasse: we cannot, accordingly, afford to get too involved with it at the very outset of our inquiries, but must put it on one side to be reconsidered later. For our purposes, fortunately, we can justifiably do so. This question is one about logical *theory*, whereas the starting-point of our studies will be logical *practice*. So let us begin by attempting to characterise the chief concepts we employ in logical practice: when this is done, the time may have come to return and ask what a 'theoretical' logic might be—what sort of a theory men might build up which could have the kind of application required.

A further precaution will be necessary. In tackling our main problems about the assessment of arguments, it will be worth while clearing our minds of ideas derived from existing logical theory, and seeing by direct inspection what are the categories in terms of which we actually express our assessments, and what precisely they mean to us. This is the reason why, in the earlier of these studies at any rate, I shall deliberately avoid terms like 'logic', 'logical', 'logically necessary', 'deductive' and 'demonstrative'. All such terms carry over from logical theory a load of associations which could prejudice one main aim of our inquiry: to see how—if at all—the formal analysis of theoretical logic ties up with the business of rational criticism. For suppose there did prove to have been a systematic divergence between the fundamental notions of logical theory and the categories operative in our practical assessment of arguments; we might then have reason to regret having committed ourselves by the use of theory-loaded terms, and find ourselves led into paradoxes which we could otherwise have avoided.

One last preliminary: to break the power of old models and analogies, we can provide ourselves with a new one. Logic is concerned with the soundness of the claims we make—with the solidity of the grounds we produce to support them, the firmness of the backing we provide for them—or, to change the metaphor, with the sort of *case* we present in defence of our claims. The legal analogy implied in this last way of putting the point can for once be a real help. So let us forget about psychology, sociology, technology and mathematics, ignore the echoes of structural engineering and *collage* in the words 'grounds' and 'backing', and take as our model the discipline of jurisprudence. Logic (we may say) is generalised jurisprudence. Arguments can be compared with law-suits, and the claims we make and argue for in extra-legal contexts with claims made in the courts, while the cases we present in making good each kind of claim can be compared with each other. A main task of jurisprudence is to characterise the essentials of the legal process: the procedures by which claims-at-law are put forward, disputed and determined, and the categories in terms of which this is done. Our own inquiry is a parallel one: we shall aim, in a similar way, to characterise what may be called 'the rational process', the procedures and categories by using which claims-in-general can be argued for and settled.

Indeed, one may ask, is this really an analogy at all? When we have seen how far the parallels between the two studies can be pressed, we may feel that the term 'analogy' is too weak, and the term 'metaphor' positively misleading: even, that law-suits are just a special kind of rational dispute, for which the procedures and rules of argument have hardened into institutions. Certainly it is no surprise to find a professor of jurisprudence taking up, as problems in his own subject, questions familiar to us from treatises on logic—questions, for instance, about causation—and for Aristotle, as an Athenian, the gap between arguments in the courts and arguments in the Lyceum or Agora would have seemed even slighter than it does for us.

There is one special virtue in the parallel between logic and jurisprudence: it helps to keep in the centre of the picture the *critical* function of the reason. The rules of logic may not be tips or generalisations: they none the less apply to men and their arguments—not in the way that laws of psychology or maxims of method apply, but rather as *standards of achievement* which a man, in arguing, can come up to or fall short of, and by which his arguments can be judged. A sound argument, a well-grounded or firmly-backed claim, is one which will stand up to criticism, one for which a case can be presented coming up to the standard required if it is to deserve a favourable verdict. How many legal terms find a natural extension here! One may even be tempted to say that our extra-legal claims have to be justified, not before Her Majesty's Judges, but before the Court of Reason.

In the studies which follow, then, the nature of the rational process will be discussed with the 'jurisprudential analogy' in mind: our subject will be the *prudentia*, not simply of *jus*, but more generally of *ratio*. The first two essays are in part preparatory to the third, for it is in Essay III that the crucial results of the inquiry are expounded. In Essay I the chief topic is the variety of the claims and arguments we have occasion to put forward, and the question is discussed, in what ways the formalities and structure of argument change and do not change, as we move from one sort of claim to another or between arguments in different 'fields': the main innovation here is a distinction between the 'force' of terms of logical assessment and the 'grounds' or 'criteria' for their use, a distinction which is taken up again later. Essay II is a study of the notion of probability, which serves here as a pilot investigation, introducing us to a number of ideas and distinctions which can throw a more general light on the categories of rational assessment.

In Essay III we reach the central question, how we are to set out and analyse arguments in order that our assessments shall be logically *candid*—in order, that is, to make clear the functions of the different propositions invoked in the course of an argument and the relevance of the different sorts of criticism which can be directed against it. The form of analysis arrived at is decidedly more complex than that which logicians have customarily employed, and forces on us a number of distinctions for which the normal analysis leaves no room; too many different things (I shall suggest) have been run together in the past under the name of 'major premisses', and a single division of arguments into 'deductive' and 'inductive' has been relied on to mark at least four different distinctions. When these various distinctions are separated out, it begins to look as though formal logic has indeed lost touch with its application, and as if a systematic divergence has in fact grown up between the categories of logical practice and the analyses given of them in logicians' textbooks and treatises.

The philosophical origins of this divergence and its implications for logic and epistemology are the subjects of the two final essays. In Essay IV the origins of the divergence are traced back to the Aristotelian ideal of logic as a formal science comparable to geometry: in the field of jurisprudence, the suggestion that we should aim to produce theories having the formal structure of mathematics has never become popular, and it turns out here that there are objections also to the idea of casting the whole of logical theory into mathematical form. Essay V traces some of the wider consequences of the deviation between the categories of working logic and the analysis of them given by philosophers and, in particular, its effect on the theory of knowledge. There, as in logic, pride of place has been given to arguments backed by entailments: wherever claims to knowledge have been seen to be based on evidence not entailing analytically the correctness of the claim, a 'logical gulf' has been felt to exist which the philosopher must find some way either of bridging or of conjuring away, and as a result a whole array of epistemological problems has grown up around scientific, ethical, aesthetic and theological claims alike. Once, however, we recognise the sources of the deviation between working logic and logical theory, it becomes questionable whether these problems should have been raised in the first place. We are tempted to see deficiencies in these claims only because we compare them with a philosopher's ideal which is in the nature of the cases unrealisable. The proper task of epistemology would be not to overcome these imagined deficiencies, but to discover what actual merits the arguments of scientists, moralists, art critics or theologians can realistically hope to achieve.

The existence of this 'double standard', this divergence between the philosopher's question about the world and the ordinary man's, is of course a commonplace: no one has expressed it better than David Hume, who recognised both habits of mind in one and the same person—namely, himself. Usually, the divergence has been treated as a matter for pride, or at any rate tolerance; as a mark (at best) of superior penetration and profundity in the thought of philosophers, or (at worst) as the result of a pardonable psychological quirk. It seems almost mean of one to suggest that it may be, in fact, a consequence of nothing more than a straightforward fallacy— of a failure to draw in one's logical theorising all the distinctions which the demands of logical practice require.

The studies which follow are, as I have said, only essays. If our analysis of arguments is to be really effective and true-to-life it will need, very likely, to make use of notions and distinctions that are not even hinted at here. But of one thing I am confident: that by treating logic as generalised jurisprudence and testing our ideas against our actual practice of argument-assessment, rather than against a philosopher's ideal, we shall eventually build up a picture very different from the traditional one. The most I can hope for is that some of the pieces whose shape I have here outlined will keep a place in the finished mosaic.

I

FIELDS OF ARGUMENT AND MODALS

Steward of Cross-Channel Packet: 'You can't be sick in here, Sir.'
Afflicted Passenger: 'Can't I?' (*Is*)

Punch

A MAN who makes an assertion puts forward a claim—a claim on
our attention and to our belief. Unlike one who speaks frivolously,
jokingly or only hypothetically (under the rubric 'let us suppose'),
one who plays a part or talks solely for effect, or one who composes
lapidary inscriptions (in which, as Dr Johnson remarks, 'a man is
not upon oath'), a man who asserts something intends his statement
to be taken seriously: and, if his statement is understood as an
assertion, it will be so taken. Just how seriously it will be taken
depends, of course, on many circumstances—on the sort of man he
is, for instance, and his general credit. The words of some men are
trusted simply on account of their reputation for caution, judgement
and veracity. But this does not mean that the question of their
right to our confidence cannot arise in the case of all their assertions:
only, that we are confident that any claim they make weightily and
seriously will in fact prove to be well-founded, to have a sound case
behind it, to deserve—have a right to—our attention on its merits.

The claim implicit in an assertion is like a claim to a right or to
a title. As with a claim to a right, though it may in the event be
conceded without argument, its merits depend on the merits of the
argument which could be produced in its support. Whatever the
nature of the particular assertion may be—whether it is a meteorologist predicting rain for tomorrow, an injured workman alleging
negligence on the part of his employer, a historian defending the
character of the Emperor Tiberius, a doctor diagnosing measles, a
business-man questioning the honesty of a client, or an art critic
commending the paintings of Piero della Francesca—in each case we
can challenge the assertion, and demand to have our attention drawn
to the grounds (backing, data, facts, evidence, considerations,
features) on which the merits of the assertion are to depend. We
can, that is, demand an argument; and a claim need be conceded

only if the argument which can be produced in its support proves to be up to standard.

Now arguments are produced for a variety of purposes. Not every argument is set out in formal defence of an outright assertion. But this particular function of arguments will claim most of our attention in the present essays: we shall be interested in justificatory arguments brought forward in support of assertions, in the structures they may be expected to have, the merits they can claim and the ways in which we set about grading, assessing and criticising them. It could, I think, be argued that this was in fact the *primary* function of arguments, and that the other uses, the other functions which arguments have for us, are in a sense secondary, and parasitic upon this primary justificatory use. But it is not important for the present investigation to justify this thesis: it is enough that the function of arguments in the business of making good claims is a significant and interesting one, and one about which it is worth getting our ideas clear.

Suppose, then, that a man has made an assertion and has been challenged for his backing. The question now is: how does he set about producing an argument in defence of the original assertion, and what are the modes or criticism and assessment which are appropriate when we are considering the merits of the argument he presents? If we put this question forward in a completely general form, there is one thing which should strike us immediately: the great range of assertions for which backing can be produced, the many different sorts of thing which can be produced as backing for assertions, and accordingly the variety of the steps from the data to conclusions which may appear in the course of justificatory arguments. This variety gives rise to the main problem we must consider in this first essay. It is the problem of deciding at what points and in what ways the manner in which we assess arguments may also be expected to vary—the question will be, what features of our assessment-procedure will be affected as we move from considering a step of one kind to considering one of another kind, and what features will remain the same regardless of the kind of step we are considering.

Let me indicate more precisely how the problem arises. A few examples will bring this out. The conclusions we come to, the assertions we put forward, will be of very different kinds, according to the nature of the problem we are pronouncing judgement about: the question may be, who will be selected to play in the American Davis Cup team against Australia, whether Crippen was justly found guilty of the murder of his wife, whether the painter Piero della Francesca fully deserves the praise which Sir Kenneth Clark bestows upon him, whether Professor Fröhlich's theory of super-conductivity is really satisfactory, when the next eclipse of the moon will take place, or the exact nature of the relation between the squares on the different sides of a right-angled triangle. In each case we may venture an opinion, expressing ourselves in favour of Budge Patty, against Crippen's conviction, sceptical of Sir Kenneth Clark's claims or provisionally prepared to accept Fröhlich's theory, citing confidently a particular date and time for the eclipse, or staking our credit upon Pythagoras' theorem. In each case, we thereby put ourselves at risk. For we may at once be asked, 'What have you got to go on?', and if challenged it is up to us to produce whatever data, facts, or other backing we consider to be relevant and sufficient to make good the initial claim.

Just what sort of facts we point to, and just what sort of argument we produce, will again depend upon the nature of the case: the recent form of the leading American tennis players, the evidence produced in court at the Crippen trial and the conduct of the proceedings, the characteristic features of Piero's paintings and the weight Clark places on them in his evaluation of the painter, the experimental findings about super-conductivity and the closeness of the fit between these findings and the predictions of Fröhlich's theory, the present and recent past positions of the earth, moon and sun or (at second hand) the printed records in the Nautical Almanac, or finally, the axioms of Euclid and the theorems proved in the earlier part of his system before the question of Pythagoras' theorem is raised. The statements of our assertions, and the statements of the facts adduced in their support, are, as philosophers would say, of many different 'logical types'—reports of present and past events, predictions about the future, verdicts of criminal guilt, aesthetic commendations, geometrical axioms and so on. The arguments which we put forward, and the steps which occur in them, will be correspondingly various: depending on the logical types of the facts adduced and of the conclusions drawn from them, the steps we take —the transitions of logical type—will be different. The step from reports of recent tennis-playing form to a predicted selection (or to the statement that a particular player deserves to be selected) is one thing, the step from evidence about clues in a murder case to the guilt of the accused party is another, that from the technical features of the pictures painted by an artist to the merits we accord him is a third, that from laboratory records and armchair calculations to the adequacy of a particular scientific theory yet another, and so one might go on. The justificatory arguments we produce may be of many different kinds, and the question at once arises, how far they can all be assessed by the same procedure, in the same sort of terms and by appeal to the same sort of standards.

This is the general problem with which we shall be concerned in this first essay. How far can justificatory arguments take one and the same form, or involve appeal to one and the same set of standards, in all the different kinds of case which we have occasion to consider? How far, accordingly, when we are assessing the merits of these different arguments, can we rely on the same sort of canons or standards of arguments in criticising them? Do they have the same sort of merits or different ones, and in what respects are we entitled to look for one and the same sort of merit in arguments of all these different sorts?

For the sake of brevity, it will be convenient to introduce a technical term: let us accordingly talk of a *field* of arguments. Two arguments will be said to belong to the same field when the data and conclusions in each of the two arguments are, respectively, of the same logical type: they will be said to come from different fields when the backing or the conclusions in each of the two arguments are not of the same logical type. The proofs in Euclid's *Elements*, for example, belong to one field, the calculations performed in preparing an issue of the *Nautical Almanac* belong to another. The argument, 'Harry's hair is not black, since I know for a fact that it is red', belongs to a third and rather special field—though one might perhaps question whether it really was an argument at all or, rather, a counter-assertion. The argument, 'Petersen is a Swede, so he is presumably not a Roman Catholic', belongs to a fourth field; the argument, 'This phenomenon cannot be wholly explained on my theory, since the deviations between your observations and my predictions are statistically significant', belongs to yet another; the argument, 'This creature is a whale, so it is (taxonomically) a mammal', belongs to a sixth; and the argument, 'Defendant was driving at 45 m.p.h. in a built-up area, so he has committed an offence against the Road Traffic Acts', comes from a seventh field, different yet again. The problems to be discussed in these inquiries are those that face us when we try to come to terms with the differences between the various fields of argument here illustrated.

The first problem we have set ourselves can be re-stated in the question, 'What things about the form and merits of our arguments are *field-invariant* and what things about them are *field-dependent*?' What things about the modes in which we assess arguments, the standards by reference to which we assess them and the manner in which we qualify our conclusions about them, are the same regardless of field (field-invariant), and which of them vary as we move from arguments in one field to arguments in another (field-dependent)? How far, for instance, can one compare the standards of argument relevant in a court of law with those relevant when judging a paper in the *Proceedings of the Royal Society*, or those relevant to a mathematical proof or a prediction about the composition of a tennis team?

It should perhaps be said at once that the question is not, how the standards we employ in criticising arguments in different fields compare in stringency, but rather how far there are common standards applicable in the criticism of arguments taken from different fields. Indeed, whether questions about comparative stringency can even be asked about arguments from different fields may be worth questioning. Within a field of arguments, questions about comparative stringency and looseness may certainly arise: we may, for instance, compare the standards of rigour recognised by pure mathematicians at different stages in the history of the subject, by Newton, Euler, Gauss or Weierstrass. How far, on the other hand, it makes sense to compare the mathematical rigour of Gauss or Weierstrass with the judicial rigour of Lord Chief Justice Goddard is another matter, and one whose consideration we must postpone.

THE PHASES OF AN ARGUMENT

What features of our arguments should we expect to be field-invariant: which features will be field-dependent? We can get some hints, if we consider the parallel between the judicial process, by which the questions raised in a law court are settled, and the rational process, by which arguments are set out and produced in support of an initial assertion. For in the law, too, there are cases of many different sorts, and the question can be raised as to how far either the formalities of the judicial process or the canons of legal argument are the same in cases of all sorts. There are criminal cases, in which a man stands charged with some offence either against common law or against a statute; civil cases, in which one man claims from another damages on account of an injury, libel or some similar cause; there are cases in which a man asks for a declaration of his rights or status, of his legitimacy (say) or his title to a peerage; cases in which one man asks the court for an injunction to restrain another from doing something likely to injure his interests. Criminal charges, civil suits, requests for declarations or injunctions: clearly the ways in which we set about arguing for legal conclusions, in these or other contexts, will be somewhat variable. So it can be asked about law-cases, as about arguments in general, how far their form and the canons relevant for their criticism are invariant—the same for cases of all types—and how far they are dependent upon the type of case under consideration.

One broad distinction is fairly clear. The sorts of evidence relevant in cases of different kinds will naturally be very variable. To establish negligence in a civil case, wilful intent in a case of murder, the presumption of legitimate birth: each of these will require appeal to evidence of different kinds. On the other hand there will, within limits, be certain broad similarities between the orders of proceedings adopted in the actual trial of different cases, even when these are concerned with issues of very different kinds. Certain broad phases can be recognised as common to the procedures for dealing with many sorts of law-case—civil, criminal or whatever. There must be an initial stage at which the charge or claim is clearly stated, a subsequent phase in which evidence is set out or testimony given in support of the charge or claim, leading on to the final stage at which a verdict is given, and the sentence or other judicial act issuing from the verdict is pronounced. There may be variations of detail within this general pattern, but the outline will be the same in most types of case. Correspondingly, there will be certain common respects in which we can assess or criticise the conduct, at any rate, of law-cases of many different kinds. For instance, to take an extreme possibility, any case in which sentence was pronounced before the verdict had been brought in would be open to objection simply on procedural grounds.

When we turn from the judicial to the rational process, the same broad distinction can be drawn. Certain basic similarities of pattern and procedure can be recognised, not only among legal arguments but among justificatory arguments in general, however widely different the fields of the arguments, the sorts of evidence relevant, and the weight of the evidence may be. Paying attention to the natural order in which we set out the justification of a conclusion, we find a number of distinct phases. To start with we have to present the problem: this can be done at best by asking a clear question, but very often by indicating only the nature of one's confused search for a question. 'When will the next eclipse of the moon take place? Who will play in the doubles in the American team for the next Davis Cup match? Were there sufficient grounds in law for condemning Crippen?' In these cases, we can formulate clear enough questions. All we may be able to do, however, is to ask, less coherently, 'What are we to think of Sir Kenneth Clark's reassessment of Piero?' or, 'How are we to make sense of the phenomenon of electrical super-conductivity at extremely low temperatures?'

Suppose, now, we have an opinion about one of these problems, and that we wish to show its justice. The case which we advance in defence of our particular solution can normally be presented in a series of stages. These, it must be remembered, do not necessarily correspond to stages in the process by which we actually reached the conclusion we are now trying to justify. We are not in general concerned in these essays with the ways in which we in fact get to our conclusions, or with methods of improving our efficiency as conclusion-getters. It may well be, where a problem is a matter for calculation, that the stages in the argument we present in justification of our conclusion are the same as those we went through in getting at the answer, but this will not in general be so. In this essay, at any rate, our concern is not with the getting of conclusions but with their subsequent establishment by the production of a supporting argument; and our immediate task is to characterise the stages into which a justificatory argument naturally falls, in order to see how far these stages can be found alike in the case of arguments taken from many different fields.

In characterising these stages, it will be convenient to connect them up with the uses of certain important terms, which have always been of interest to philosophers and have come to be known as modal terms: the present essay will consist largely of a study of their practical uses. These terms—'possible', 'necessary' and the like—are best understood, I shall argue, by examining the functions they have when we come to set out our arguments. To mention the first stage first: in dealing with any sort of problem, there will be an initial stage at which we have to admit that a number of different suggestions are entitled to be considered. They must all, at this first stage, be admitted as candidates for the title of 'solution', and to mark this we say of each of them, 'It may (or might) be the case that. ...' At this stage, the term 'possibility' is properly at home, along with its associated verbs, adjective and adverb: to speak of a particular suggestion as a *possibility* is to concede that it has a right to be considered.

Even at this early stage, different suggestions may have stronger or weaker claims on our attention: possibilities, as we say, are more or less *serious*. Still, to regard something as being a possibility at all is, among other things, to be prepared to spend *some* time on the evidence or backing bearing for it or against it; and the more serious one regards a possibility as being the more time and thought will need to be devoted to these considerations—in the case of the more remote possibilities, less will suffice. The first stage after the stating of the problem will be concerned, therefore, with setting out the possible solutions, the suggestions demanding our attention, or at any rate the serious possibilities, which demand our attention most urgently.

One thing had better be said straight away. In connecting up the words 'possible', 'possibly', 'may' and 'might' with this initial stage in the presentation of an argument, I do not see myself as presenting a formal analysis of the term 'possible'. The word is, I imagine, one of a sort for which it would be difficult to give any strict dictionary equivalent, certainly in the terms in which I am now trying to elucidate it. But there is no need to go so far as to say that, as a matter of definition, the statement 'This is a possible solution of our problem' means the same as 'This solution of our problem must be considered'. No formal equivalence need be aimed at, and there is probably no place here for a formal definition: yet the philosophical point involved can nevertheless be stated fairly cogently.

Suppose, for instance, that a man is required to defend some claim he has made; that a counter-suggestion is made to him, and he replies, 'That is not possible'; and yet that he proceeds on the spot to pay close attention to this very suggestion—and does so, not at all in an unfulfilled-conditional manner (covering himself by the clause 'If that had been possible, then...'), but with the air of one who regards the suggestion as entitled to his respectful consideration. If he behaves in such a manner, does he not thereby lay himself open to a charge of inconsistency, or perhaps of frivolity? He *says* that this suggestion is not possible, yet he *treats* it as possible. In the same way, if when a particular suggestion comes up he says, 'That is possible' or 'That might be the case', and yet does not thereupon pay any attention whatever to the suggestion, a similar situation arises: once again he must be ready to defend himself against a charge of inconsistency. There will, of course, in suitable cases be a perfectly good defence. He may, for instance, have reason to believe that this particular suggestion is one of the more remote possibilities, which there will be time enough to consider after we have found grounds for dismissing those which at present appear more serious. But, by allowing that a particular suggestion is 'possible' or 'a possibility', he at any rate allows it a claim on his attention in due course: to call something 'possible' and then to ignore it indefinitely without good reason is inconsistent. In this way, though we may not be in a position to give a strict dictionary definition of the words 'possible' and 'possibility' in terms of arguing-procedures, a close connection can all the same be recognised between the two things. In this case, at any rate, we can begin elucidating the meaning of a family of modal terms by pointing out their place in justificatory arguments.

So much for the initial phase. Once we begin to consider those suggestions which have been acknowledged to deserve our attention, and ask what is the bearing on these suggestions of any information we have in our possession, a number of things may happen. In each of the resulting situations further modal terms come into the centre of the picture.

There are, for instance, occasions when the claims of one of the candidates are uniquely good. From all the possibles with which we began, we find ourselves entitled to present one particular conclusion as unequivocally the one to accept. We need not concern ourselves for the moment with the question what sort of tests have to be satisfied for us to reach this happy state. We are familiar enough with its happening, and that is enough to be going on with: there is one person whose current form demands his inclusion in a tennis team, the evidence leaves no doubt that the man in the dock committed the crime, a watertight proof of a theorem is constructed, a scientific theory passes all our tests with flying colours.

In some fields of dispute, no doubt, this happens rarely, and it is notoriously difficult to establish the pre-eminent claims of one particular candidate above all others: in these fields, more often than in most, the answers to questions remain matters of opinion or taste. Aesthetics is an obvious field in which this is liable to happen, though even there it is easy to exaggerate the room for reasonable disagreement, and to overlook the cases in which only one informed opinion can seriously be maintained—e.g. the superiority as a landscape painter of Claude Lorraine over Hieronymus Bosch. At any rate, when we do for once find ourselves in a situation in which the information at our disposal points unequivocally to one particular solution, we have our characteristic terms with which to mark it. We say that the conclusion 'must' be the case, that it is 'necessarily' so—a 'necessity' of the appropriate sort. 'Under the circumstances', we say, 'there is only one decision open to us; the child *must* be returned to the custody of its parents.' Or alternatively, 'In view of the preceding steps in the argument, the square on the hypotenuse of a right-angled triangle *must* be equal to the sum of the squares on the other two sides.' Or again, 'Considering the dimensions of the sun, moon and earth and their relative positions at the time concerned, we see that the moon *must* be completely obscured at that moment.' (Once again, there is no question here of giving dictionary definitions of the words 'must', 'necessarily', and 'necessity'. The connection between the meaning of these words and the sort of situation I have indicated is intimate, but not of a sort which could be adequately expressed in the form of a dictionary definition.)

Needless to say, we are not always able to bring our arguments to this happy termination. After taking into account everything of whose relevance we are aware, we may still not find any one conclusion unequivocally pointed to as the one to accept. However, a number of other things may happen. We may at any rate be able to dismiss certain of the suggestions initially admitted to the ranks of 'possibilities' as being, in the light of our other information, no longer deserving of consideration: 'After all,' we say, 'it *cannot* be the case that such-and-such.' One of the original suggestions, that is, may turn out after all to be inadmissible. In such a situation further modal terms find a natural use—'cannot', 'impossible', and the like—and to these we shall pay special attention shortly.

Sometimes, again, having struck out from our list of 'possible' solutions those which our information entitles us to dismiss entirely and finding ourselves left with a number of other, undismissible possibilities on our hands, we may nevertheless be able to grade these survivors in order of comparative trustworthiness or credibility —having regard to our information. Though we may not be justified in presenting any one suggestion as being uniquely acceptable, some of the survivors may, in the light of our data, be more deserving than others. Starting from what we know, we may accordingly be entitled to take the step to one of the conclusions with more confidence than the step to others: this conclusion, we say, is more 'probable' than the others. This is only a hint: the whole subject of probability is a complicated one, to which a later essay will be devoted.

There is one last type of situation which is worth mentioning at the outset: sometimes we are able to show that one particular answer would be *the* answer, supposing only we were confident that certain unusual or exceptional conditions did not apply in this particular case. In the absence of a definite assurance of this, we must qualify our conclusion. A man is entitled to a declaration of legitimacy in the absence of positive evidence of illegitimacy; one can suppose that the regular chairman took the chair at a meeting of a committee, unless there is some record to the contrary in the minutes; only a few exceptional bodies, such as balloons filled with hydrogen gas, rise instead of falling when released above the ground. Here too we have a characteristic way of marking the special force of our conclusions: we speak of a man's legitimacy as a 'presumption', we say that the regular chairman was 'presumably' in the chair at that meeting, or infer from the information that a body was released from a height that it can be 'presumed' to have fallen to the ground.

In all this, one thing should be noted: in characterising the different situations which may arise in the setting-out of a justificatory argument, one can rely on finding examples in many different sorts of field. The various phases—first, of setting out the candidate-solutions requiring consideration; then, of finding one particular solution unequivocally indicated by the evidence, ruling out some of the initial possibilities in the light of the evidence, and the rest— may be encountered equally whether our argument is concerned with a question of physics or mathematics, ethics or law, or an everyday matter of fact. In extra-judicial as well as in judicial arguments, these basic similarities of procedure hold good throughout a wide range of fields; and, in so far as the form of the argument we present reflects these similarities of procedure, the form of argument in different fields will be similar also.

IMPOSSIBILITIES AND IMPROPRIETIES

We can now get a little closer to solving our first main problem: that of distinguishing the features of arguments in different fields which are field-invariant from those that are field-dependent. We can elicit the answer, by taking one of the modal terms already mentioned and seeing what remains the same and what changes when we consider its characteristic manner of employment, first in one field of argument and then in others. Which term shall we choose to examine? It might seem natural, in view of their long philosophical history, to choose either the notion of 'necessity' or that of 'probability'; but for our present purposes this long history is a handicap rather than a help, for it gives rise to theoretical preconceptions which may get in our way now that we are trying, not to establish any point of theory, but simply to elucidate the use these concepts have in the workaday business of assessing arguments. So let us begin by considering a modal term not hitherto much regarded by philosophers—the verb 'cannot'. (As will be seen shortly, the application of the verbal form 'cannot' is rather wider than that of the abstract noun 'impossibility', so we can afford to concentrate on the verb.) The first questions we must ask are, under what circumstances we make use of this particular modal verb, and what we are understood to indicate by it. When we have found the answers to these questions in a number of fields of argument, we must go on to ask how far the implications of using such a verb and the criteria for deciding that it can appropriately be used vary from field to field.

Let us, therefore, start off with a batch of situations in which the word 'cannot' is naturally used. The first step in dealing with our problem will be to compare these situations. 'You cannot', we might tell someone on one occasion or another, 'lift a ton single-handed, get ten thousand people into the Town Hall, talk about a fox's tail, or about a sister as male, smoke in a non-smoking compartment, turn your son away without a shilling, force defendant's wife to testify, ask about the weight of fire, construct a regular heptagon or find a number which is both rational and the square root of two.' We must run over a string of such examples, and see what is achieved in each case by using the word 'cannot'. (One point in passing—I have deliberately omitted from this batch of examples some which are philosophically of great importance: namely, those involving 'formal' impossibilities. The present set is confined to fairly familiar 'can'ts' or 'cannots', concerned with straightforward practical, physical, linguistic and procedural impossibilities and improprieties. My reason for doing so is this: in cases of formal impossibility, one or more of these simpler sorts of impossibility and impropriety is commonly involved as well, the relative importance of the formal and non-formal impossibilities varying from case to case. We must sort out the non-formal impossibilities and improprieties, and see what they involve, before introducing the extra element of formal impossibility. We shall in any case be returning to this topic in a later essay.)

In studying these examples, how shall we begin? We can take a tip from the *Punch* joke quoted as a superscription at the beginning of this essay. Clearly, a man who says 'X can't do Y' is in some cases understood to imply that X has not recently done Y, is not doing so now, and will not do so in the near future; whereas some uses of 'cannot' carry no such implication whatever. With this difference in mind, it will be worth asking, about each of our examples, what we should think if the man to whom we said 'You can't do X' were to reply 'But I have'; and we can add to this the further question, what sorts of grounds entitle us in any particular case to say 'You can't do X'—what would have to be different for our claim to have to be rejected, and for it to prove, after all, to have been unjustified. The examples may be taken in turn.

(*a*) A large piece of metal falls from a lorry on to the road. The driver, a pale, seedy-looking young man, gets down from his cab and makes towards it as if to pick it up. We see this and say to him, 'You can't lift that weight single-handed: hang on a moment, while I get help or some lifting-tackle.' He replies, 'Bless you, I've done the like often enough', and going up to it hoists it deftly back on to the lorry again.

Some implications of our statement can be brought out at once. By doing what he does, the driver surprises us, and his action irremediably falsifies what we previously said. We had under-estimated his strength, and had thought him physically incapable of the task: it demanded, we thought, someone of stronger physique, and this was implied in our remark. What was only implicit in the actual statement can be made explicit by re-writing it in the form:

'Your physique being what it is, you can't lift that weight single-handed—to attempt to do so would be vain.'

It may be asked whether there is really an argument here at all. Not an elaborate or fully-fledged one, certainly: but the essentials are there. For our implied claim is not only that the man *will* not lift the weight single-handed, but that we have reasons for thinking his doing so out of the question. If our claim is challenged, we have grounds, backing, to point to in order to indicate what leads us to reach this particular conclusion and rule out this particular possibility. He will not lift the weight single-handed: that is the conclusion, and we put it forward on account of his physique. We may be mistaken about his actual physique, but this does not affect the question of relevance: the physique we take him to have is certainly relevant when we ask the question whether he will—indeed *can*— lift the weight alone.

(*b*) A friend is arranging a public meeting in the Town Hall, and sends out pressing invitations to ten thousand people. On inquiry, we find that he professes to expect the majority of them to turn up on the day. Fearing that he may have overlooked one practical objection to this project, we say, 'You can't get ten thousand people into the Town Hall.'

This time, of course, we are sceptical not about his personal powers or capabilities, as in the case of the seedy Hercules who surprised us by lifting the large lump of metal, but rather on account of the seat-capacity of the Town Hall. If our friend replies, 'But I have!' we may feel like retorting that it certainly cannot be done; and, if he insists, we shall become suspicious and suspect him of resorting to some kind of verbal trickery. We may accordingly ask in return, 'What do you mean?'—but by the time we come to ask this, the example will have changed its character, and the considerations relevant will now be quite different. These complications apart, we can re-write our statement, more explicitly, in the words:

'The seating-capacity of the Town Hall being what it is, you can't get ten thousand people into it—to attempt to do so would be vain.'

In this case, too, it may be objected that we are not considering a genuine argument. But the bones of an argument are indeed here: the conclusion is that our friend will not succeed in getting ten thousand people into the Town Hall even if he tries, and the grounds for this conclusion are the facts about the seating-capacity of the building—these facts being what they are, his project must be ruled out.

(c) These first two examples have been rather alike, but here is a contrasting one. A townsman returns from the country and describes a rustic spectacle which he has watched. 'A troop of cavalry in red jackets were thudding along,' he explains, 'and in front of them a herd of dogs was strung out across the field, shouting noisily as they gradually reduced the distance separating them from the tail of a miserable fox.' One of his hearers, a devotee of blood-sports, corrects his description scornfully, saying, 'My dear fellow, you can't talk about a fox's tail; and as for the "dogs", I suppose you mean the hounds; and the "cavalry in red jackets" were hunts-men in their pink coats.'

In this example, of course, there is no question of any of the things mentioned in the story being insufficient in some respect for the impossible to be possible: indeed, the man who is told that he *cannot* talk about a fox's tail has in fact just done so. The point at issue in this case is accordingly different, and the word 'cannot' indicates not so much a physical impossibility as a terminological *impropriety*. By talking of the fox's tail, the speaker does not falsify the belief of his hearers, but instead is guilty of a linguistic solecism. We must therefore amplify this statement rather differently:

'The terminology of hunting being as it is, you can't talk about a fox's tail—to do so is an offence against sporting usage.'

(d) We are asked to read the manuscript of a new novel, and on doing so find one of the characters referred to in some places as being another person's sister, and elsewhere as 'he'. Wishing to save the author from the mockery of literary sleuths, we point this out to him, saying, 'You can't have a male sister.'

Now what precisely is at issue in this case? On the one hand, there is no question here about anybody's personal capacities or constitution. This is not, directly at any rate, a matter of physiology, for, our nomenclature remaining what it is, not even the most drastic physiological changes would enable a sister to be male: any change of sex, for instance, which transformed her into a male would *ipso facto* make her a brother, and so not a sister any longer. At the same time, one must hesitate to say that this is a purely linguistic example, as the previous one clearly is. One could hardly say that talking of a 'male sister' was just bad English, like talking of a fox's caudal appendage as a 'tail' instead of as a 'brush'. The townsman's description of a fox-hunt was perfectly intelligible and its defects were no more than linguistic solecisms, but an author who wrote about one of his characters both as a sister and as male would risk more than the ridicule of hunting types, since he would not even be understood. What matters here, we are impelled to say—though the statement may be obscure—is not just the usage of the terms 'male', 'female', 'brother' and 'sister'; it is the meaning.

If we are asked to explain why our author had better not include a 'male sister' in his novel, we therefore have to refer both to the terminologies of sexes and relationships, and to the second-order reasons why these terminologies take the forms they do. No doubt a sufficient change in the facts of life—e.g. a striking increase in the proportion of hermaphrodites—might lead us to revise our nomenclature, and so create a situation in which references to 'male sisters' would no longer be unintelligible. But as things in fact are, our nomenclature being as it is, the phrase 'male sister' has no meaning; and this of course is the consideration we have in mind when we tell our author that he cannot write about one.

Accordingly, if he replies, 'But I can have a male sister', surprise or scepticism will be entirely out of place. These reactions were all very well in the case of the man who insisted that he could lift the heavy weight, but if a man says, 'I can have a male sister', one can only reply by saying, 'What do you mean?' Put into our usual form, this example becomes:

'The nomenclature of sexes and relationships being what it is, you can't have a male sister—even to talk of one is unintelligible.'

About these first four examples, two remarks can be made. To begin with, one might think that there was an unbridgeable gulf, a hard and fast line, separating the first two from the second two: in practice, however, they often shade into one another. Someone may, for instance, say to me, 'You think that one can't lift a ton single-handed? That shows how much you know. Why today I watched a man lifting a hundred tons single-handed!' If this happens, my proper reaction will be no longer one of surprise, but rather one of incomprehension: the first type of example shades over, therefore, into the fourth. For I shall suspect that, in this case, the phrase 'lifting...single-handed' is being given a fresh meaning. Presumably what the speaker saw was (say) a man operating a large mechanical excavator at an open-cast mining site. No doubt a hundred tons was being moved at a time through the agency of one man alone, but he had a vast machine to help him, or something similar. Likewise with the second example: a man who says he can get ten thousand people into the Town Hall may again be playing a linguistic trick with us: when we say, 'What do you mean?', his response may be to produce a calculation showing that the whole population of the world can be got into a cube half a mile in each direction, and *a fortiori* that a mere ten thousand could easily be packed into the volume of the Town Hall. And of course, if their survival were no consideration, a great many more than ten thousand people could no doubt be got into the Town Hall.

The second point, to be mentioned here only in passing, will be important when we turn later to consider the nature of formal and theoretical impossibilities. Scientific theories include a number of very fundamental principles which refer to 'theoretical impossibilities': for instance, the famous impossibility of reducing entropy —the so-called second law of thermodynamics. Now in discussing the philosophical implications of such theories, one is tempted at first to compare them with the four sorts of 'cannot' which we have examined up to now. One starts by feeling, that is, that such impossibilities must be either solid, physical impossibilities (like those involved in the first two examples) or else disguised terminological improprieties (like the second pair). Philosophers of physics are, accordingly, divided between those who consider that such impossibilities report general features of Nature or Reality and those who consider that the propositions concerned are at bottom analytic propositions, the 'cannot' involved being therefore a terminological impropriety rather than a real, physical impossibility. The origin of such a theoretical impossibility is accordingly sought for in only two places: either in the nature of the universe-as-a-whole (the character of things-in-general), or alternatively in the terminology adopted by theoretical physicists when building up their theories. At this point in the argument, I want to remark only that the four examples discussed up to now are not the sole possible objects of comparison. This topic, too, will concern us again in a later essay.

(e) A guard on a train finds a passenger in a non-smoking compartment smoking a cigarette while an old lady in the compartment coughs and weeps under the influence of the tobacco-smoke. In exercise of his authority, he says to the passenger, 'You can't smoke in this compartment, Sir.'

By saying this the guard implicitly invokes the Railway Company's regulations and bye-laws. There is no suggestion that the passenger is incapable of smoking in this compartment, or that any feature of the compartment will prevent his doing so—the case is accordingly different from both (a) and (b). Nor is the guard concerned, as in (c) and (d), with questions of language or meaning. What he draws attention to is the fact that smoking in this particular compartment is an offence against the regulations and bye-laws, which set aside certain compartments for those who find tobacco smoke obnoxious: this is not the proper place for smoking, and the passenger had better go elsewhere. The sense of the guard's remark is:

'The bye-laws being as they are, you can't smoke in this compartment, Sir—to do so would be a contravention of them and/or an offence against your fellow passengers.'

(f) A stern father denounces his son as a dissolute wastrel, and turns him out of the house. A friend intercedes on the son's behalf, saying, 'You can't turn him away without a shilling!'

As in the *Punch* example, the man addressed may be tempted to reply, 'Can't I? You just watch me!'; and nothing about the man addressed or about his son will as a matter of fact be certain to prevent his doing so. Alternatively he may answer, 'Not only can I, I must: it is my sorry duty so to do'; and this reply reminds us of the true force of the original protest or appeal. The question raised in this case is a moral one, concerned with the man's obligations towards his son. The friend's intercession can be written more explicitly in the words:

'Standing in the relationship you do to this lad, you can't turn him away without a shilling—to do so would be unfatherly and wrong.'

These examples are varied enough to show a general pattern emerging. We could of course go on to consider others, which involved not so much physical impossibilities, linguistic solecisms, legal or moral offences, but rather improprieties of judicial procedure ('You can't force defendant's wife to testify'), conceptual incongruities ('You can't ask about the weight of fire'), or mathematical impossibilities—and about this last type we shall have something to say in a moment. But the common implication of all these statements, marked by the use of the word 'cannot', should be clear by now. In each case, the proposition serves in part as an injunction to *rule out* something-or-other—to dismiss from consideration any course of action involving this something-or-other—to rule out, for example, courses of action which would involve lifting a ton single-handed, talking about a fox's tail, or forcing defendant's wife to testify. These courses of action, it is implied, are ones against which there are conclusive reasons; and the word 'cannot' serves to locate each statement at this particular place in an argument, as concerned with the ruling out of one relevant possibility.

What counts as 'ruling out' the thing concerned varies from case to case; the implied grounds for ruling-out, and the sanction risked in ignoring the injunction, vary even more markedly; nor need there be any formal rule by reference to which the ruling-out is to be justified. Still, subject to these qualifications, what is common to all the statements remains. Each of them can be written in the following pattern so as to bring out the implications involved:

'P being what it is, you must rule out anything involving Q: to do otherwise would be R, and would invite S.'

The form is common to all the examples: what vary from case to case are the things we have to substitute for P, Q, R and S. Q is in each case the course of action actually specified in the statement: lifting a ton single-handed, talking about a fox's tail, turning one's son away without a shilling, asking about the weight of fire, or constructing a regular heptagon. P will be, in different cases, the lorry driver's physique, fox-hunter's jargon, a father's relationship with his son, the concepts of physics and chemistry, or the axioms of geometry and the nature of geometrical operations: these are the grounds relied on in each case. The offence involved (R) and the penalties risked (S) also vary from case to case: to ignore a physical impossibility will be vain, and will lead to disappointment; to ignore a point of terminology will result rather in a solecism, carrying with it the risk of ridicule; to ignore moral injunctions is (say) wicked and unfatherly but, virtue being its own reward, no specific sanction is attached to them: while, finally, a question involving a contradiction or a conceptual incongruity (like 'the weight of fire' or 'a male sister') is as it stands unintelligible, so that in asking it one runs the risk of incomprehension.

FORCE AND CRITERIA

At this point a distinction can be made, which will prove later of great importance. The meaning of a modal term, such as 'cannot', has two aspects: these can be referred to as the *force* of the term and the *criteria* for its use. By the 'force' of a modal term I mean the practical implications of its use: the force of the term 'cannot' includes, for instance, the implied general injunction that something-or-other has to be ruled out in this-or-that way and for such-a-reason. This force can be contrasted with the criteria, standards, grounds and reasons, by reference to which we decide in any context that the use of a particular modal term is appropriate. We are entitled to say that some possibility has to be ruled out only if we can produce grounds or reasons to justify this claim, and under the term 'criteria' can be included the many sorts of things we have then to produce. We say, for instance, that something is physically, mathematically or physiologically impossible, that it is terminologically or linguistically out of order, or else morally or judicially improper: it is to be ruled out, accordingly, *qua* something or other. And when we start explaining '*qua* what' any particular thing is to be ruled out, we show what criteria we are appealing to in this particular situation.

The importance of the distinction between force and criteria will become fully clear only as we go along. It can be hinted at, perhaps, if we look for a moment at the notion of mathematical impossibility. Many theorems in geometry and pure mathematics state impossibilities of one sort or another: they tell us, e.g., that it is impossible to construct a regular heptagon using ruler and compass, and that you cannot find a rational square root of 2. Such a construction or such a square root is, we are told, a mathematical impossibility.

Now what is involved in saying this? What precisely is signified by this phrase 'mathematical impossibility?' It is easy to give too simple an answer, and we must not be in a hurry. The natural thing to look at first is the procedure mathematicians have to go through in order to prove a theorem of this sort—to show, for instance, that there cannot be a rational square root of 2. When we inquire what they establish in such a proof, we find that one thing is of supreme importance. The notion of 'a rational square root of 2' leads us into contradictions: from the assumption that a number x is rational and that its square is equal to 2, we can by brief chains of argument reach two mutually contradictory conclusions. This is the reason, the conclusive reason, why mathematicians are led to consider the idea that any actual number x could have both these properties an impossible one.

Having remarked on this, we may be tempted to conclude at once that we have the answer to our question—namely, that the phrase 'mathematically impossible' just means 'self-contradictory, or leading to self-contradictions'. But this is too simple: to understand the notion properly, one must pay attention, not only to what mathematicians do before reaching the conclusion that something is impossible, but also to what they do after reaching this conclusion and *in consequence of* having reached it. The existence of a mathematical impossibility is not only something which requires proving, it is also something which has implications. To show the presence of the contradictions may be all that is required by a mathematician if he is to be justified in saying that the notion x is a mathematical impossibility—it may, that is, be a conclusive demonstration of its impossibility—but the force of calling it impossible involves more than simply labelling it as 'leading to contradictions'. The notion x involves one in contradictions and is *therefore* or *accordingly* an impossibility: it is impossible *on account of* the contradictions, impossible *qua* leading one into contradictions. If 'mathematically impossible' meant precisely the same as 'contradictory', the phrase 'contradictory and so mathematically impossible' would be tautologous—'contradictory and so contradictory'. But this will not do: to say only, 'This supposition leads one into contradictions or, to use another equivalent phrase, is impossible', is to rob the idea of mathematical impossibility of a crucial part of its force, for it fails to draw the proper moral—it leaves the supposition un-ruled out.

Even in mathematics, therefore, one can distinguish the criterion or standard by reference to which the rational square root of 2 is dismissed *as* impossible from the force of the conclusion that it *is* impossible. To state the presence of the contradictions is not thereby to dismiss the notion as impossible, though from the mathematicians' point of view this may be absolutely all we require in order to *justify* its dismissal. Once again, the force of calling the number *x* an 'impossibility' is to dismiss it from consideration and, since we are to dismiss it from consideration from the mathematical standpoint, the grounds for doing so have to be of a kind appropriate to mathematics, e.g. the fact that operating with such a conception leads one into contradictions. Contradictoriness can be, mathematically speaking, a *criterion* of impossibility: the implied *force* or *moral* of such an impossibility is that the notion can have no place in subsequent mathematical arguments.

To insist on this distinction in the case of mathematical impossibility may seem to be mere hair-splitting. Mathematically, the consequences of the distinction may be negligible: philosophically, however, they are considerable, especially when one goes on (as we shall do in a later essay) to make the parallel distinction in the case of 'logical impossibility'. For this distinction between 'force' and 'criteria' as applied to modal terms is a near-relation to distinctions which have recently been made in other fields with great philosophical profit.

Let us look at this parallel for a moment. Philosophers studying the general use of evaluative terms have argued as follows:

A word like 'good' can be used equally of an apple or an agent or an action, of a volley in tennis, a vacuum-cleaner or a Van Gogh: in each case, to call the fruit or the person or the stroke or the painting 'good' is to commend it, and to hold it out as being in some respect a praiseworthy, admirable or efficient member of its class—the word 'good' is accordingly defined most accurately as 'the most general adjective of commendation'. But because the word is so general, the things we appeal to in order to justify commending different kinds of thing as 'good' will themselves be very different. A morally-good action, a domestically-good vacuum-cleaner and a pomiculturally-good apple all come up to standard, but the standards they all come up to will be different—indeed, incomparable. So one can distinguish between the commendatory force of labelling a thing as 'good', and the criteria by reference to which we justify a commendation.

Our own discussion has led us to a position which is, in effect, only a special case of this more general one. For the pattern is the same whether the things we are grading or assessing or criticising are, on the one hand, apples or actions or paintings or, on the other, arguments and conclusions. In either case we are concerned with judging or evaluating, and distinctions which have proved fruitful in ethics and aesthetics will do so again when applied to the criticism of arguments. With 'impossible' as with 'good': the use of the term has a characteristic force, of commending in one case, of rejecting in the other; to commend an apple or an action is one thing, to give your reasons for commending it is another; to reject a suggestion as untenable is one thing, to give your reasons for rejecting it is another, however cogent and relevant these reasons may be.

What is the virtue of such distinctions? If we ignore them in ethics, a number of things may happen. We may, for instance, be tempted to think that the standards which a thing has to reach in order to deserve commendation are all we need point to in explaining what is meant by calling it 'good'. To call a vacuum-cleaner good (we may conclude) is just to say that its efficiency, in terms of cubic-feet-of-dust-sucked-in per kilowatt-of-electricity-consumed and the like, is well above the average for machines of this type. (This is like thinking that the phrase 'mathematically impossible' just *means* 'involving self-contradictions' and no more.) Such a view, however, leads to unnecessary paradoxes. For it may now seem that the terms of commendation and condemnation in which we so frequently express our judgements of value have as many meanings as there are different sorts of thing to evaluate, and this is a very unwelcome suggestion. As a counter to this, it has to be recognised that the *force* of commending something as 'good' or condemning it as 'bad' remains the same, whatever sort of thing it may be, even though the criteria for judging or assessing the merits of different kinds are very variable.

But this is not the only way in which we may be led astray, or indeed the most serious way. Having recognised that, in the meaning of evaluative terms, a multiplicity of criteria are linked together by a common force, and that to evaluate something normally involves both grading it in an order of commendability and also referring to the criteria appropriate to things of its kind, we may nevertheless wish to take a further step. For, being preoccupied with some particular type of evaluation, we may come to feel that one particular set of criteria has a unique importance, and accordingly be tempted to pick on the criteria proper for the assessment of things of some one sort as the proper or unique standards of merit for all sorts of thing, so dismissing all other criteria either as misconceived or as unimportant. One may suspect that something of this kind happened to the Utilitarians, who were so whole-hearted and single-minded in their concern for questions of legislation and social action that they came to feel that there was only one problem when evaluating things of all kinds: all one had to do was determine the *consequences* which could be associated with or expected from things of any kind.

The dangers of such single-mindedness become apparent when philosophers of this kind begin to generalise: preoccupied as they are with some one type of valuation, they blind themselves to the special problems involved in other sorts—to all the difficulties of aesthetic judgement, and to many of the issues facing one in the course of one's moral life. There are many sorts of assessment and grading besides the appraisal of legislative programmes and social reforms, and standards which may be wholly appropriate when judging the worthiness of a Bill before Parliament can be misleading or out-of-place when we are concerned with a painting, an apple or even our individual moral quandaries.

The same dangers can arise over arguments. The use of a modal term like 'cannot' in connection with arguments from quite different fields involves, as we have seen, a certain common force, like the common force recognisable in a wide range of uses of the word 'good'. Yet the criteria to be invoked to justify ruling out conclusions of different types are very different. Here, as in ethics, two conclusions are tempting, both of which must be avoided. On the one hand, it will be wrong to say, merely on account of this variation in criteria, that the word 'cannot' means quite different things when it figures in different sorts of conclusions: not for nothing are physical, linguistic, moral and conceptual 'cannots' linked by the use of a common term. It will also be a mistake, and a more serious one, to pick on some one criterion of impossibility and to elevate it into a position of unique philosophical importance. Yet in the history of recent philosophy both of these conclusions have been influential—the latter, I shall argue, disastrously so.

Before returning to our main question, there is one further caution. We have already, for the purposes of this present investigation, renounced the use of the word 'logical'; it will be as well to renounce now the use of the word 'meaning' and its associates also. For the distinction which we have here drawn between force and criteria is one which cuts across the common use of the term 'meaning', and we need, for our present purposes, to operate with finer distinctions than the term 'meaning' ordinarily allows one to draw. It is not enough to speak about the meaning or use of such terms as 'good' or 'impossible' as though it were an indivisible unit: the use of such terms has a number of distinguishable *aspects*, for two of which we have introduced the words 'force' and 'criteria'. Until we make this distinction, the false trails of which I have spoken will remain tempting, for, when we are asked whether the differences between all the varied uses of the words 'good', 'cannot' and 'possible' do or do not amount to differences in meaning, we shall inevitably find ourselves pulled in opposite directions. If we say that there *are* differences in meaning, we seem committed to making as many different entries in our dictionaries as there are sorts of possibility or impossibility or merit—indeed, as many entries as there are different kinds of thing to be possible or impossible or good—a ridiculous conclusion. On the other hand, to say that there is *no* difference in meaning between these varied uses suggests that we can expect to find our standards of goodness or possibility or impossibility proving field-invariant, and this conclusion is no better. If, however, we make the further distinction between the force of assessments and the criteria or standards applicable in the course of them, we can avoid giving any crude 'yes or no' answer to the coarse-grained question, 'Are the meanings the same or different?' As we shift from one use to another, the criteria may change while the force remains the same: whether or no we decide to *call* this a change of meaning will be a matter of comparative indifference.

THE FIELD-DEPENDENCE OF OUR STANDARDS

We are now in a position to see the answer to our first major question. When one sets out and criticises arguments and conclusions in different fields, we asked, what features of the procedure we adopt and of the concepts we employ will be field-invariant, and what features will be field-dependent? For impossibilities and improprieties, we saw, the answer was clear enough. The *force* of the conclusion 'It cannot be the case that...' or '...is impossible' is the same regardless of fields: the *criteria* or sorts of ground required to justify such a conclusion vary from field to field. In any field, the conclusions that 'cannot' be the case are those we are obliged to rule out—whether they are concerned with lifting a ton single-handed, turning one's son away without a shilling, or operating mathematically with a rational square root of 2: on the other hand, the criteria of physiological incapacity are one thing, standards of moral inadmissibility are another, and those of mathematical impossibility a third. We must now check more briefly that in this respect the terms 'cannot' and 'impossible' are typical of modal terms generally, and that what is true of these samples is true likewise of other modal terms and terms of logical assessment.

Let us take a quick look at the notion of 'possibility'. What is meant by calling something a possibility, whether mathematical or other? From the standpoint of mathematics, we may be justified in treating some notion as a possibility simply in the absence of any demonstrable contradiction—this is the converse of contradictoriness, the mathematical criterion of impossibility. In most cases, however, to call something a possibility is to claim much more than this. For instance the statement, 'Dwight D. Eisenhower will be selected to represent the U.S.A. in the Davis Cup match against Australia', certainly makes sense, and involves one in no demonstrable contradictions. Yet nobody would say that President Eisenhower was a *possible* member of the team: no one, that is, would think of introducing his name for consideration when genuinely discussing its composition. For to put him forward as a possibility would be to imply that he at any rate deserved our attention—that it was necessary, at the very least, to state arguments *against* the view that he would be selected—whereas, in fact, if his name were introduced into a serious discussion of the question, it would be dismissed not with an argument but with a laugh, since one cannot even begin to consider the chances of a man who has effectively no tennis-playing form to be taken into account.

In order for a suggestion to be a 'possibility' in any context, therefore, it must 'have what it takes' in order to be entitled to genuine consideration *in that context*. To say, in any field, 'Such-and-such is a possible answer to our question', is to say that, bearing in mind the nature of the problem concerned, such-and-such an answer deserves to be considered. This much of the meaning of the term 'possible' is field-invariant. The criteria of possibility, on the other hand, are field-dependent, like the criteria of impossibility and goodness. The things we must point to in showing that some-thing is possible will depend entirely on whether we are concerned with a problem in pure mathematics, a problem of team-selection, a problem in aesthetics, or what; and features which make something a possibility from one standpoint will be totally irrelevant from another. The form that makes a man a possibility for the Davis Cup is one thing; the explanatory power that makes Professor Fröhlich's theory a possible explanation of super-conductivity is another; the features of Piero's painting of the Resurrection which make it possibly the finest picture ever painted are a third; and there is no question of weighing these possibilities all in the same scale. They are all possibilities of their kinds, all (that is) suggestions entitled to respectful consideration in any serious discussion of the problems to which they are relevant; but, because they are possibilities of *different* kinds, the standards by which their claims to our attention are judged will vary from case to case.

This is not to deny that possibilities of different kinds can be compared in *any* way. In every field of argument, there can be some very strong possibilities, other more or less serious ones, and others again which are more and more remote; and, in comparing possi-bilities from different fields, we can set against each other the comparative degrees of strength or remoteness which each possibility has in its own field. This cannot normally be done at all precisely—there are not in general exact measures of 'degree of possibility'—yet some sort of rough comparison is open to us, and indeed familiar enough. A hostile physicist might say, 'Fröhlich's theory is no more a possible theory of super-conductivity than Dwight D. Eisenhower is a possible member of the U.S. Davis Cup team', and this would be, I take it, a contemptuous way of dismissing Fröhlich's theory from consideration; but to say such a thing will not be to imply that one can measure Fröhlich's theory and Dwight D. Eisenhower against a common standard. Rather, it will be to set against one another the degrees to which each of them comes up to the standards of possibility appropriate to things of the kind in question.

'Can' and 'possible' are, accordingly, like 'cannot' and 'impossible' in having a field-invariant force and field-dependent standards. This result can be generalised: all the *canons* for the criticism and assessment of arguments, I conclude, are in practice field-dependent, while all our terms of assessment are field-invariant in their *force*. We can ask, 'How strong a case can be made out?' —whether for expecting Budge Patty to be a member of the U.S. Davis Cup team, or for accepting Sir Kenneth Clark's reassessment of Piero della Francesca, or for adopting Fröhlich's theory of superconductivity—and the question we ask will be how strong each case is when tested against its own appropriate standard. We may even ask, if we please, how the three cases compare in strength, and produce an order of merit, deciding (say) that the case for selecting Patty is watertight, the case for Fröhlich's theory strong but only provisional, and the case for Piero somewhat exaggerated and dependent upon a number of debatable matters of taste. (In saying this I do not imply that *all* aesthetic arguments are looser, or more dependent on matters of taste, than *all* scientific or predictive arguments.) But in doing this we are not asking how far the cases for the three conclusions measure up to a common standard: only, how far each of them comes up to the standards appropriate to things of its kind. The form of question, 'How strong is the case?', has the same force or implications each time: the standards we work with in the three cases are different.

QUESTIONS FOR THE AGENDA

This result may seem a rather slender outcome for so laborious an inquiry. It may also seem a trifle obvious; and certainly we must avoid exaggerating either its magnitude or its immediate philosophical importance. Nevertheless, if we take its implications seriously, we shall see that it does force on us certain questions which are of undoubted importance for philosophy, and particularly for our understanding of the scope of formal logic. In this last part of the present essay, let me indicate what these questions are, since they will be high on our agenda in subsequent essays.

To begin with, we must ask: are the differences between the standards we employ in different fields *irreducible*? Must the things which, in practice, make a conclusion possible, probable, or certain —or an argument shaky, strong or conclusive—vary as we move from one field of argument to another? This, one might think, was not an unavoidable feature of the ways in which we assess and criticise arguments; and certainly it is a feature with which professional logicians have been unwilling to come to terms. So far from accepting it, they have always hoped that it would prove possible to display arguments from different fields in a common form, and to criticise arguments and conclusions as weak, strong or conclusive, possible, probable or certain, by appeal to a single, universal set of criteria applicable in all fields of argument alike. Quite consistently, logicians can admit that, in actual practice, we do not employ any universal battery of criteria, and yet maintain unabated their ambition to discover and formulate—theoretically, if no more—such a set of universal standards: the actual differences between the criteria we employ in one field or another they will regard, not as something inevitable and irreducible, but rather as a challenge. Acknowledging these differences for what they are, they may at the same time make it their aim to develop methods of assessment more general and standards of judgement more universal than those which we customarily employ in the practical criticism of everyday arguments.

This is only the first hint of a wider divergence which we shall find ourselves having to face more and more as we proceed, between the attitudes and methods of professional logicians and those of everyday arguers. At the moment there is nothing about it that leads to any serious disquiet. The logicians' ambition to produce a system of logic field-invariant both in the forms it employs and in the criteria it sets out for the criticism of arguments is at first sight a wholly reasonable ambition: one would not easily hit on any immediate reason for dismissing it as unrealisable. All we can do at this stage, therefore, is to state the general question which is raised for logic by the adoption of this programme: it is the question, 'How far is a *general* logic possible?' In other words, can one hope, even as a matter of theory alone, to set out and criticise arguments in such a way that the form in which one sets out the arguments and the standards by appeal to which one criticises them are both field-invariant?

A second question of general importance for philosophy arises out of our inquiry in the following way. Philosophers have often held that arguments in some fields of inquiry are intrinsically more open to rational assessment than those in others: questions of mathematics and questions about everyday matters of fact, for instance, have been considered by many to have a certain priority in logic over (say) matters of law, morals or aesthetics. The court of reason, it has been suggested, has only a limited jurisdiction, and is not competent to adjudicate on questions of all kinds. In our inquiry, no contrast of this sort has so far turned up: there is, for all that we have seen, a complete parallelism between arguments in all these different fields, and no grounds are yet evident for according priority to mathematical and similar matters. In considering, for example, the different grounds on which something may have to be ruled out in the course of an argument, we found plenty of differences on going from one field to another, but nothing which led us to conclude that any special field of argument was intrinsically non-rational, or that the court of reason was somehow not competent to pronounce upon its problems. So the question arises, just what lies behind the desire of many philosophers to draw distinctions of this particular kind between different fields of arguments.

Probably we all have some sympathy for this philosophical doctrine. If we look again at the batch of sample conclusions ruled out with a 'cannot' from arguments in different fields, we may quite naturally feel, to begin with, that some of the examples have more right to be labelled with this word than others. That one 'cannot' lift a ton single-handed, or get ten thousand people into the Town Hall; or again, that one 'cannot' have a male sister—these sorts of impossibility, over which trying is bound to be vain even where to speak of trying is itself intelligible, do certainly seem to us to be more real, more authentic, than some of the other examples at which we looked. They overshadow especially those examples in which the grounds for ruling out a conclusion are only grounds of illegality or immorality—though why, we may at once ask, does one feel inclined to say, '*Only* grounds of illegality or immorality'?

The question now has to be asked, whether there is anything more to this difference than a *feeling* of authenticity. Has this feeling of authenticity, which attaches to the impossibilities of physical incapacity and linguistic incoherence, but not to such things as moral impropriety, anything more in the way of a backing than a psychological one? Can it really be said that there is any difference, from the point of view of logic, between these two classes of inquiry; or is the difference between them no more than we have so far recognised?

Certainly, on looking at the different circumstances in which we use modal terms such as 'cannot', we do find differences—there may be many reasons, indeed many kinds of reason, for stopping and reconsidering something one is doing, about to do, or thinking of doing; or else for calling on someone else to stop and think in the same way. The fact that an action would be illegal is one perfectly good reason for reconsidering it, the fact that it would be unjudicial is in some circumstances a second, the knowledge that the very attempt would inevitably be vain is a third good reason for hesitation, that it would involve a linguistic solecism or an ungrammatical utterance are two more, and so on. What is not at first apparent is any logical ground for saying that certain of these sorts of reason are *really* reasons, while others are not. Logically speaking, the cases appear on a par.

Logically speaking, the penalties a man risks by ignoring different impossibilities and improprieties are also at first sight entirely on a par: by ignoring a legal provision one runs a risk of prosecution, by ignoring the rules of judicial procedure that of public outcry or a successful appeal, by ignoring one's physical capacities the risk of disappointment, by ignoring the need to respect the conventions of language in one's utterances that of not being understood. The grounds, offences and sanctions in question may not be the same in different fields, but it is hard to see from this inquiry alone why some fields need be more 'logical' or 'rational' than others. So here is one general question of undoubted philosophical importance, which we must add to our agenda for later discussion: what sort of priority in logic, if any, can matters of fact (say) claim over such things as matters of morals?

This inquiry has, I hope, illustrated one thing: namely, the virtues of the parallel between procedures of rational assessment and legal procedures—what I called earlier the jurisprudential analogy. In deciding both questions of law and questions about the soundness of arguments or the groundedness of conclusions, certain fundamental procedures are taken for granted. The uses we make of terms of modal qualification, which we have examined at some length in the present essay, are only one illustration of this. But there is one further possibility that the analogy suggests, which we have not yet faced explicitly. Although in the conduct of law-cases of all kinds the procedures observed share certain common features, there are some respects in which they will be found to vary: the conduct of a civil case, for instance, will not be parallel in every single feature to that of a criminal case. Now we must bear it in mind that similar differences may be found in the case of rational procedures also. It may turn out, for instance, not only that the sorts of grounds to which we point in support of conclusions in different fields are different, but also that the ways in which these grounds bear on the conclusions—the ways in which they are capable of supporting conclusions—may also vary as between fields. There are indications that this may actually be so: e.g. the fact that, though in many cases we speak quite happily of our grounds for putting forward some conclusion as 'evidence', in other cases this term would be quite out of place—a man who pointed out the features of a painting which, in his view, made it a masterpiece would scarcely be spoken of as presenting 'evidence' that it was a great work of art.

This kind of difference need not surprise us: after all, the distinctions we have made so far are very broad ones, and a closer examination could certainly bring to light further more detailed distinctions, which would improve our understanding of the ways in which arguments in different fields are related. Perhaps at this point we might begin to see more clearly what makes people feel that questions of mathematics, meteorology and the like are somehow more rational than—say—aesthetic questions. It would be worth considering, indeed, whether there are not even crucial differences between the procedures appropriate to aesthetic questions on the one hand, and moral ones on the other. But all this would lead us off on to another equally laborious investigation, and the problem must be left for another place.

One of the questions on which the jurisprudential analogy focuses attention we shall, however, have to take very seriously, and it will serve as the starting-point for our central essay: that is the question, what it means to speak about *form* in logic. If it is said that the validity of arguments depends upon certain features of their form, what precisely is meant by this? One of the chief attractions of the mathematical approach to logic has always been that it alone gave anything like a clear answer to this question. If one thinks of logic as an extension of psychology or sociology, the notion of logical form remains impenetrably obscure—indeed, it can be explained only in terms of even more mysterious notions, being accounted for as a structure of relations between psychic entities or social behaviour-patterns. The mathematical approach to logic has always appeared to overcome this particular obscurity, since mathematicians have long studied pattern and shape in other branches of their science, and the extension of these ideas to logic has seemed entirely natural. Mathematical ratios and geometrical figures carry with them a clear enough idea of form; so no wonder the doctrine that logical form could be construed in the same way has proved extremely attractive.

The analogy between rational assessment and judicial practice presents us with a rival model for thinking about the idea of logical form. It now appears that arguments must not just have a particular shape, but must be set out and presented in a sequence of steps conforming to certain basic rules of procedure. In a word, rational assessment is an activity necessarily involving *formalities*. When we turn in the third essay to consider the layout of arguments, we shall accordingly have a definite question to start from: we must ask how far the formal character of sound arguments can be thought of *more geometrico*, as a matter of their having the right sorts of shape, and how far it needs to be thought of, rather, in procedural terms, as a matter of their conforming to the formalities which must be observed if any rational assessment of arguments is to be possible.

II

PROBABILITY

> So terrified was he [my eldest brother] of being caught, by
> chance, in a false statement, that as a small boy he acquired
> the habit of adding 'perhaps' to everything he said. 'Is that
> you, Harry?' Mama might call from the drawing-room. 'Yes,
> Mama—perhaps.' 'Are you going upstairs?' 'Yes, perhaps.'
> 'Will you see if I've left my bag in the bedroom?' 'Yes, Mama,
> perhaps—p'r'haps—paps!'
>
> ELEANOR FARJEON, *A Nursery in the Nineties*

THESE FIRST two studies are both, in different ways, preliminary
ones. The aim of the first was to indicate in broad outline the
structure our arguments take in practice, and the leading features
of the categories we employ in the practical assessment of these
arguments. By and large, I aimed throughout it to steer clear of
explicitly philosophical issues and leave over to be discussed later
the relevance of our conclusions for philosophy. The method of this
second study will be rather different. We shall in the course of it
carry our analysis of modal terms rather further; yet at the same time
a secondary aim will be to indicate how the results of such an inquiry
can be relevant to philosophical questions and problems; and certain
broad conclusions will be suggested which will have to be established
more securely and in more general terms in subsequent essays.

This difference in aim is reflected in the type of examples chosen
for discussion. In the first study I wished to bring out clearly what
actual functions our modal terms perform in the course of practical
arguments, without being distracted by philosophical preconceptions
and disputes which we were not yet ready to face: I therefore chose
to concentrate on the terms 'possible' and 'impossible', together
with their cognate verbs and adverbs. In recent years, at any rate,
philosophers have theorised about these particular terms comparatively little, and this made them admirable examples for our
purpose. On the other hand, a great deal of attention has been paid
lately to some other modal terms, especially to the words 'probable'
and 'probability': these latter terms will accordingly be our concern

now. Bearing in mind the general distinctions which have already come to light, let us turn and see what philosophers have recently had to say on the subject of probability, and to what extent these discussions have done justice to the practical functions of the terms 'probably', 'probable' and 'probability' in the formulation and the criticism of arguments.

If we do this, we are in for a disappointment. The subject of probability is one in which the prolegomena are as neglected as they are important. Anyone who sets out to expound the subject as it has traditionally been handled finds so much that is expected of him, so much that is beguiling to discuss—philosophical theses of considerable subtlety, a mathematical calculus of great formal elegance, and fascinating side-issues, like the legitimacy of talking about 'infinite sets'—that he is tempted to cut short the preliminary stating of the problem in order to get on to 'the real business in hand'. This is thought of as requiring continual refinement at the level of theory, and the practical aspects of the subject have as a result been inadequately studied.

Among recent writers on the subject both Mr William Kneale and Professor Rudolf Carnap are open to criticism on this count, despite the fact that their books, *Probability and Induction* and *Logical Foundations of Probability*, have become standard works on the subject. The same difficulties arise over Kneale's book as over so many others: a reader who is interested in the application of logic to actual arguments will find it unclear what, in practical terms, are the questions under discussion, and particularly, what connection they are supposed to have with the sorts of everyday situation in which words like 'probably', 'likely' and 'chance' are used. For Kneale writes almost exclusively in terms of such abstractions as 'probability', 'knowledge' and 'belief'. He accepts as straight-forward (and states his problems in terms of) notions which are surely patent metaphors—even his initial description of probability, as 'the substitute with which we try to make good the shortcomings of our knowledge, the extent of which is less than we could wish', being a metaphor taken from the trade in commodities.

This might not matter, if he gave a thorough account of the way in which his theoretical discussion is to be related to more familiar things: it would then be a legitimate and effective literary device. But he does not; and, if we reconstruct one for ourselves, we shall discover two things. First, we shall come to see that an abstract account of the relations between probability, knowledge and belief, such as Kneale gives, cannot help failing in a number of essential respects—these abstract nouns are too coarse-grained to serve as material for a satisfactory analysis of our practical notions, which figure more often in the form of verbs, adverbs and adjectives— 'I shall probably come', 'It seemed unlikely', 'They believe' and 'He didn't know'. Furthermore, it will become evident how far the puzzles about probability at present fashionable are given their seeming point by just this sort of over-reliance on abstract nouns: when we ask the questions, 'What *is* probability? What are probability statements *about*? What do they *express*?', prematurely and in too general a form, we in fact help to set the discussion of the subject off along the traditional, well-oiled, well-worn rails, and succeed in hiding even from ourselves the man-made origins of the puzzles and the reasons for their perennial insolubility.

Carnap presents a rather more elusive target. The system of ideas he presents is so elaborate, and the theories accompanying it are so sophisticated, that it is difficult to see what he would himself regard as a valid objection against them. Kneale, at any rate, is prepared to take some account of the ways in which the notion of probability is actually applied. 'In the theory of probability', he says, 'the business of the philosopher is not to construct a formal system with consistency and elegance for his only guides. His task is to clarify the meaning of probability statements made by plain men, and the frequency theory [to mention only one of the current theories of probability] must be judged as an attempt to carry out this under-taking.'[1] And again, he says, 'No analysis of the probability relation can be regarded as adequate, i.e. as explaining the ordinary usage of the word 'probability', unless it enables us to understand why it is rational to take as a basis for action a proposition which stands in that relation to the evidence at our disposal.'[2] So far as Kneale's account is demonstrably untrue to practical life—so far, that is, as one can catch him misrepresenting the notion of probability as a category of applied logic—one can press home objections against his theory.

Carnap is more cavalier about objections of this kind, and pro-fesses to find allusions to the everyday use of the notion of 'proba-bility' uninteresting and irrelevant—indeed he counter-attacks, and

---

[1] *Probability and Induction*, § 32, p. 158.   [2] *Ibid.* § 6, p. 20.

justifies his dismissal of such appeals on the grounds that they are
'pre-scientific'. (Whether anything which is pre-scientific is necessarily also *un*-scientific is another matter, to which we shall have to
return at the close of this essay.) Still, though he would claim to
despise the unsophisticated study of the pre-scientific term 'probable'
and its cognates, we can afford to look and see what he has to say
about more up-to-date kinds of probability. One conclusion he
presents will be of particular interest to us: he is led to insist that
the very word 'probability' is through-and-through ambiguous, and
the reasons which he gives for insisting on the point will prove
illuminating. Far from allowing that this is a proper conclusion, I
shall argue that it is a paradox, and is forced on him just *because* he
dismisses so cavalierly all questions about 'probability' in a less
technical sense. When such considerations are re-introduced, the
paradoxes into which he finds himself driven can be resolved.

The programme of this essay will be roughly as follows. I shall
begin by analysing the most primitive origins of the notion of
probability, and work by stages towards its more sophisticated and
technical refinements. In doing this, I shall be aiming to bring out
clearly the relations between the term 'probability' and the general
family of modal terms. As the analysis proceeds, I shall compare
the results obtained against the philosophical theories of Kneale and
Carnap, showing where, in my opinion, they go astray through
failing to attend sufficiently to the practical function of modal terms.
Some of the distinctions and conclusions which the inquiry will
bring to light will be clarified and more fully worked out in the three
remaining essays.

I KNOW, I PROMISE, PROBABLY

Let us examine first what we all learn first, the adverb 'probably':
its force can best be shown with the help of some elementary
examples.

There comes a moment in the life of a well-brought-up small boy when
he finds himself in a quandary. For the last week he has come every day
after tea to play with the little girl who lives in the next street, and he has
begun to value her esteem. Now bed-time is near, Mother has come to
fetch him away, and his companion says, with bright eyes, 'You *will* come
to-morrow, won't you?' Ordinarily he would have answered 'Yes'
without a qualm, for every other evening he has fully intended to come

next day, and known of nothing to stand in his way. But...but there was some talk at home of a visit to the Zoo to-morrow; and what if that, and tea in a tea-shop afterwards, and the crowds in the Tube, meant that they were late getting home, and that he was to fail, after saying 'Yes'? ...How difficult life is! If he says 'Yes' and then cannot come, she will be entitled to feel that he has let her down. If he says 'No', and then is back in time after all, she will not be expecting him and he won't be able, decently, to come; and so he will have deprived himself, by his own word, of his chief pleasure. What is he to say? He turns to his mother for help. She, understanding the dilemma, smiles and presents him with a way out: 'Tell her that you'll *probably* come, darling. Explain that you can't *promise*, since it depends on what time we get home, but say that you'll come if you possibly can.' Thankful for the relief, he turns back and utters the magic word: 'Probably'.

The important difference to notice here is that between saying 'I shall come' and saying 'I shall probably come'. This difference is similar in character, though opposite in sense to that which Professor J. L. Austin has discussed, between saying 'S is P' or 'I shall do A', and saying 'I know that S is P' or 'I promise that I shall do A'. On this subject, let me quote Austin's paper:

When I say 'S is P', I imply at least that I believe it, and, if I have been strictly brought up, that I am (quite) sure of it: when I say 'I shall do A', I imply at least that I hope to do it, and, if I have been strictly brought up, that I (fully) intend to. If I only believe that S is P, I can add 'But of course I may (very well) be wrong': if I only hope to do A, I can add 'But of course I may (very well) not'. When I only believe or only hope, it is recognised that further evidence or further circumstances are liable to make me change my mind. If I say 'S is P' when I don't even believe it, I am lying: if I say it when I believe it but am not sure of it, I may be misleading but I am not exactly lying. If I say 'I shall do A' when I have not even any hope, not the slightest intention of doing it, then I am deliberately deceiving; if I say it when I do not fully intend to, I am misleading but I am not deliberately deceiving in the same way.

But now, when I say 'I promise', a new plunge is taken: I have not merely announced my intention, but, by using this formula (performing this ritual), I have bound myself to others, and staked my reputation, in a new way. Similarly, saying 'I know' is taking a new plunge. But it is *not* saying 'I have performed a specially striking feat of cognition, superior, in the same scale as believing and being sure, even to being merely quite sure': for there *is* nothing in that scale superior to being quite sure. Just as promising is not something superior, in the same scale as hoping and intending, even to merely fully intending: for there *is* nothing in that scale superior to fully intending. When I say 'I know', *I give others my word: I give others my authority for saying that* 'S is P'.[1]

Our small boy's difficulty can be put as follows. If, in reply to his companion's appeal 'You *will* come to-morrow, won't you?', he says 'Yes, I'll come', he commits himself. For to utter the words 'Yes, I'll come', is to *say* you'll come, and this, while not being as solemn and portentous as a promise, is in some ways all but one. ('I didn't promise': 'Maybe not, but you *as good as* promised.') By saying, 'Yes, I'll come', he not only leads her to expect him (i.e. to anticipate, to make preparations for, his arrival). He also ensures that coming to-morrow will be something that is expected of him: he gives her reason to reproach him if he does not turn up, though not of course reason to reproach him in such strong terms as she would be entitled to use if he were to fail after having promised— i.e. after having solemnly said, 'I promise that I'll come'. To say 'Yes', when there was any reason to suppose that he might be prevented from coming, would therefore be laying up trouble for himself.

The point of the word 'probably', like that of the word 'perhaps', is to avoid just this trouble. By saying 'I know that S is P' or 'I promise to do A', I expressly commit myself, in a way in which I also do—though to a lesser degree and only by implication—if I say 'S is P' or 'I shall do A'. By saying, 'S is probably P' or 'I shall probably do A', I expressly avoid unreservedly committing myself. I insure myself thereby against some of the consequences of failure. My utterance is thereby 'guarded'—that is, in the words of the *Pocket Oxford Dictionary*, 'secured by stipulation from abuse or misunderstanding'. But the insurance is not unlimited; the nature of the stipulation must, in normal cases, be made quite clear ('It depends on what time we get home'), and the protection afforded by the use of the word 'probably' extends in the first place only to those contingencies which have been expressly stipulated. To say 'I'll probably come, but it depends on what time we get back from the Zoo', and then not to go in spite of being back in plenty of time, would be (even if not deliberate deceit) at any rate 'taking advantage'; as misleading as saying unreservedly 'I'll come', and then not going. You are again committed, and therefore again responsible: to attempt

---

[1] 'Other Minds' in *Logic and Language*, 2nd series, pp. 143-4.

to excuse yourself by saying, 'But I only told you I'd *probably* come', would be a piece of bad faith.

Nor of course is anyone who uses the word 'probably' in this way permitted to fail either always or often, even though he may have 'covered' himself expressly every time. By saying 'probably' you make yourself answerable for fulfilment, if not on all, at least on a reasonable proportion of occasions: it is not enough that you have an excuse for each single failure. Only in some specialised cases is this requirement tacitly suspended—'When a woman says "Perhaps", she means "Yes": when a diplomat says "Perhaps", he means "No".'

Finally, and in the nature of the case, certain forms of words are prohibited. To follow Austin again, 'You are prohibited from saying "I know it is so, but I may be wrong", just as you are prohibited from saying "I promise I will, but I may fail." If you are aware you may be mistaken (have some concrete reason to suppose that you may be mistaken in this case), you oughtn't to say you know, just as, if you are aware you may break your word, you have no business to promise.'[1] In the same way, and for the same reasons, you are prohibited from saying 'I'll probably come, but I shan't be able to'; for to say this is to take away with the last half of your utterance what you gave with the first. If you know that you will not be able to go, you have no right to say anything which commits you in any way to going.

In this first example, we see how the word 'probably' comes to be used as a means of giving guarded undertakings and making qualified declarations of one's intentions. Philosophers, however, have been concerned less with this sort of use of the word than they have with its use in scientific statements and especially, in view of the traditional connection between the problems of probability and induction, with its use in predictions. It is important, therefore, to illustrate the everyday use of the word 'probably' in such a context, and we may choose for this purpose a typical extract from a weather forecast:

A complex disturbance at present over Iceland is moving in an easterly direction. Cloudy conditions now affecting Northern Ireland will spread to N.W. England during the day, probably extending to the rest of the country in the course of the evening and night.

[1] *Loc. cit.* pp. 142–3.

All the features characteristic of our previous example are to be found here also. The Meteorological Office's forecasters are prepared to commit themselves unreservedly to the first of their predictions (that the cloudy conditions will spread to N.W. England during the day), but they are not prepared to do this in the case of the second (that the cloud will extend to the rest of the country during the evening and night); and they know that, the M.O. being the M.O., we have to go by what they say. If they unreservedly forecast cloud later today and the skies remain clear, they can justifiably be rounded on by the housewife who has put off her heavy wash on account of their prediction. If they say '...will certainly spread...' or 'We know that cloudy conditions will spread...', there will in case of failure be even more cause for complaint; though, as it is the M.O.'s business to know and they are the authorities on the subject of the weather, we tend to take for granted in their case the introductory formula 'We know...'. In the present state of their science, how-ever, they cannot safely—cannot without asking for trouble, that is—always commit themselves to unqualified predictions for more than an extremely limited time ahead: what then are they to say about the coming night?

Here again the word 'probably' comes into its own. Just as it finds a place as a means of giving guarded and restricted under-takings, so it can be used when we have to utter guarded and res-tricted predictions—predictions to which, for some concrete reason or other, we are not prepared positively to commit ourselves. Once again, however, the use of the word 'probably' insures one against only some of the consequences of failure. If the forecasters say 'probably extending', they cover themselves only within those limits which have to be recognised as reasonable in the present state of meteorology. If clouds do not turn up over the rest of the country sooner or later, we are entitled to ask why. And if in reply to this inquiry they refuse to offer any explanation, such as they might give by saying, 'The anti-cyclone over Northern France persisted for longer than is usual under such circumstances', but try to excuse themselves with the words, 'After all we only said the clouds would *probably* extend', then they are hedging, taking refuge, quibbling, and we are entitled to suspect that their prediction, even though guarded and restricted, was an improper one—i.e. one made on inadequate grounds. (At this point the use of the modal term 'probably' to mark the sub-standard quality of the *evidence* and *argument* at the speaker's disposal begins to enter the picture.)

Further, if you use the word 'probably' in predictions correctly, you are not permitted to prove mistaken either always or often, even though you may be expressly covered every time. In predictions as in promises, by saying 'probably' you make yourself answerable for fulfilment on a reasonable proportion of occasions: it is not enough that you have an explanation of each single failure. In predictions, again, certain forms of words must be ruled out. 'The cloud will probably extend to the rest of the country, but it won't' is no more permissible than 'I'll probably come, but I shan't be able to', 'I promise I will, but I may fail' or 'I know it is so, but I may be mistaken'. For a guarded prediction, though distinct from a positive prediction, is properly understood as giving the hearer reason to expect (hope for, prepare for, etc.) that which is forecast, even though he is implicitly warned not to bank on it; and to utter even a qualified prediction is incompatible with flatly denying it.

One distinction needs to be remarked on at this point, since neglect of it can lead one into philosophical difficulties here as elsewhere. What an utterance actually states is one thing: what it implies, or gives people to understand, is another. For instance, giving someone reason to expect something is not necessarily the same as explicitly saying, 'I expect it', or even, 'I expect it with reason'. The M.O. forecasters are not, as some philosophers have suggested, *saying* that they are quite certain that the cloud will reach N.W. England today but only fairly confident that it will extend to the rest of the country before the night is out; though they are of course *implying*, and giving one to understand this, since it is their business as weather forecasters not to say 'will spread' unless they are sure, or to say 'probably extending' unless they are fairly confident. What they are talking about is the weather: what we infer about their expectations is only implied by their actual utterances. 'Saying "I know"', as Professor Austin points out, 'is *not* saying "I have performed a specially striking feat of cognition, superior, in the same scale as believing and being sure, even to being merely quite sure": for there *is* nothing in that scale superior to being quite sure.... When I say "I know", *I give others my word: I give others my authority for saying* that "S is P".' So also, saying 'S is probably P' is *not* saying

'I am fairly confident, but less than certain, that S is P', for 'probably' does not belong in this series of words either. When I say 'S is probably P', I commit myself guardedly, tentatively or with reservations to the view that S is P, and (likewise guardedly) lend my authority to that view.

'IMPROBABLE BUT TRUE'

In the light of these examples, let me turn to the difficulties which one may find in connecting the statements about probability in Kneale's book with the kinds of everyday use we make of the family of words, 'probably', 'probable', 'probability', 'likely', 'chance' and so on.

The first difficulty consists in seeing in concrete terms what Kneale is claiming, when he uses the abstract noun 'probability' or his own neologisms 'probabilify' and 'probabilification', instead of more familiar locutions. This difficulty could probably be overcome, at least in part, by careful attention to the context, so for the moment I shall do little more than mention it. Certainly many of the things he expresses in terms of the noun 'probability' could be put in more concrete terms. For instance, in saying 'Probability often enables us to act rationally when without it we should be reduced to helplessness', he presumably has in mind this kind of fact: that to say of a man that he knows that it will probably rain this afternoon implies that he knows enough to be well advised to expect and prepare for rain this afternoon, though not enough to be seriously surprised if it holds off for once; whereas to say that he does not even know that much implies that he has nothing very definite to go on when it comes to predicting and preparing for the afternoon's weather—to describe him as 'reduced to helplessness' is however too strong. (I am less sure what we ought to make of the word 'probabilification' and we shall have to return to this question later.)

The second difficulty is more serious. For in several places in Kneale's introductory chapter, he not only misrepresents the familiar terms he is analysing and explaining, but in each instance *insists* on doing so, specifically claiming as good sense (despite appearances) something which is a manifest solecism—and a solecism for reasons which turn out to be philosophically important.

Three passages may be quoted in which this happens:

(i) 'Probability is relative to evidence; and even what is known to be false may be described quite reasonably as probable in relation to a certain selection of evidence. We admit this in writing history. If a general, having made his dispositions in the light of the evidence at his disposal, was then defeated, we do not necessarily say that he was a bad general, i.e. that he had a poor judgement about probabilities in military affairs. We may say that he did what was most sensible in the circumstances, because in relation to the evidence which he could and did obtain it was probable that he would win with those dispositions. Similarly what is known to have happened may be extremely improbable in relation to everything we know except that fact. "Improbable but true" is not a contradiction in terms. On the contrary, we assert just this whenever we say of a fact that it is strange or surprising.'[1] Against this argument four objections can be made. To begin with, what is known *by me* to be false may be spoken of quite reasonably as probable *by others*, having regard to the evidence at their disposal: I can, at most, speak of it as 'having seemed probable until it was discovered to be false'. Again, if we say that the general did what was most sensible in the circumstances, we do so because in relation to the evidence which he could and did obtain it must have seemed probable, and was perfectly reasonable to suppose, that he would win with those dispositions. The form of words 'It *was* probable that he would win...' can be understood here and now only as a report, in *oratio obliqua*, of what the general may reasonably have thought at the time. In the third place, what is now known to have happened may earlier have seemed extremely improbable, having regard to everything we then knew; and it may yet seem so, with reason, to one who knows now only what we knew then. But while he may properly, though mistakenly, speak of it as 'improbable', we who know what actually happened may not.

Finally, no one person is permitted, in one and the same breath, to call the same thing both improbable and true, for reasons we have already seen: to do this is to take away with one hand what is given with the other. So the form of words 'improbable but true' is ruled out—except as a deliberate shocker. One can perhaps imagine a newspaper columnist's trading on the queerness of this form of

[1] *Probability and Induction*, § 3, pp. 9–10.

words by using it as the title of a column similiar to Ripley's *Believe It or Not*, and no doubt this is the kind of possibility Kneale refers to in his last sentence; but in such a context the phrase 'Improbable but true' is an effective substitute for 'surprising' just because it is a contraction of '*seems* improbable but is true', rather than of '*is* improbable but is true'. (Whether or no we should say that 'improbable but true' is an actual contradiction is another question, and one that might get us into deep water, though I think a strong case could be made out for calling it one.) Certainly we can speak of a tale as improbable-sounding but true, and in the course of a conversation one person might speak of something as improbable until the other person assured him that it was true—after that, the sceptic would be limited to saying, 'It still *seems* to me most improbable', or more baldly, 'I don't believe it', since there is no place any longer for the words 'It *is* improbable'.

(ii) 'If I say "It is probably raining", I am not asserting in any way that it is raining, and the discovery that no rain was falling would not refute my statement, although it might render it useless.'[1] In this case it is unclear what Kneale would accept, or refuse to accept, as 'asserting something in *any* way'; and unclear also what exactly is the force of his distinction between rendering a statement useless and refuting it. But surely, if I say 'It is probably raining' and it turns out not to be, then (*a*) I was mistaken, (*b*) I cannot now repeat the claim, and (*c*) I can properly be called upon to say what made me think it was raining. (Answer, for instance: 'It sounded as though it was from the noise outside, but I see now that what I took to be rain was only the wind in the trees.') Does this not amount to refutation? Indeed, once we have found out for certain either that it is, or that it is not raining, the time to talk of probabilities at all is past: I cannot any longer say even that it is probably *not* raining—the guard is out of place.

(iii) 'We know now that the stories which Marco Polo told on his return to Venice were true, however improbable they may have been for his contemporaries.'[2] Kneale quotes this example on the very first page of his book, and places a good deal of weight on it: it is, he says, 'worth special notice, because it shows that what is improbable may nevertheless be true.' Yet it contains a vital ambiguity; and we cannot place any weight on it at all until this

---

[1] *Ibid.* § 2, p. 4. [2] *Ibid.* § 1, p. 1.

ambiguity is resolved. For are we to understand the words 'however improbable they may have been for his contemporaries' as being in direct or in indirect speech? If the latter, if for instance they report in *oratio obliqua* the reaction at the time of Marco Polo's fellow-countrymen, then the example may be perfectly well expressed, but it does not in any way show 'that what is improbable may nevertheless be true'—i.e. that what is properly spoken of as improbable may by the same person and in the same breath be properly spoken of as true. If on the other hand it is intended to be in direct speech, as it must be if it is to prove what Kneale claims that it proves, then it is expressed very loosely. However improbable the stories which Marco Polo told on his return to Venice may have seemed to his contemporaries, we know now that they were substantially true: we therefore have no business to describe them as ever having been improbable, since for us to do this tends in some measure to lend our authority to a view which we know to be false.

In each of these passages, Kneale skates over one or both of two closely-related distinctions, which are implicit in our ordinary manner of speaking about probabilities and essential to the meaning of the notion. The first of these is the distinction between saying that something is or was probable or improbable (e.g. 'This man's stories of a flourishing empire far away to the east are wildly improbable', or 'The idea that theirs was by far the richest empire in the world had become so ingrained in the Venetians that tales of one yet richer were not likely to be believed'), and saying that it seems or seemed probable or improbable ('Though substantially true, Marco Polo's stories of a flourishing empire far away to the east *seemed* to the Venetians of his time wildly incredible and improbable'). The second concerns the difference in the backing required for claims that something is probable or improbable, when these claims are made by different people or at different times: at several places in the passages I have quoted, it is left unstated by whom or on what occasion the claim that 'probably so-and-so' is made, although it makes a vital difference to the grammar and sense how one fills in the blanks.

Neglected though they have been, these two distinctions are of central importance for the subject of probability, and they are more subtle than is usually recognised. We must spend a little time getting them straight, before we can hope to see more clearly the nature of the problems with which philosophers of probability concern themselves.

IMPROPER CLAIMS AND MISTAKEN CLAIMS

We can throw into relief these features of probability ('probably', 'it seemed probable', etc.) by setting them alongside the corresponding features of knowledge ('I know', 'He knew', 'I didn't know', 'He thought he knew', etc.).

The chief distinction to examine for these purposes is that between saying of someone 'He claimed to know so-and-so, but he didn't', and saying 'He thought he knew, but he was mistaken'. Suppose that I am trying to grow gentians on my rock-garden, and that they are not doing at all well. A plausible neighbour insists on giving me his advice, telling me what in his view is the cause of the trouble, and what must be done to remedy it. I follow his advice, and afterwards the plants are in a worse condition than ever. There are at this stage two subtly, but completely different things I can say about him and his advice: I can say 'He thought he knew what would put matters right, but he was mistaken' or I can say 'He claimed to know what would put matters right, but he didn't.'

To see the differences between these two sorts of criticism, consider what kinds of thing would be proper responses to the challenge, 'Why (on what grounds) do you say that?' If I say 'He thought he knew what would put matters right, but he was mistaken', and I am asked *why* I say that, there is only one thing to do in reply namely, to point to the drooping gentians. He prescribed a certain course of treatment, and it was a failure: that settles the matter.

If however I say instead, 'He claimed to know what would put matters right, but he didn't', the complaint is quite a different one. When asked why I say so, I shall give some such answer as, 'He has no real experience of gardening', or 'He may be an expert gardener in his own line, but he doesn't understand alpines', or 'He only looked at the plants: with gentians you have to start by testing the soil', or 'He may have tested the soil, but he tested it for the wrong things', ending up, in each case, '...so he *didn't* know (was in no position to know) what would put matters right'. I am now attacking, not the prescription itself, but one of two wholly other things: either the man's credentials, as in the first two answers, or his grounds for prescribing what he did, as in the second two. Indeed, the condition of the gentians is actually irrelevant, except as an indication of these other things: one might say, 'He didn't know...' even in a case where his prescription was in fact successful ('It was only a lucky guess'). Equally, when I claim that he was mistaken, the quality of his credentials and reasoning is irrelevant: 'He thought he knew what would put matters right, and no one could be better qualified or in a better position to say, but he was mistaken nevertheless.'

To put this briefly: the phrase 'He didn't know' serves to attack the claim *as originally made*, whereas the phrase 'He was mistaken' serves to correct it *in the light of subsequent events*. In practice, we recognise a clear distinction between an 'improper' claim to know something, and a claim which subsequently turns out to be 'mistaken'. Criticism designed to attack (discredit, cancel out) a claim to know or to have known something, as opposed to correcting (modifying, revising) it in the light of events, must proceed in the first place by attacking, not the conclusion claimed as known, but the argument leading up to it or the qualifications of the man making the claim. Showing that a claim to know something proved in the event a mistaken one may do nothing at all towards showing that it was at the time an improper claim to make.

The distinction between 'It *seemed* probable, but it turned out otherwise' and 'It *was* probable, though we failed to realise it' is a parallel one. An insurance company may be prepared to ask only a small premium from a man of thirty whom they understand from their inspecting doctor to have chronic heart trouble, in exchange for an annuity policy maturing at age 80; for they will argue, reasonably enough, that he is very unlikely to live that long. But what if he does? What are they to say on his 80th birthday, as the chief accountant adds his signature to the first of many sizeable cheques?

This depends on the circumstances: two possibilities in particular must be remarked on. It may be that advances in medical science, unforeseen and unforeseeable at the time when the policy was issued, have in the course of the intervening fifty years revolutionised the treatment of this type of heart disease, and so (as we might in fact put it) increased the man's chances of living to eighty. In this case, the directors of the company will cast no aspersions on the data and computations originally employed in fixing the premium if they admit to having under-estimated his chances of living so long, saying, 'It seemed to us at that time, for the best possible reasons, extremely improbable that he would live that long; but in the event our estimate has proved mistaken.' Looking back over the recent records of the company, they may now produce a revised estimate, corresponding to the estimate they would originally have made, could they have known then all that we are in a position to know now about the progress medicine was to make in the intervening years— this they will refer to as the chance he actually was to have of living to eighty, as opposed to that which at the time it seemed he would. (This case is like the ones in which we say, 'He thought he knew, but he was mistaken', when we revise and correct a past claim without seeking to criticise its propriety.)

Alternatively, that which was responsible for the discrepancy between their expectation and the event may have been, not so much the advance of medicine, as some fault in the original data or computation. On looking into the matter, they may be led to any of several conclusions: for instance, that he bribed the doctor to say he had chronic heart disease when he had not, or that the doctor's report referred to another man of the same name and got on to his file by mistake, or that his was an exceptional, sub-acute form of the disease which it is hard to tell from the normal one, or, in other cases, that the clerk looked at the wrong page of figures when working out his chances, or that their tables for farm-workers were based on too small a sample.

In these circumstances, the directors will have to criticise the estimate as originally made, and admit that the company failed to recognise at the time just how large his chances of survival were: 'His chances of living to eighty were really quite good; but, being misled by the doctor, the clerk or the records, we failed to recognise this.' (The present case is like those in which we say, 'He claimed to know, but he didn't': the propriety of the original claim is being attacked, and the fact that it also proved mistaken in the event is only incidental.)

To sum up: over claims that something is probable, as over claims to know something, we recognise in practice a difference between attacking a claim as originally made, and correcting it in the light of subsequent events. Once again, we distinguish a claim which was improper at the time it was made from one which subsequently turned out to have been mistaken; and criticism directed against the claim as originally made must attack the backing of the claim or the qualifications of the man who made it—showing that in the event it proved mistaken may do nothing to establish that it was at the time an improper claim to make.

Before we go on to discuss the philosophical importance of these distinctions, we must take a look at another distinction closely related to them: between the grounds required as backing for a claim, either to know something or that something is probable, when this claim is made and considered *on different occasions*.

When my neighbour makes his claim to know what will set my gentians right, then, if his claim is to be a proper one, he must be sure of three things: that he has enough experience, of flowers in general and of alpines in particular, to be in a position to speak; that he has made all the observations and performed all the tests which can reasonably be demanded of him; and that the judgement he bases on these observations is a reasonably considered one. Provided that these conditions are fulfilled, he has done what we are entitled to require to ensure that his judgement is a trustworthy one, one which provides a fit basis for action. He is then entitled to make the claim, 'I know...' and, unless we mistrust his judgement, we can equally properly take his word for it and say, 'He knows...'. The fact that the gerundive forms 'trust*worthy*' and '*fit* basis' are naturally used here is important.

The same considerations apply to the insurance company's claim that their prospective client is very unlikely to live to eighty. They are required to satisfy themselves that their records are sufficiently comprehensive to provide a reliable guide, that the data about the client on which their estimate is based are complete and correct, and that the computation is done without slips. Given these things, we can accept their claim as a proper one, for they too have ensured that, in the present state of knowledge, the estimate is a trustworthy one.

Whether a prediction is uttered with all your authority ('I know that p') or with reservations ('Probably p'), the situation is the same. If you have shown that there is *now* no concrete reason to suppose that this particular prediction will prove mistaken, when so many others like it have stood the test of time, all that can now be required of you before making the claim, 'I know that p' or 'Probably p', has been done. If anyone is ever to attack the *propriety* of your prediction, or say with justice, 'He claimed to know, but he didn't' or 'He failed to see how small the chances were', it is this claim which he will have to discredit.

This is a perfectly practical claim, and it must not be confused with another, and clearly futile one—the claim that your prediction can remain, despite the passage of time, beyond all reach of possible future amendment; that you can see to it now that there will never be any question of asking, in the light of future events, whether after all you were not mistaken. For, as time passes, the question whether the prediction *remains* a trustworthy one can always be reopened. Between the time of the prediction and the event itself, fresh considerations may become relevant (new discoveries about gentians, new treatments for heart trouble) and the backing which must be called for, if the predictions are to be repeated, may in consequence become more stringent. Furthermore, after the event itself has taken place, one can check what actually happened. So, however proper the original claim to know may have been, when uttered, the retrospective question, 'Was he right?', can always be reconsidered in the light of events, and the answer may in course of time have to be modified.

All this seems natural enough, if one comes to it without irrelevant preconceptions. After all, if it is the *trustworthiness* of a prediction that we are considering, the standards of criticism which are appropriate (the grounds which it is reasonable to demand in support of it) must be expected to depend on the circumstances in which it is being judged, as well as on those in which it was originally uttered. At the time a prediction is uttered, it does not even make sense to include 'eye-witness accounts of the event itself' among the evidence demanded in support of it: if this did make sense, it would be wrong to call the utterance a prediction. But if we ask ourselves retrodictively, after the event, whether the claim actually provided a fit and proper basis for action, it is only reasonable for us to demand that it should in fact have been fulfilled.

Has this discussion a moral? If we are to keep clear in our minds about knowledge and probability, we must remember always to take into account the occasion on which a claim is being judged, as well as that on which it was uttered. It is idle to hope that what is true of claims of the forms, 'I know', He knows' and 'It is probable', will necessarily be true of claims of the forms, 'I knew', 'He knew' and 'It was probable'; or that what is true of such claims when considered before the event will necessarily be true of them when reconsidered in the light of events. Claims of this kind cannot be considered and judged *sub specie aeternitatis*, 'from outside time' as it were: the superstition that they can may play havoc with the most careful arguments. Just those vital differences are liable to be overlooked, and just this superstition fostered, if one discusses probability, knowledge and belief in terms of abstract nouns, instead of considering the verbs and adverbs from which they derive their meaning.

THE LABYRINTH OF PROBABILITY

There can be no doubt, therefore, of the philosophical relevance of the distinctions to which I drew attention in criticising Kneale's opening chapter, and tried to map out in the last section—distinctions which are firmly rooted in our everyday ways of thinking, but which Kneale goes out of his way to deny. The questions we must now ask are, first, what is the special importance of these distinctions for the philosophy of probability; and secondly, whether the direction of Kneale's conceptual eccentricities throws any light on the things he says about probability and 'probabilification'.

I think it is possible to see, in outline at any rate, how the attention of philosophers discussing this subject has come to be focused on the wrong questions—and not just on the wrong ones, but on *wrong 'uns*. In recent philosophical discussions about probability, the chief bogy has been subjectivism: that is to say, the view that statements expressed in terms of probability are not about the outside world, but about the speaker's attitude to, and beliefs about, the world. The object of the philosophers' quest has therefore been to formulate a watertight definition of the notion in sufficiently objective terms; and the questions from which discussion has begun have been questions like, 'What *is* Probability?' 'What are probability-statements *about*?' 'What is the true *analysis* of probability-statements?' and 'What do they *express*?' Kneale evidently feels that, though the subjectivist's position is grossly paradoxical, the case for this position is *prima facie* a strong one, for he makes its refutation his first business; and he has no doubts about the proper starting-point:

If, as seems natural, we start by contrasting probability-statements with statements in which we express knowledge, the question immediately arises: 'What then do we express by probability-statements?'[1]

And indeed, when this kind of question is asked, we are at first at a loss, not knowing quite what to point to, quite where to look. Let us see why this happens.

If you ask me what the weather is going to do, and looking up at the sky I reply, 'There will be rain this evening', the question what my statement is about, or refers to, gives rise to no particular philosophical difficulty. The common-sense answer, 'The evening's weather', is acceptable to all, and if I turn out to have been right (spoken truly, predicted correctly) this seems very happily accounted for by saying that what I predicted was a fact—indeed was 'a fact', a perfectly definite 'fact' about the evening's weather: namely, its raining this evening. But if I reply instead, 'There will *probably* be rain this evening', philosophy and common-sense tend to part company. Though the common-sense answer to the question what I am talking about remains 'the evening's weather', philosophers feel scruples about accepting this as an answer. For if we try to answer the question in an infinitely specific way, what are we to pick on? By using the word 'probably', I explicitly avoid tying myself down positively to any particular prediction (e.g. that it *will* rain this evening) and so, it seems, to any particular 'fact'; even if it does not rain, I may find some let-out ('The clouds were piling up all the evening, but didn't actually discharge till they got a bit further inland: still, it was touch-and-go the whole time'); so we are apparently unable to point to any one 'thing' about the evening's weather such that, if it happens, I spoke truly and, if it does not happen, I was wrong. This discovery makes us feel that the 'link with the future', which we think of—though to our jeopardy—as present in the case of positive predictions, has in the case of guarded predictions been irreparably severed; and we are uncomfortable about saying any longer that my statement refers to, is about, or is concerned with the evening's weather, still more about saying that

[1] *Op. cit.* § 2, p. 3.

it expresses a future fact. We dread the metaphysician's challenge to say *what* fact it expresses.

Having reached this point, we are wide open to the subjectivist's attack. He has noticed one thing (perhaps the only one) which is always the case whenever the word 'probably', or one of its derivatives, is used correctly: everyone who says and means 'Probably *p*' does *believe confidently* that *p*. And if this is the only thing which is always the case, he argues, it must likewise be the only fact which the word 'probability' can refer to or denote. In advancing his doctrine that the real topic of probability-statements is the speaker's 'strong belief that *p*', he can therefore challenge us to point to anything else: 'If what we mean by "probability" isn't *that*, what is it?'

This question puts us in a quandary. Obviously there is something extremely queer about the subjectivist's doctrine. Degrees of belief cannot be all that matter, for over most issues belief of one degree is more reasonable (is more justified, ought rather to be held) than belief of another. As Kneale puts it, 'When a man sees a black cat on his way to a casino and says, "I shall probably win today: give me your money to place on your behalf", we decline the invitation if we are prudent, even although we believe the man to be honest.'[1] Whatever probability is, we want to say, it must be more objective than the subjectivist can allow: 'The essential point is that the thinking which leads to the formation of rational opinion, like any other thinking worth the name, *discovers* something independent of thought. We think as we ought to think when we think of things as they are in reality; and there is no other sense in which it can be said that we ought to think so-and-so.' Instead of suspecting the propriety of the questions, what *exactly* my statement was about (as opposed, of course, to the common-sense answer), and what *exactly* it is that we mean by this word 'probability', we press onwards into the murk: it seems vital to find an answer of some kind to these questions for, if we fail to do so, shall we not be letting the case go to the subjectivist by default?

When we begin looking around to see what exactly to say probability-statements are about, simply in virtue of being probability-statements, several candidates present themselves. The frequency with which events of the kind we are considering happen in such circumstances: if we bear in mind what goes on in life insurance

[1] *Op. cit.* § 2, p. 7.

offices, this seems to have strong claims. The proportion which the event under consideration represents of the number of alternative possible happenings: when we remember the calculations we did at school about dice, packs of playing-cards, and bags full of coloured balls, this in its turn seems an attractive suggestion. The philosophy of probability, as traditionally presented, is largely a matter of canvassing and criticising the qualifications of these and other candidates. For once, however, let us refrain from plunging any deeper into the labyrinth: if we return the way we came, we can find reasons for believing that our present dilemma, which gives the search for the 'real' subject-matter of probability-statements its appearance of importance, is one of our own making.

These reasons are of two kinds. In the first place, the abstract noun 'probability'—despite what we learnt at our kindergartens about nouns being words that stand for things—not merely has no tangible counterpart, referent, *designatum* or what you will, not merely does not name a thing of whatever kind, but is a word of such a type that it is nonsense even to talk about it as denoting, standing for, or naming anything. There are therefore insuperable objections to any candidate for the disputed title; and in consequence, over the question what probability-statements are about, common-sense has the better of philosophy. There can be probability-statements about the evening's weather, about my expectation of life, about the performance of a race-horse, the correctness of a scientific theory, the identity of a murderer—in fact, any subject on which one can commit oneself, with reservations, to an opinion —quite apart from the guarded undertakings, cautious evaluations, and other sorts of qualified statement in which the word 'probability' can equally properly appear: e.g. 'Andrea Mantegna was, in all probability, the most distinguished painter of the Paduan School.'

Conversely, there is no special thing which all probability-statements must be about, simply in virtue of the fact that they are probability-statements. By refusing not only to produce anything as the universal answer to this question but even to countenance the production of other answers, we do not, accordingly, leave the subjectivist in possession of the field: for the thing which he puts up as a candidate is in as bad a case as all the others. It is true that the subjectivist misses the point of probability-statements and that they are, in some sense, more objective than he will allow, but two other points must be remarked on—first, that the objectivity which the subjectivist fails to provide is not of the kind which philosophers have sought; and second, that the discovery of a tangible *designatum* for the word 'probability', quite apart from being a delusory quest, would in no way help to fill the gap.

These last two points must be argued in order for, if I understand his argument aright, Kneale recognises some of the force of the first point but entirely misses the second.

PROBABILITY AND EXPECTATION

Consider, first, in what kinds of context the noun 'probability' enters our language. Sometimes the Meteorological Office, instead of saying, 'Cloud will *probably* extend to the rest of the country during the night', may say, 'Cloud will *in all probability* extend...'. By choosing this form of words instead of the shorter 'probably', they are understood to weaken the force of the tacit reservation, implying that the indications are now very nearly clear enough for one to make a positive prediction; and they thereby make it necessary for themselves to produce a more elaborate explanation if the cloud fails to turn up as predicted. Promises and predictions of the form 'In all probability *p*', as opposed to 'Probably *p*', must be fulfilled not only on a reasonable proportion of occasions, but on nearly all: if we have to fall back at all often on excuses or explanations, we can be told to be more careful before committing ourselves so far. Apart from this, however, there is little difference between the two forms: the phrase 'in all probability' serves *as a whole* a purpose of the same kind as the single word 'probably'.

Likewise with such phrases as, 'The balance of probabilities suggests that cloud will extend...' and 'The probability that cloud will extend...is high': in either case, the word 'probability' gets its meaning as a part of a phrase which serves *as a whole* a similar purpose to 'probably'. Each of the metaphorical turns of phrase, suggesting, e.g., that a pair of weighing-scales would be needed in order to answer so open a question, is taken as weakening or strengthening the force of the implicit reservations, so making the assertion itself either more or less positive and failure in fulfilment correspondingly less or more excusable. Whatever else it does, it certainly does not imply the existence of a thing or stuff called 'probability' which can literally be weighed in a balance. (How, then, is it that one can express probabilities numerically? This is a question we shall return to shortly.)

If we consider only phrases like 'in all probability' and 'the balance of probabilities', there seems little point in talking about probability and probabilities in isolation; and, if the word 'probability' never appeared except in phrases which were obviously either unities or metaphors, there might be less temptation than there is to ask what—taken by itself—that word denotes. But the situation is more complicated. Sentences like 'The probability of their coming is negligible' remind us of other sentences, such as 'The injuries he sustained are negligible'; and we are therefore inclined to talk as though probabilities could be discussed in isolation quite as sensibly as injuries.

This resemblance is, however, misleading. If we say, 'The injuries he sustained are negligible', we mean that *the injuries themselves* can safely be neglected; and, if asked how we know or on what grounds we say this, we can appeal to experience, explaining that *experience has shown* that injuries of this type will heal themselves without complications. On the other hand, if we say, 'The probability of their coming is negligible', we mean something of a different kind. What may safely be neglected in this case is not the probability of their coming for, when compared with the wholly unmysterious statement, 'It is safe to neglect his injuries', the statement, 'It is safe to neglect "the probability of their coming"', is hardly even grammatical English: rather, what may safely be neglected is the *preparations against* their coming—and this is surely what we are meant to understand. The sentence, 'The probability of their coming is negligible', is in practice less like 'The injuries he sustained are negligible' than it is like 'The *danger from* his injuries is negligible.' Both sentences must be understood by reference to their practical implications, namely, that his injuries are such that complications need not be feared or guarded against, or that under the circumstances their coming is something that need not be expected, feared or prepared for. The word 'danger', like 'probability', is most at home in whole phrases—e.g. *danger of* complications, death by drowning or bankruptcy, *from* injuries, a mad bull or high-tension cables, *to* life and limb, peace or navigation.

When we are talking about the implications of probabilities, as opposed to those of injuries, an appeal to experience is neither needed nor even meaningful. We can talk of experience teaching us that there is no need to dress superficial grazes, or to expect shade temperatures of 105° F in England; but we cannot speak of experience teaching us that there is no need to expect the extremely unlikely, nor of experience teaching us that things having high probabilities are more to be expected than those with low ones. Correspondingly, one can ask why, under what circumstances, or how we know that there is no need to dress superficial grazes; but not why, under what circumstances or how we know that there is no need to expect the extremely unlikely. Such questions do not arise about truisms.

This last fact provides us with a test with which we can rule out a large proportion of the suggested definitions of 'probability': if a definition is to be acceptable, it must share at least this characteristic with the word defined. Any analysis of 'probability' which neglects this requirement commits the general fallacy which G. E. Moore has recognised in the field of ethics, and christened 'the naturalistic fallacy'. Just as it becomes clear that 'right' cannot be analysed in terms of (say) promise-keeping alone, when one sees that the questions 'But *is* promise-keeping right?' and 'But *ought* one to keep one's promises?' are at any rate not trivial; and that 'impossible' cannot, even in mathematics, be analysed solely in terms of contradictoriness, because the statement that contradictory suppositions are to be ruled out is more than a tautology; so also it becomes clear that 'probability' cannot be analysed in terms of (say) frequencies or proportions of alternatives alone, when one notices that it is certainly not frivolous to ask whether, or why, or over what range of cases, observed frequencies or proportions of alternatives do *in fact* provide the proper backing for claims about probabilities—i.e. claims about what is to be expected, reckoned with, and so on. To attempt to define what is meant by the probability of an event in terms of such things is to confuse the meaning of the term 'probability' with the grounds for regarding the event as probable, i.e. with the grounds for expecting it; and, whatever we do or do not mean by 'probability', whether or no the word can properly stand on its own, these two things are certainly distinct. As with so many of those abstract nouns formed from gerundive adjectives which have puzzled philosophers down the ages—nouns like 'goodness', 'truth', 'beauty', 'rightness', 'value' and 'validity' —the search for a tangible counterpart for the word 'probability', once begun, is bound to be endless: whatever fresh candidate is proposed, Moore's fatal questions can be asked about that also.

To say that the term 'probability' cannot be analysed in terms of frequencies or proportions of alternatives is not, however, to say that the role of these things in the practical discussion of probabilities is not an important one, and one which needs clarification. Rather the reverse; for it shows that they are to be regarded, not as rival claimants to a tinsel crown—each claiming to be the real *designatum* of the word 'probability'—but as different types of grounds, either of which can properly be appealed to, in appropriate contexts and circumstances, as backing for a claim that something is probable or has a probability of this or that magnitude.

This at once raises the very interesting question, what it is about some cases and contexts that makes observed frequencies the relevant kinds of grounds to appeal to, and why proportions of alternatives are the things to look for in others. The distinction has something to do with the difference between *objets trouvés* and events beyond our control on the one hand, and the products of manufacture on the other. The 'perfect die' of our algebraic calculations is both a theoretical ideal and a manufacturers' specification. In applying the results of our calculations about ratios of alternatives to an actual die, we take for granted that the makers succeeded near enough in reaching this ideal, and this assumption is usually close enough for practical purposes. But if all our dice grew on trees, instead of being made by skilled engineers, we might well feel it necessary to test them in the laboratory before use and so end up talking about the chances with dice, too, as much in terms of frequencies as in terms of proportions of alternatives.

While we are on this point we can afford to inquire why the definitions in terms of frequencies and proportions of alternatives have proved so attractive. In part, this seems to be the result of an excessive respect for mathematics; so it is worth reminding ourselves that the sums we did in algebra about 'the probability of drawing two successive black balls from a bag' were as much *pure* sums as those others about 'the time taken by four men to dig a ditch 3 ft. × 3 ft. × 6 ft.'. The former have no more intimate a connection with probability, and throw no more light on what we *mean* by the term, than the latter have to do with time or its metaphysical status.

The attempt to find some 'thing', in terms of which we can analyse the solitary word 'probability' and which all probability-statements whatever can be thought of as really being about, turns out therefore to be a mistake. This does not imply that no meaning can be given to the term: 'probability' has a perfectly good meaning, to be discovered by examining the way in which the word is used in everyday and scientific contexts alike, in such phrases as 'there is a high probability, or a probability of 4/5, that...' and 'in all probability'. It is with such an examination that we must begin the philosophy of 'probability', rather than with questions like 'What is Probability?' and 'What do probability-statements express?', if we are not to start off on the wrong foot. To say that a statement is a probability-statement is *not* to imply that there is some one thing which it can be said to be about or express. There is no single answer to the questions, 'What do probability-statements express? What are they about?' Some express one thing: some another. Some are about to-morrow's weather: some about my expectation of life. If we insist on a unique answer, we do so at our own risk.

The way in which a false start can queer our pitch comes out if we consider the second point: the problem of objectivity in proba-bility-statements. There are certainly important reasons why the subjectivist's account is deficient and why we find it natural to describe probability (as Kneale does) as something objective, in-dependent of thought, which has to be 'discovered'. But so long as we begin by looking for the *designatum* of the term 'probability', we are liable to suppose that it is this which must be found if we are to preserve the objectivity of probability-statements. The problem of justifying our description of such statements as objective thus gets entangled from the start with the vain search for the feature of the world we refer to by the word 'probability'. This is quite unnecessary, for the objectivity we actually require is of a very different kind.

What it is, we can remind ourselves if we recall how an insurance company comes to distinguish between an estimate of probability which can reasonably be relied on and a faulty or incorrect one. If the doctor lies, or the computer misreads the tables, or the data themselves are inadequate, then the estimate which the company will make of a client's chances of living to the age of eighty will not be as trustworthy a one as they think, nor as trustworthy a one as they are capable of producing. When the error comes to light, therefore, they can distinguish between the client's 'real' chance of living to eighty and their first, faulty estimate. Again, we saw how as the years pass and the relevant factors alter they come further to distinguish between the best possible estimate which was, or indeed could have been made when the policy was issued, and the estimate which they now see in the light of subsequent events would have been more trustworthy. Medicine makes unexpectedly rapid strides and this type of heart disease is mastered, so their client's expectation of life increases: they therefore distinguish the chance he 'actually had', or was to have, of living to eighty from the chance which in the first place he seemed reasonably enough to have. In either case, they do so because it is their business to produce estimates which can be relied on, and what immediately concerns them is the *trustworthiness* of their estimates. Trustworthiness, reliability, these are what distinguish an 'objective' estimate of the chances of an event from a mere expression of confident belief. And it is in ignoring the need for estimates of probability to be *reliable* that the subjectivist (who talks only about degrees of belief) is at fault. What factors are relevant, what kind of classification will in fact prove most reliable, these are things which insurance companies and actuaries can discover only in the course of time, from experience. But whatever the answers to these questions, we certainly need not delay asking them until we have found out definitely what it is that the word 'probability' denotes—if we were to do that we should never be in a position to ask them.

PROBABILITY-RELATIONS AND PROBABILIFICATION

Let us return to the first chapter of Kneale's *Probability and Induction*. We can now see how, in seeking to prove that probability possesses a kind of almost tangible objectivity which it neither can have nor needs, Kneale sacrifices even the possibility of that other objectivity which we in practice demand and which makes the notion of probability what it is.

Kneale sees clearly enough that one cannot treat probability as an intrinsic character, possessed by every proposition or event which

can ever properly be spoken of as probable: 'No proposition (unless
it is either a truism or an absurdity) contains in itself anything to
indicate that we ought to have a certain degree of confidence in it'[1]
—after all, one person may properly, though mistakenly, regard as
probable what another equally properly says is untrue. He therefore
abandons the demand for some *single* thing, which can be called '*the*
probability of an event'. But, rather than appear to surrender to the
subjectivist, rather than give up as vain the search for that which all
probability-statements express, he cuts his losses, and defines 'probability' as a 'relation' between the proposition guardedly asserted
and the grounds for asserting it. A 'probability-relation' is said to
exist between the evidence and the proposition, and the evidence is
said to 'probabilify' the proposition to some degree or other. The
probability which we talk of an event as possessing is thus still thought
of as being in the nature of a 'thing' (sc., an objective relation), but
it is now any of a large number of different 'things', according to
the evidence at one's disposal. If this comes as a surprise, that, he
says, is because 'our probability statements are commonly elliptical'
and the particular batch of evidence understood to be relevant 'is
not immediately recognizable'.[2]

Kneale's suggestion is an unhappy one, for several reasons. Quite
apart from the conceptual eccentricities which it encourages, it leads
him to deny to probability the very kind of objectivity which really
does matter. When an insurance company obtains fresh information
about a client and in the light of this information a new estimate is
made of his expectation of life, this estimate is commonly spoken
of as being a more accurate (i.e. more trustworthy) estimate, a closer
approximation to his actual chance of survival. This piece of usage
Kneale recognises but condemns: 'Sometimes in such a case we
speak as though there were a single probability of the man's surviving to be sixty, something independent of all evidence, and our
second estimate were better in the sense of being nearer to this
single probability than our first. But this view is surely wrong.'[3]
He is forced to condemn this mode of expression because, in his
view, after discovering fresh evidence, the insurance company is
no longer concerned with the *same* probability-relation—and so
cannot strictly correct its estimate. This is only one special case
of the general paradox into which he is driven by his doctrine that

[1] *Op. cit.* § 2, p. 8.   [2] *Ibid.* § 3, p. 9.   [3] *Ibid.* § 3, p. 10.

'probability is relative to evidence'. According to him, whenever two people are in possession of different evidence, they cannot be said to contradict one another about the probability of an event *p*— cannot quarrel, apparently, as to how far one should be prepared to act as though, and commit oneself to the assertion that, *p*—for they are talking about different probability-relations!

Kneale's doctrine does not even escape the 'naturalistic fallacy', though this fact is partly obscured by his terminology. For there are two possible interpretations of what he says, one of them innocent, the other fallacious, and he seems committed to the latter. In the first place, one might suppose that he intended us to regard 'recognizing that a large degree of probabilification exists between, e.g., the evidence that a man of thirty has chronic heart disease, and the proposition that he will not live to eighty' as meaning the *same* as 'coming correctly to the conclusion that, in view of his physical condition, we cannot expect him to live that long (though we must bear in mind that 1 in 1000 of such cases does stagger on)'. If that were the proper interpretation, no objection could arise, for then he would be presenting us with a possible, though roundabout way of explaining the meaning of phrases like 'there is a small probability that' and 'in all probability'. But this does not seem to be his intention, for, if it were, then one could not even *ask* the question which, according to him, any adequate analysis of the probability-relation must answer: namely, the question, 'Why is it rational to take as a basis for action a proposition (that he will not survive) which stands in that relation (of being highly probabilified) to the evidence at our disposal?' For this would be to query a truism, being only an elaborate way of asking, 'Why need we not expect that which is extremely unlikely?'

The probability-relations of which Kneale writes are therefore to be thought of as *distinct* entities, coming logically between detailed evidence of the prospective client's age and physical condition and the practical moral that he need not be expected to survive (though of course one in a thousand does). At once all the objections to a naturalistic definition recur. Even if certain entities always were found 'between' the evidence and the conclusions we base on it, we could presumably only discover *from experience* that, in some or all circumstances, they can reasonably be relied on as a guide to the future, like the green cloud out at sea presaging a gale. The words 'probability', 'probably' and 'in all probability' could no more be analysed in terms of such entities as these than in terms of frequencies or proportions of alternatives, and for the same reasons. In that case we could properly ask the question Kneale regards as important —why, when our knowledge is less than we could wish, it is reasonable to rely on probability-relations but not on mere belief. This question would now be no more trivial than the question why, when butter and sugar are short, it is reasonable to rely on margarine but not on saccharine. In each case, however, the question would have to be answered by appeal either to direct experience or to independent information, such as that margarine contains enough fats and vitamins to be a nourishing as well as palatable substitute for butter, whereas saccharine, though it tastes sweet, has no nutritive value. Does Kneale intend us to regard probability-relations as the vitamins of probability? Only if that is how he sees them does his crucial question amount to more than a truism; but in that case there is no hope of their providing us with an *analysis of the term* 'probability'. No amount of talk about vitamins, calories, proteins and carbohydrates alone will serve to analyse what the word 'nourishing' *means*.

One question Kneale leaves very obscure: namely, what sort of room he sees for anything to come between the facts about a situation and the chances we can allot to any future event in view of these facts. He appears to believe that there are two substantial inferences between the evidence and the moral, not just one, and certain features of our usage do, it is true, suggest this: we say, e.g., 'He's got chronic heart-disease at thirty, *so* the probability that he'll live to eighty is low, *so* we needn't reckon on his living that long.' But, if asked what grounds we have for ignoring the possibility of his surviving, we point immediately to his age and physical condition and to the statistics: nothing substantial is added by saying instead, 'There is no need to reckon on his surviving, *because* the probability of his doing so is low, *because* he's got chronic heart-disease at thirty.' To put our reasons like this would be to present an artificially elaborate argument, like saying, 'Your country needs Y-O-U, and Y-O-U spells *you*.'

IS THE WORD 'PROBABILITY' AMBIGUOUS?

The criticisms which have been directed here against Kneale's views on probability may seem to be unnecessarily minute. Minute they perhaps are; but I shall try to show both now and subsequently how important it is for philosophers to recognise and respect the distinctions which we have here been pressing. Kneale's book is as patient and clear-headed a contribution to the recent controversy about the philosophy of probability as one could ask, yet it should be clear, I hope, how far the very problems with which he concerns himself arise as a result of misapprehending the true character of modal terms like 'probably', 'probable' and 'probability'. Once one has recognised how such terms serve, characteristically, to qualify the force of our assertions and conclusions, it is difficult any longer to take seriously the pursuit of a *designatum* for them. The whole interminable dispute, one cannot help thinking, keeps going only for so long as one construes these terms, not as the modal terms they are, but as something else.

This conclusion is forced on one even more strongly if one looks at the writings of Professor Rudolf Carnap on this subject. In his book, *Logical Foundations of Probability*, he constructs an elaborate mathematical system for handling the concept of probability and its close relations, and also gives us his views about the leading philosophical problems to which this notion gives rise. From the philosophical part of his book, two things in particular need to be discussed: a central distinction which he makes and insists on between two senses of the word 'probability' which in his view are unfortunately 'designated by the same familiar but ambiguous word', and also the arguments which he offers against allowing psychological considerations to enter into the discussion of probability and related subjects—arguments which he would undoubtedly consider told very strongly against the point of view adopted in this essay.

In advancing his first point, Carnap finds many allies. Kneale himself talks of there being 'two species of probability... two senses of "probability", one applicable in matters of chance, and the other applicable to the results of induction'.[1] Professor J. O. Urmson, too, has written a paper about 'Two Senses of "Probable"', advocating

[1] *Op. cit.* § 3, p. 13; § 6, p. 22.

a similar distinction, and some such division has often been hinted at by philosophers from F. P. Ramsey on.

It is easy enough, of course, to show that the classes of situation in which we make use of the word 'probability' and its affiliates are many and varied. But does this mean that the word has a correspondingly large number of meanings? We foresaw in the first of these essays, apropos of impossibility and possibility, the dangers of jumping too quickly to this type of conclusion, and it is a conclusion which Urmson has himself explicitly rejected in the case of the word 'good'. No doubt when I say, 'It is highly probable that, if you throw a dice twenty times, the sequence you get will include at least one six', I mean something different from what I do if I say, 'It is highly probable that Hodgkin's explanation of the role of phosphorus in nervous conduction is the correct one.' But are not the differences between these two statements fully accounted for by the differences between the sorts of inquiry in question?

By insisting, in addition, that two senses of 'probable' are involved, nothing is gained and something is lost. If you are considering the correctness or incorrectness of a scientific hypothesis, the sort of evidence to appeal to is of course different from that bearing on a prediction about dice-throwing: in particular, there is a place for sums in the latter case of a kind which could hardly come into the former. But, unless we are once again to confuse the grounds for regarding something as probable with the meaning of the statement that it is probable, we need not go on to say that there are, in consequence, a number of different senses of the words 'probable' and 'probability'. Nor indeed *should* we say this, for the word 'probable' serves a similar purpose in both sentences: in each case, what is at issue is the question how far one ought to take it, and commit oneself to the statement, either that Hodgkin's explanation is correct, or that a six will turn up. Suppose instead that one said, 'I know that Hodgkin's explanation is correct', or 'I know that if you throw this dice twenty times, a six will turn up at least once.' Here again, the sorts of evidence relevant to the two claims will be very different, but will it therefore follow that one is now using the word 'know' in two different senses? And in yet another, if one says, as a matter of mathematics, 'I know that the square root of 2 is irrational'? Surely the plea of ambiguity is in both cases too easy a way out.

In itself, then, there is nothing unprecedented in Carnap's claim that one should distinguish two senses of the word 'probability', two different concepts of probability, to be referred to respectively as 'probability$_1$' and 'probability$_2$'. On the one hand, he says, we have a *logical* concept, 'probability$_1$', which represents the degree of support that a body of evidence gives to an hypothesis; on the other hand, we have an *empirical* concept, 'probability$_2$', which is simply concerned with the relative frequency of events or things having one particular property among the members of the class of events or things having another property. What are novel are the exact ways in which Carnap understands this distinction, and the length to which he is prepared to carry it. For instance, he insists that we are here concerned, not with complementary aspects of a single conception, but with two quite distinct senses of the word 'probability'—a plain ambiguity, though one of which an etymological explanation can perhaps be given. He invites us to conclude that philosophers who have puzzled over the notion of probability were simply misled by this ambiguity—talking about different things, as in the celebrated dispute about the nature of *vis viva* between Leibniz and Descartes who (we can now see) were maintaining in opposition to one another perfectly compatible truths, the one about momentum, the other about kinetic energy. One may agree that a measure of cross-purposes enters into most disputes over probability, and yet feel that Carnap over-states his case. Not every distinction which needs drawing in philosophy can properly be presented as a distinction between different senses of a word; such a presentation, indeed, often conceals the real source of philosophical difficulty, and leaves one feeling that one's authentic problem has been conjured out of sight.

Carnap's account of the way in which evidence can support a scientific theory needs to be considered separately. For the moment, let us concentrate on his alleged distinction between probability$_1$ and probability$_2$, and see whether the two things are really as different as he paints them. To begin with probability$_2$: the key question we must ask is whether the word 'probability' is ever in fact used in practice to *mean* simply a ratio or relative frequency. No doubt it has been the practice to *say* this: von Mises, for instance, declares that the limiting value of the relative frequency of things of class B among things of class A is called the 'probability' of an A's being a B, and Carnap follows him in this. But a glance at the way in which probability theory is given a practical application should be enough to raise doubts about this dictum.

To test the view, we may consider the following table:

	I	II	III
a	25,785	2821	0·109
b	32,318	2410	0·075
c	16,266	785	0·047

Let the figures in the first column represent the numbers of people in the United Kingdom in specified categories '*a*', '*b*' and '*c*', alive on 1 January 1920; and the figures in the second column the numbers of these same people dying before 1 January 1930. In column III are shown the ratios of the figures in the two previous columns. The question which now needs to be asked is: 'What heading are we to put at the top of column III?' What, to use von Mises' word, are we to *call* these ratios?

The answer is that there is no uniquely appropriate heading. We are not obliged to call the ratios there tabulated by any one name: what we shall in fact call them will depend on our reasons for being interested in them, and in particular on the sort of moral we wish to draw from them. Consider three possibilities. We may be statisticians; the table shown may be, for us, just a sample table of vital statistics; and we may be interested in drawing no morals from it other than mathematical ones. In that case, a natural heading for column III will be 'Proportionate mortality over the decade 1920–9'. Alternatively, we may be engaged on research in social medicine; the table may be providing us with a way of assessing the physical condition of people in the classes '*a*', '*b*' and '*c*' a year after the end of the First World War; and we may accordingly be interested in drawing from the table morals *looking backwards* to the beginning of the decade. Since we are now taking the tabulated ratios as a measure of physical condition at this time, a natural heading will be 'Susceptibility of members of given class at 1. 1. 20'. Again, we may be actuaries; the table shown will then be a part of our Life Tables; and we shall be interested in it for the sake of the morals we can draw from it of a *forward-looking* kind. The ratios listed in column III will be taken as a measure of the chances which members of each class have of surviving a further ten years, and the natural heading will be, e.g., 'Probability of survival till 1. 1. 40'.

The term 'probability', that is to say, is not in practice allotted to ratios or relative frequencies *as such*: frequencies will be spoken of as probabilities only so far as we are using them as *measures* of probability when drawing morals about matters of fact at present unknown. Indeed, even to speak of ratios as probabilities is already to have taken the vital logical step towards the drawing of such a moral; the knowledge that only a minute fraction of sufferers from the disease which Jones has contracted live ten years is certainly the best of reasons for saying that we are not warranted in expecting him to survive that long, but the information that the probability of his surviving that long is minute *entails* that conclusion. Accordingly, we can pull von Mises up for declaring that his limiting ratios are simply *called* 'probabilities': if this is intended as an analysis of our existing notion of probability, it is faulty, and, if it is intended as a stipulative definition, it is a most unhappy one—he should say, rather, that these ratios are a *measure of* the probability of, say, an *A*'s being a *B*. It is interesting to remark that Laplace, in expounding the classical theory of probability, avoided this trap. He introduced the ratio 'favourable/total number of cases' not as a definition of probability, but as giving a measure of degree of probability and hence of our *espérance morale*; and though he did refer to this expression as a definition later in his treatise, he made it clear that the word was intended in a wide sense, to mark it off as an operational definition or 'measure' rather than as a philosophical analysis or dictionary entry.

The second leg of Carnap's distinction is therefore shaky. Frequencies are called probabilities only when used as supports for qualified predictions, practical policies and the like, so that 'frequency' is not a sense of the term 'probability' at all, and his account of probability$_2$ is unacceptable. Even where all our calculations are conducted in terms of frequencies, the conclusion, 'So the probability of *h* is so-and-so', does more than report the answer to a sum: its point is to draw from the sum the practical moral, 'So one is entitled to bank on *h* to such-an-extent', and the phrase 'bank on' can here be read in a more or less literal or figurative manner, according as the consequent policies are of a financial kind—as with actuaries and punters—or otherwise.

Difficulties also arise over Carnap's discussion of probability$_1$. Like Kneale, he considers that statements of the form 'The probability of h is so-and-so' are elliptical, since they omit all explicit reference to the batch of evidence in the light of which the probability was estimated. Like Kneale again, he prefers to reserve the term probability for the relation between an hypothesis, h, and the evidence bearing on it, e, and treats the term as a function of two separate variables, e and h.

This is one of the eccentricities we remarked on earlier in discussing Kneale's views: as we saw then, the probability of an event is normally regarded as one thing, the support which a particular batch of evidence gives to the view that the event will take place as another, and Kneale's account conceals the differences between them. To talk about evidential support is *of course* to talk both about hypothesis and about evidence, and different batches of evidence lend different degrees of support to the same hypothesis. Unlike probability as we normally understand it, the notion of support necessarily involves two variables: there is always that which supports and that which is supported. So it is not surprising that Carnap has to use such words as 'support' in the course of his explanation of probability$_1$. This fact is suggestive. Much confusion and cross-purposes would have been avoided if Carnap's probability$_1$, and the corresponding relations in treatises from Keynes onwards to Kneale, had been labelled 'support-relations' and not 'probability-relations' at all. This change would in no way affect the mathematical and formal side of the discussions; but it would make their interpretation a thousand times more felicitous. Many of us will never agree that probability is relative to evidence in any more than an epigrammatic sense; but we would agree instantly that *support* was, in the nature of the case, a function as much of evidence as of conclusion. If anything here is elliptical, it is not so much the everyday word 'probable' as the jargon phrases 'probability-calculus', 'probability-relation' and 'probabilification'. As Kneale himself has recognised, the formal properties of a calculus alone cannot entitle it to the name of 'the probability-calculus': it must rather be the calculus suitable for use in estimating probabilities—in estimating, that is, how much reliance we are entitled to place on this or that hypothesis.

In this respect support-relations are in the same boat as frequencies. We do not in practice give the name of 'probabilities' to degrees of support and confirmation as such: only so far as we are interested in hypothesis h, and the total evidence we have at our disposal is e, does the support-relation having *h* and *e* as its arguments become a measure of the probability we are entitled to allot to *h*. With support-relations as with frequencies, the conclusion we come to about *h* in the light of the evidence at our disposal, *e*, namely, that we are entitled to bank so far on *h*, is no mere repetition of the support which *e* gives to *h*: it is once again a *moral drawn from it*. The effect of writing the evidence into all probability-estimates is to conceal the vital logical step, from a hypothetical statement about the bearing of *e* on *h* to a categorical conclusion about *h*—from the inference-licence, 'Evidence *e*, if available, would suggest very strongly that *h*', to an argument in which it is actually applied, namely '*e*; so very likely *h*'. We are, of course, at liberty if we choose to *call* the bearing of *e* on *h* by the name of 'probabilification'; but it is as well to realise the dangers we expose ourselves to by such a strained—not to say elliptical—choice of terms.

Once we have distinguished the probability of *h* from the bearing of *e* on *h* or the support which *e* gives to *h*, we can see the saying that 'Probability is Relative to Evidence' for the epigram it is. Certainly the most reasonable estimate a man can make of the probability of some hypothesis depends in every case on the evidence at his disposal —not just any batch he chooses to consider, but *all* the relevant evidence he has access to—but equally, it depends on the same body of evidence whether he can reasonably conclude that a given state-ment is *true*. To put the point in other words, it depends on the evidence a man has at his disposal which of the possibilities he considers are to be accepted with complete trust (accepted as true) and what weight he is entitled to put on the others (how probable he should consider them). In each case, the reasonable conclusion is that which is warranted by the evidence, and the terms 'bearing', 'support' and the like are the ones we use to mark the relation be-tween the statements cited as evidence and the possibilities whose relative credibilities are being examined. However, all that goes here for 'probable' goes also for 'true'; so if we accept 'Probability is Relative to Evidence' as more than an epigram, then we are saddled with 'Truth is Relative to Evidence' as well. If this has been over-looked, it is because of the unhappy practice which has grown up among philosophers of using the word 'probability' interchange-ably with the words 'support' and 'bearing', and attributing to the first notion all the logical features characteristic of the other two.

The fundamental mistake is to suppose that the evidence in the light of which we estimate the likelihood of some view must always be written into the estimate we make, instead of being kept in the background and alluded to only implicitly. In fact, there are very good reasons for keeping it in the background. To begin with, the arguments for writing the evidence into probability-estimates, once accepted, must be extended: 'The truth of his statement is beyond doubt' must be supplanted on Carnap and Kneale's principles by 'The truth-value of his statement, on the available evidence, is 1' and a statement will have to be attributed as many truths as there are possible bodies of evidence bearing on it.

Carnap himself regards truth as exempt from the relativity to evidence which he attributes to probability$_1$. His reasons for treating them so differently are illuminating, for they illustrate his extremely literal interpretation of the principle of verifiability. This exposes him to the full rigours of the fatal question, 'What fact precisely do probability-statements express?', and springs presumably from his determination to deal only in concepts 'admissible for empiricism and hence for science'. Our use of 'probability$_1$-statements', he explains, is ostensibly inconsistent with the principle of verifiability; for, if we regard the statement 'The chances of rain tomorrow are one in five' as a variety of prediction, we can specify no happening which would conclusively verify or falsify it. Accordingly his principles compel him to conclude, either that this is 'a factual (synthetic) sentence without a sufficient empirical foundation' and so inadmissible, or else that it is not really a factual prediction at all, but rather a purely logical (analytic) sentence, and so of a kind which 'can never violate empiricism'. Carnap chooses the latter alternative and it leads him into paradoxes. But need he really have embraced either conclusion?

The way of escape from his dilemma we have already recognised. Of course one cannot specify any happening which would conclusively verify or falsify a prediction held out as having only a certain probability; for this is just what probability-terms are used to ensure. Yet such a statement need be none the less respectable and none the less of a prediction. It cannot be said to *fail* to obtain the highest honours (namely, *veri*fication) since it is not even a candidate for them. In the nature of the case, the evidence required to justify a prediction qualified by the adverb 'probably' or an affiliate is less than would be needed for a positive one, and the consequences to which one is committed by making it are weaker—to say that the chances of rain tomorrow are one in five is not to say *positively* that it either will or will not rain. Only statements which are held out as the positive truth need be criticised for straight unverifiability: predictions made with an explicit qualification, such as 'probably', 'the chances are good that' or 'five to one against' must therefore be exempted.

So much for Carnap's alleged distinction between the two concepts probability$_1$ and probability$_2$. We can see now why it is far too strong for him to talk of the word 'probability' as ambiguous, and to suggest that philosophical disputes about the nature of probability are futile and unnecessary for the same reasons as the *vis viva* dispute. Actually, statements about the probability of p are concerned, in practice, with the extent to which we are entitled to bank on, take it that, subscribe to, put our weight and our shirts on p, regardless of whether the phrase is used in a way Carnap would speak of in terms of probability$_1$ or in terms of probability$_2$. His decision whether to use the term 'probability$_1$' or the term 'probability$_2$' seems indeed to depend, not on the sense in which the word 'probability' is being used, for this is the same in both cases, but rather on whether he is paying attention to the formal or the statistical aspects of the arguments in support of p.

'Probable', like 'good' and 'cannot', is a term which keeps an invariant force throughout a wide variety of applications. It is closely connected with the idea of evidential support, but is distinct from that idea, for the same reasons that a categorical statement 'A, so B' is distinct from a hypothetical one 'If A, then B', or the conclusion of an argument from its backing. If we go to the length of *identifying* support with probability, then and only then will the latter term become ambiguous; but good sense will surely forbid us to do this. A mathematician who really identified impossibility and contradictoriness would have no words with which to rule out contradictions from his theorising; and by making probabilities identical with evidential support we should rob ourselves of the very terms in which we at present draw practical conclusions from supporting evidence.

PROBABILITY-THEORY AND PSYCHOLOGY

Why has the attention of philosophers been distracted from the characteristic modal functions of words like 'probable'? and why have they allowed themselves to be sidetracked in this way into the discussion of irrelevant disputes? One important factor, it appears, is their perennial fear of lapsing into psychology. One can find evidence of this motive at work in the writings both of Kneale and of Carnap. As we saw, the starting-point of Kneale's argument is the danger of subjectivism—the thing we must above all be at pains to avoid, he implies, is the conclusion that to talk about probabilities is to talk about one's actual strength of belief, and a main virtue of 'probability-relations' for him is the hope that appealing to these relations will rescue him from the subjectivist's pit. For Carnap, too, psychology presents an ever-looming danger; but its dangers for the theory of probability are, in his view, only one side of a more general danger which it presents to logic as a whole. At all costs, he asserts, the logician must avoid the dangers of 'psychologism', and in making good his escape from this wider peril he is driven once again into extravagances which Kneale avoids.

Let us look and see what Kneale has to say first.[1] He rejects, rightly enough, the view that statements in terms of probability have to be understood as telling us simply about the present strength of the speaker's beliefs: unfortunately, he thinks that in dismissing this jejune theory he is obliged to reject certain other points of view also. For instance, he discusses very briefly one 'traditional treatment' of sentences containing words like 'probably'—namely, that in terms of 'modes or manners of assertion'; this he feels bound to dismiss on the grounds that it too is 'a subjectivist theory'. But name-calling gets one nowhere, and the label must be justified. His only positive argument against this point of view depends upon the idea that 'if I say, "it is probably raining", the discovery that no rain was falling would not refute my statement', a remark which we criticised earlier both as paradoxical and as inconsistent with our common ways of thinking. Our own inquiries in these essays, on the other hand, strongly reinforce the view that 'probably' and its cognates are, characteristically, modal qualifiers of our assertions: so the question for us must be, why Kneale should object to such

[1] *Op. cit.* § 2, p. 3.

an account as a subjectivist one or see it as confusing logic with psychology.

This idea seems to be the result of a plain misunderstanding: let me indicate where this lies. Earlier in this essay, we distinguished between the things which an utterance positively *states*, and those which are not so much stated by it as *implied in* it. Neglect of this distinction regularly leads one into philosophical difficulties, and Kneale's present objections appear to arise from this very source. When the forecasters assert that it will rain tomorrow, what they are talking about is tomorrow's weather and not their own beliefs, though no doubt one can safely infer from their utterance that they do have beliefs of a certain kind. Likewise if they say, 'It will *probably* rain tomorrow', what they say is something about the weather, and what we can infer about their beliefs is only implied. The view that the function of words like 'probably' is to qualify the mode of one's assertions or conclusions is one thing: a proposal that one should analyse the statement 'It will probably rain tomorrow' as equivalent to 'I am on the whole inclined to expect that it will rain tomorrow' would be something quite different.

To say 'Probably p' is to assert guardedly, and/or with reservations, that p; it is *not* to assert that you are tentatively prepared to assert that p. If our present account of 'probably' and its cognates is to be criticised as subjectivist, one might as well level the same criticism against the doctrine that a man who says, honestly and sincerely, 'p', makes the assertion that p. For although a man who says 'p' does not positively assert that he is prepared to assert that p, he does thereby *show* that he is, and he thereby enables us to infer from what he says something about his present beliefs as surely as does a man who says, not 'p', but 'Probably p'. Either assertion, whether positive or guarded, is about the world or about the state of mind of the speaker as much as the other: if it is a mistake to regard the positive assertion as a statement about the speaker's state of mind then it is also a mistake to regard the qualified assertion in this way. In fact, either assertion 'p' or 'Probably p' is surely safe against Kneale's objection: whether the assertion is qualified or un-qualified, it is equally paradoxical to think of it as about the speaker's state of mind. We can, of course, infer things about the states of mind of our fellow-men from all the things they say, but it does not follow that all their statements are really autobiographical remarks.

Carnap's crusade against psychologism is more drastic: he detects this fallacy very widely, both in inductive and in deductive logic. It consists in essence, he says, of the view that 'logic is...the art of thinking, and the principles of logic...principles or laws of thought. These and similar formulations refer to thinking and hence are of a subjectivist nature.'[1] Being framed in psychological terms, he argues, they ignore the discoveries of Frege and Husserl, and can be labelled as 'psychologistic'. His position looks at first glance like a familiar one, but as we read on a certain extravagance shows itself; the flame-thrower with which, for instance, Frege gave such a well-merited scorching to the doctrine that numbers are a variety of mental image is employed by Carnap on some quite undeserving victims.

Primitive psychologism, the view that statements in logic are about actual mental processes, Carnap admits to be very rare. F. P. Ramsey toyed with a definition of 'probability' in terms of actual degrees of belief, but soon withdrew his support for it. The only unqualified instance Carnap thinks he can cite is a discussion of 'probability-waves' in quantum mechanics in Sir James Jeans's book *Physics and Philosophy*. The reference is an unhappy one. Jeans is rated severely for speaking of the quantum theorist's picture of the atom as one whose ingredients 'consist wholly of mental constructs'; and the rating is most unjust, since he is not calling probability a subjective concept but only speaking of the Schrödinger functions as theoretical fictions—which may or may not be a correct description of them, but is certainly a very different sort of story.

A great many logicians and mathematicians, from Bernoulli through Boole and de Morgan to Keynes, Jeffreys and Ramsey, are none-the-less convicted of 'qualified psychologism'. 'Still clinging to the belief that there must somehow be a close relation between logic and thinking, they say that logic is concerned with correct or rational thinking.' This mistake Carnap corrects:

> The characterisation of logic in terms of correct or rational or justified belief is just as right but not more enlightening than to say that mineralogy tells us how to think correctly about minerals. The reference to thinking may just as well be dropped in both cases. Then we say simply: mineralogy makes statements about minerals, and logic makes statements about logical relations. The activity in any field of knowledge involves, of course,

[1] *Logical Foundations of Probability*, § 11, p. 39.

thinking. But this does not mean that thinking belongs to the subject matter of all fields. It belongs to the subject matter of psychology but not to that of logic any more than to that of mineralogy.[1] One thing in this account is undoubtedly correct. There is certainly no reason why mental words should figure at all prominently in books on logic; especially if one thinks of belief, with Russell, as something having as one aspect 'an idea or image combined with a yes-feeling'. The important thing about drawing a proper conclusion is to be ready to *do* the things appropriate in view of the information at one's disposal: an actuary's respect for logic is to be measured less by the number of well-placed yes-feelings he has than by the state of his profit-and-loss account.

Nevertheless, Carnap's account reveals some important misconceptions. He talks, first, as though the meaning of the phrase 'logical relations' were transparent, and says that 'the formulation [of logic] in terms of justified belief is derivable from' that in terms of logical relations.[2] Secondly, he treats all logical relations, and hence all justified beliefs, all evidential support and all satisfactory explanations as relying for their validity on considerations of semantics alone. Waismann has criticised Frege for thinking that the statements of logic represent 'little hard crystals of logical truth': it is curious, therefore, that Carnap, following Frege, should put logical relations on a footing with minerals.

From our point of view, a characterisation of logic in terms of justified beliefs, actions, policies, and so on is unavoidable. For if logic is to have any application to the practical assessment of arguments and conclusions, these references are bound to come in. This is not at all the same as saying that thinking is the *subject-matter* of logic, as Carnap supposes: not even Boole, who chose the name *Laws of Thought* for his major logical treatise, can have meant that. The laws of logic are not generalisations about thinkers thinking, but rather standards for the criticism of thinkers' achievements. Logic is a critical not a natural science. To put the point bluntly: logic does not describe a subject-matter, and is not *about* anything— at any rate, in the way in which natural sciences such as mineralogy and psychology are about minerals or the mind. So Carnap's dictum, 'Logic makes statements about logical relations', is misleading as well as unrevealing.

[1] *Ibid.* § 11, pp. 41–2.   [2] See *ibid.* § 11, p. 41.

The form of Carnap's argument is worth noticing. He begins by setting up a bogy, primitive psychologism, whose actual existence he fails to establish. He next points to a single resemblance between the writings of each of the logicians whom he puts into the dock and this bogy, namely that they contain such words as 'thought', 'belief', 'reasoning' and 'confidence'. The logicians are then lectured on the dangers of keeping bad company, and threatened with a verdict of guilt by association—'All this has a psychologistic sound'; but in view of their otherwise good records they are let off with a caution. Finally, since nobody has actually been found guilty, Carnap remarks that 'It cannot, of course, be denied that there is also a subjective, psychological concept for which the term "probability" may be used and sometimes is used.' But no instance of this alleged usage is cited, apart from one bare and unconvincing formula: 'The probability or degree of belief of the prediction h at the time t for X.'

This last barbarism is symptomatic. For the meaning of the term 'probability' outside the special sciences does not seem to interest Carnap at all. Not only does he want to turn logic into the mineralogy of logical relations. He also regards all but scientific probability-statements as vague, inexact, in need of explication—in his own word, 'prescientific'. This belief relieves him of the arduous task of establishing just what these extra-scientific uses are: he would agree with the view that, once the scientific uses have been examined, 'the probability-statements of plain men should prove fairly easy to describe, since, when not fallacious, they would presumably be found to be approximations to those of the scientists'.

If precedents are anything to go on, however, this is a most unsafe thing to presume. For the two philosophical problems most resembling the problem of probability are that engaged in by Berkeley on the subject of points, and that which burned fiercely during the nineteenth century around the dynamical notion of force. In both these cases the problem was solved, not by developing a single mathematically-precise use of the term concerned, and dismissing the extra-scientific uses as obsolete, because pre-scientific. It was the very attempt to equate the old and the new uses of the words 'point' and 'force' that started the trouble, leading Berkeley, for instance, to ask about the mathematicians' point, 'What it is— whether something or nothing; and how it differs from the *Minimum*

Sensibile', and thereafter into his speculations about the *Minima Sensibilia* of cheese-mites. The solution came rather from analysing and expounding carefully *all* the uses of the terms 'point' and 'force', both those inside geometry or dynamics and those outside, without favour to either one or the other. Only when this had been done, and the differences noted, did the philosophical questions which had seemed so perplexing cease to ask themselves.

In the philosophy of probability, too, it causes only trouble if one thinks of the scientific applications of the term as the sole satisfactory ones. The everyday uses, though not numerical, are none-the-less perfectly definite; and the scientific ones grow out of them in a more complicated manner than Carnap realises. It is one thing to point out the comparative precision—i.e. numerical exactness— of statements in the mathematical sciences, and the comparative absence of this kind of precision in extra-scientific talk. But to interpret this absence of numerical exactness as a lack of precision, in the sense of definiteness, and to criticise extra-scientific discourse as essentially vague and hazy, is to take a highly questionable further step. Statements expressed in numerically-exact terms are not the only ones to be perfectly definite and unambiguous.

THE DEVELOPMENT OF OUR PROBABILITY-CONCEPTS

At this point I must try to draw together the threads of this essay. It has consisted, in part, of an attempt to bring to light the manner in which we in practice operate with the concept of probability and its close relations; and, in part, of an attempt to show how the current controversies about the philosophy of probability have tended to misrepresent the nature of the concept. The general philosophical points we have come across will be coming up for reconsideration again later: what I want to do here is to bring together the more practical observations we have made about the functions of our probability-terms, and to summarise them briefly, showing how the concept develops from its elementary beginnings to its most sophisticated scientific and technical applications.

To begin with, I argued, the adverb 'probably' serves us as a means of qualifying conclusions and assertions, so as to indicate that the statement is made something less than positively, and must not be taken as committing the speaker to more than a certain extent. Thus, a man may give a preliminary indication of his intentions or a guarded undertaking by saying, 'I shall probably do so-and-so.' Or he can make a tentative prediction, on the basis of evidence which is insufficient for a more positive one, by saying, 'So-and-so will probably happen.' Or again, he can make a cautious evaluation which he presents (perhaps) as subject to reconsideration in the light of a more detailed study, by saying, 'This painting is probably the finest product of the whole Paduan School.' At this stage, there is nothing to choose between evaluations, promises and predictions: all of them equally can contain the word 'probably', and its force in each case is the same—even though the sorts of evidence needed for a tentative as opposed to a positive meteorological prediction will, in the nature of the case, be very different from the sorts of grounds justifying a cautious as opposed to an outright ascription of genius to a painter, and from the reasons which oblige a man to give only a qualified and not a fully-committal undertaking or statement of his intentions.

Just how far we are entitled to commit ourselves depends on the strength of the grounds, reasons or evidence at our disposal. We may, like Eleanor Farjeon's brother, hesitate in an excess of caution ever to commit ourselves at all, and so feel obliged to add to all our statements a qualifying 'probably', 'possibly' or 'perhaps'. But if we are prepared to commit ourselves, whether positively or under comparatively weak guards, then we can be challenged to produce the backing for our commitment. We may not say, 'I shall probably come', if we have strong reasons for thinking that we shall be prevented; or say, 'This is probably his finest painting', when it is the only one of the artist's works that we have ever seen; or say, 'It will probably rain tomorrow', in the absence of fairly solid meteorological evidence. Our probability-terms come to serve, therefore, not only to qualify assertions, promises and evaluations themselves, but also as an indication of the strength of the backing which we have for the assertion, evaluation or whatever. It is the quality of the *evidence* or *argument* at the speaker's disposal which determines what sort of qualifier he is entitled to include in his statements: whether he ought to say, 'This must be the case', 'This may be the case', or 'This cannot be the case'; whether to say 'Certainly so-and-so', 'Probably so-and-so', or 'Possibly so-and-so'.

By qualifying our conclusions and assertions in the ways we do, we authorise our hearers to put more or less faith in the assertions or conclusions, to bank on them, rely on them, treat them as correspondingly more or less trustworthy. In many fields of discussion, this is as far as we can go: for instance, we can present an aesthetic judgement with all the weight of our authority behind it, or in a more or less qualified manner—'Monet has a strong claim to be regarded as the outstanding member of the Impressionist School'— but there is little room here for laying bets or allotting numerical values to the strength of claims or to the degrees of confidence one can place in conclusions or assertions. With predictions, on the other hand, a new possibility emerges, especially where a particular kind of event is liable to recur at intervals in very much the same form; we may now be able to indicate the trust a proposition is entitled to, and the extent to which we should be prepared to bank on it, not just in a general, qualitative way but in numerical terms. At this point mathematical methods can enter into the discussion of probabilities. When the question at issue has to do with the winner of a forthcoming horse-race, with the sex of an unborn baby, or the number on which the ball will settle next time the roulette-wheel is spun, then it becomes meaningful to talk about numerical probabilities in a way in which in aesthetics it probably never will. 'Five to one on the *Madonna of the Rocks*', 'The chances that the *Marriage of Figaro* is Mozart's finest opera are three to two', and the like: it is not easy to see how arithmetic could ever enter into the assessment of probabilities in such a field as this.

Still, logically, little is altered by the introduction of mathematics into the discussion of the probability of future events. The numerical discussion of probabilities becomes, no doubt, sophisticated and somewhat complex, but unless a calculus provides a means of estimating how far propositions are entitled to our trust or belief, it can hardly be called a 'calculus of probabilities' at all. The development of the mathematical theory of probability accordingly leaves the *force* of our probability-statements unchanged; its value is that it greatly refines the *standards* to be appealed to, and so the morals we can draw about the degree of expectability of future events.

It would be too strong to say that—logically speaking—the development of mathematical statistics and the theory of chances left our talk about probability entirely unaltered. Within the mathematical theory itself, abstraction does its usual work, and we can make general statements about the odds or chances of this or that kind of event which appear to have, in themselves, none of the 'guarding' or 'qualifying' character of their particular applications. Particular probability-statements, again, can call for correction on occasions when general statements about odds can be left uncorrected. Thus, the odds against a steam-roller running over a Lord Mayor of London are enormous; and with this generality in mind we can say, predictively, 'The present Lord Mayor of London will, in all probability, not die during his term of office beneath the wheels of a steam-roller.' Supposing, however, the incredible happens, we shall be forced to confess our particular prediction mistaken; yet we shall maintain unamended the general statement by which we should have defended it—the odds against such an accident are certainly not diminished by its having happened once, and it remains as reasonable as before to discount entirely the danger of its occurrence.

Theoretical calculations of odds and 'probabilities', in the mathematical sense, can accordingly be taught and performed, without the modal function of their practical applications ever attracting attention. Still, for all the differences in degree of corrigibility and so on between such general considerations and our guarded predictions, the logical affiliations remain. The guarded prediction, 'Such an accident will probably never happen', remains an application of the general assurance that 'The odds against such an accident are enormous.'

Our probability-terms—'probably', 'chance', 'the odds are', 'in all probability'—show in practice, therefore, many of the features which we discovered in the first essay to be characteristic of modal terms. In this respect, the mathematical treatment of 'probability' represents a natural extension of the term's more elementary and everyday uses.

Some philosophers nevertheless have an ineradicable suspicion of our everyday forms of thought. It seems to them that the ways we employ words like 'force', 'motion', 'cause' and so on in the workaday affairs of life only too likely rest on mistaken assumptions, and that our extra-scientific use of the term 'probability' may well harbour gross fallacies also. In their view, the development of science, and the displacement of all our ordinary, pre-scientific ideas by the more refined notions of the theoretical sciences, hold out the only hope of salvation from incoherence, fallacy and intellectual confusion. Ordinary concepts are vague and inexact, and have to be replaced by more precise ones, and the scientist is entitled to disregard the pre-scientific significations of the terms he employs. In the field of probability, this prognostication has turned out to be unnecessarily gloomy. There is, after all, no radical discontinuity between the pre-scientific and the scientific uses of our probability-terms. Some philosophers have, indeed, talked as though there were such a discontinuity: they have rather welcomed the idea that they were discrediting long-standing fallacies, and replacing vague and muddled ideas by precise and exact ones. As we have seen, this picture of themselves as scientific crusaders will stand up to examination only so long as one fails to distinguish between precision in the sense of 'exactness' and precision in the sense of 'definiteness'. Outside the betting-shop, the casino and the theoretical physicist's study, we may have little occasion to introduce numerical precision into our talk about probabilities, but the things we say are none-the-less definite or free from vagueness. Were one, in fact, to cut away from the theory of mathematical probability all that it owes to our pre-scientific ways of thought about the subject, it would lose all application to practical affairs. The punter and the actuary, the physicist and the dice-thrower are as much concerned with degrees of acceptability and expectation as the meteorologist or the man-in-the-street: whether backed by mathematical calculations or no, the characteristic function of our particular, practical probability-statements is to present *guarded* or *qualified* assertions and conclusions.

III

THE LAYOUT OF ARGUMENTS

AN ARGUMENT is like an organism. It has both a gross, anatomical structure and a finer, as-it-were physiological one. When set out explicitly in all its detail, it may occupy a number of printed pages or take perhaps a quarter of an hour to deliver; and within this time or space one can distinguish the main phases marking the progress of the argument from the initial statement of an unsettled problem to the final presentation of a conclusion. These main phases will each of them occupy some minutes or paragraphs, and represent the chief anatomical units of the argument—its 'organs', so to speak. But within each paragraph, when one gets down to the level of individual sentences, a finer structure can be recognised, and this is the structure with which logicians have mainly concerned themselves. It is at this physiological level that the idea of logical form has been introduced, and here that the validity of our arguments has ultimately to be established or refuted.

The time has come to change the focus of our inquiry, and to concentrate on this finer level. Yet we cannot afford to forget what we have learned by our study of the grosser anatomy of arguments, for here as with organisms the detailed physiology proves most intelligible when expounded against a background of coarser anatomical distinctions. Physiological processes are interesting not least for the part they play in maintaining the functions of the major organs in which they take place; and micro-arguments (as one may christen them) need to be looked at from time to time with one eye on the macro-arguments in which they figure; since the precise manner in which we phrase them and set them out, to mention only the least important thing, may be affected by the role they have to play in the larger context.

In the inquiry which follows, we shall be studying the operation of arguments sentence by sentence, in order to see how their validity or invalidity is connected with the manner of laying them out, and what relevance this connection has to the traditional notion of 'logical form'. Certainly the same argument may be set out in quite a number of different forms, and some of these patterns of analysis will be more candid than others—some of them, that is, will show the validity or invalidity of an argument more clearly than others, and make more explicit the grounds it relies on and the bearing of these on the conclusion. How, then, should we lay an argument out, if we want to show the sources of its validity? And in what sense does the acceptability or unacceptability of arguments depend upon their 'formal' merits and defects?

We have before us two rival models, one mathematical, the other jurisprudential. Is the logical form of a valid argument something quasi-geometrical, comparable to the shape of a triangle or the parallelism of two straight lines? Or alternatively, is it something procedural: is a formally valid argument one *in proper form*, as lawyers would say, rather than one laid out in a tidy and simple *geometrical* form? Or does the notion of logical form somehow combine both these aspects, so that to lay an argument out in proper form necessarily requires the adoption of a particular geometrical layout? If this last answer is the right one, it at once creates a further problem for us: to see how and why proper procedure demands the adoption of simple geometrical shape, and how that shape guarantees in its turn the validity of our procedures. Supposing valid arguments can be cast in a geometrically tidy form, how does this help to make them any the more cogent?

These are the problems to be studied in the present inquiry. If we can see our way to unravelling them, their solution will be of some importance—particularly for a proper understanding of logic. But to begin with we must go cautiously, and steer clear of the philosophical issues on which we shall hope later to throw some light, concentrating for the moment on questions of a most prosaic and straightforward kind. Keeping our eyes on the categories of applied logic—on the practical business of argumentation, that is, and the notions it requires us to employ—we must ask what features a logically candid layout of arguments will need to have. The establishment of conclusions raises a number of issues of different sorts, and a practical layout will make allowance for these differences: our first question is—what are these issues, and how can we do justice to them all in subjecting our arguments to rational assessment?

Two last remarks may be made by way of introduction, the first of them simply adding one more question to our agenda. Ever since

Aristotle it has been customary, when analysing the micro-structure of arguments, to set them out in a very simple manner: they have been presented three propositions at a time, 'minor premiss; major premiss; *so* conclusion'. The question now arises, whether this standard form is sufficiently elaborate or candid. Simplicity is of course a merit, but may it not in this case have been bought too dearly? Can we properly classify all the elements in our arguments under the three headings, 'major premiss', 'minor premiss' and 'conclusion', or are these categories misleadingly few in number? Is there even enough similarity between major and minor premisses for them usefully to be yoked together by the single name of 'premiss'?

Light is thrown on these questions by the analogy with jurisprudence. This would naturally lead us to adopt a layout of greater complexity than has been customary, for the questions we are asking here are, once again, more general versions of questions already familiar in jurisprudence, and in that more specialised field a whole battery of distinctions has grown up. 'What different sorts of propositions', a legal philosopher will ask, 'are uttered in the course of a law-case, and in what different ways can such propositions bear on the soundness of a legal claim?' This has always been and still is a central question for the student of jurisprudence, and we soon find that the nature of a legal process can be properly understood only if we draw a large number of distinctions. Legal utterances have many distinct functions. Statements of claim, evidence of identification, testimony about events in dispute, interpretations of a statute or discussions of its validity, claims to exemption from the application of a law, pleas in extenuation, verdicts, sentences: all these different classes of proposition have their parts to play in the legal process, and the differences between them are in practice far from trifling. When we turn from the special case of the law to consider rational arguments in general, we are faced at once by the question whether these must not be analysed in terms of an equally complex set of categories. If we are to set our arguments out with complete logical candour, and understand properly the nature of 'the logical process', surely we shall need to employ a pattern of argument no less sophisticated than is required in the law.

THE PATTERN OF AN ARGUMENT: DATA AND WARRANTS

'What, then, is involved in establishing conclusions by the production of arguments?' Can we, by considering this question in a general form, build up from scratch a pattern of analysis which will do justice to all the distinctions which proper procedure forces upon us? That is the problem facing us.

Let it be supposed that we make an assertion, and commit ourselves thereby to the claim which any assertion necessarily involves. If this claim is challenged, we must be able to establish it—that is, make it good, and show that it was justifiable. How is this to be done? Unless the assertion was made quite wildly and irresponsibly, we shall normally have some facts to which we can point in its support: if the claim is challenged, it is up to us to appeal to these facts, and present them as the foundation upon which our claim is based. Of course we may not get the challenger even to agree about the correctness of these facts, and in that case we have to clear his objection out of the way by a preliminary argument: only when this prior issue or 'lemma', as geometers would call it, has been dealt with, are we in a position to return to the original argument. But this complication we need only mention: supposing the lemma to have been disposed of, our question is how to set the original argument out most fully and explicitly. 'Harry's hair is not black', we assert. What have we got to go on? we are asked. Our personal knowledge that it is in fact red: that is our datum, the ground which we produce as support for the original assertion. Petersen, we may say, will not be a Roman Catholic: why?: we base our claim on the knowledge that he is a Swede, which makes it very unlikely that he will be a Roman Catholic. Wilkinson, asserts the prosecutor in Court, has committed an offence against the Road Traffic Acts: in support of this claim, two policemen are prepared to testify that they timed him driving at 45 m.p.h. in a built-up area. In each case, an original assertion is supported by producing other facts bearing on it.

We already have, therefore, one distinction to start with: between the *claim* or conclusion whose merits we are seeking to establish (C) and the facts we appeal to as a foundation for the claim—what I shall refer to as our *data* (D). If our challenger's question is, 'What have you got to go on?', producing the data or information on which the claim is based may serve to answer him; but this is only one of the ways in which our conclusion may be challenged. Even after we have produced our data, we may find ourselves being asked further questions of another kind. We may now be required not to add more factual information to that which we have already provided, but rather to indicate the bearing on our conclusion of the data already produced. Colloquially, the question may now be, not 'What have you got to go on?', but 'How do you get there?'. To present a particular set of data as the basis for some specified conclusion commits us to a certain *step*; and the question is now one about the nature and justification of this step.

Supposing we encounter this fresh challenge, we must bring forward not further data, for about these the same query may immediately be raised again, but propositions of a rather different kind: rules, principles, inference-licences or what you will, instead of additional items of information. Our task is no longer to strengthen the ground on which our argument is constructed, but is rather to show that, taking these data as a starting point, the step to the original claim or conclusion is an appropriate and legitimate one. At this point, therefore, what are needed are general, hypothetical statements, which can act as bridges, and authorise the sort of step to which our particular argument commits us. These may normally be written very briefly (in the form 'If D, then C'); but, for candour's sake, they can profitably be expanded, and made more explicit: 'Data such as D entitle one to draw conclusions, or make claims, such as C', or alternatively 'Given data D, one may take it that C.'

Propositions of this kind I shall call *warrants* (W), to distinguish them from both conclusions and data. (These 'warrants', it will be observed, correspond to the practical standards or canons of argument referred to in our earlier essays.) To pursue our previous examples: the knowledge that Harry's hair is red entitles us to set aside any suggestion that it is black, on account of the warrant, 'If anything is red, it will not also be black.' (The very triviality of this warrant is connected with the fact that we are concerned here as much with a counter-assertion as with an argument.) The fact that Petersen is a Swede is directly relevant to the question of his religious denomination for, as we should probably put it, 'A Swede can be taken almost certainly not to be a Roman Catholic.' (The step involved here is not trivial, so the warrant is not self-authenticating.) Likewise in the third case: our warrant will now be some such statement as that 'A man who is proved to have driven at more than 30 m.p.h. in a built-up area can be found to have committed an offence against the Road Traffic Acts.'

The question will at once be asked, how absolute is this distinction between data, on the one hand, and warrants, on the other. Will it always be clear whether a man who challenges an assertion is calling for the production of his adversary's data, or for the warrants authorising his steps? Can one, in other words, draw any sharp distinction between the force of the two questions, 'What have you got to go on?' and 'How do you get there?'? By grammatical tests alone, the distinction may appear far from absolute, and the same English sentence may serve a double function: it may be uttered, that is, in one situation to convey a piece of information, in another to authorise a step in an argument, and even perhaps in some contexts to do both these things at once. (All these possibilities will be illustrated before too long.) For the moment, the important thing is not to be too cut-and-dried in our treatment of the subject, nor to commit ourselves in advance to a rigid terminology. At any rate we shall find it possible in *some* situations to distinguish clearly two different logical functions; and the nature of this distinction is hinted at if one contrasts the two sentences, 'Whenever A, one *has found* that B' and 'Whenever A, one *may take it* that B.'

We now have the terms we need to compose the first skeleton of a pattern for analysing arguments. We may symbolise the relation between the data and the claim in support of which they are produced by an arrow, and indicate the authority for taking the step from one to the other by writing the warrant immediately below the arrow:

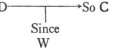

Or, to give an example:

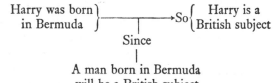

As this pattern makes clear, the explicit appeal in this argument goes directly back from the claim to the data relied on as foundation:

the warrant is, in a sense, incidental and explanatory, its task being simply to register explicitly the legitimacy of the step involved and to refer it back to the larger class of steps whose legitimacy is being presupposed. This is one of the reasons for distinguishing between data and warrants: data are appealed to explicitly, warrants implicitly. In addition, one may remark that warrants are general, certifying the soundness of *all* arguments of the appropriate type, and have accordingly to be established in quite a different way from the facts we produce as data. This distinction, between data and warrants, is similar to the distinction drawn in the law-courts between questions of fact and questions of law, and the legal distinction is indeed a special case of the more general one—we may argue, for instance, that a man whom we know to have been born in Bermuda is presumably a British subject, simply because the relevant laws give us a warrant to draw this conclusion.

One more general point in passing: unless, in any particular field of argument, we are prepared to work with warrants of *some* kind, it will become impossible in that field to subject arguments to rational assessment. The data we cite if a claim is challenged depend on the warrants we are prepared to operate with in that field, and the warrants to which we commit ourselves are implicit in the particular steps from data to claims we are prepared to take and to admit. But supposing a man rejects all warrants whatever authorising (say) steps from data about the present and past to conclusions about the future, then for him rational prediction will become impossible; and many philosophers have in fact denied the possibility of rational prediction just because they thought they could discredit equally the claims of all past-to-future warrants.

The skeleton of a pattern which we have obtained so far is only a beginning. Further questions may now arise, to which we must pay attention. Warrants are of different kinds, and may confer different degrees of force on the conclusions they justify. Some warrants authorise us to accept a claim unequivocally, given the appropriate data—these warrants entitle us in suitable cases to qualify our conclusion with the adverb 'necessarily'; others authorise us to make the step from data to conclusion either tentatively, or else subject to conditions, exceptions, or qualifications—in these cases other modal qualifiers, such as 'probably' and 'presumably', are in place. It may not be sufficient, therefore, simply to specify our data, warrant and claim: we may need to add some explicit reference to the degree of force which our data confer on our claim in virtue of our warrant. In a word, we may have to put in a *qualifier*. Again, it is often necessary in the law-courts, not just to appeal to a given statute or common-law doctrine, but to discuss explicitly the extent to which this particular law fits the case under consideration, whether it must inevitably be applied in this particular case, or whether special facts may make the case an exception to the rule or one in which the law can be applied only subject to certain qualifications.

If we are to take account of these features of our argument also, our pattern will become more complex. Modal qualifiers (Q) and conditions of exception or rebuttal (R) are distinct both from data and from warrants, and need to be given separate places in our layout. Just as a warrant (W) is itself neither a datum (D) nor a claim (C), since it implies in itself something about both D and C —namely, that the step from the one to the other is legitimate; so, in turn, Q and R are themselves distinct from W, since they comment implicitly on the bearing of W on this step—qualifiers (Q) indicating the strength conferred by the warrant on this step, conditions of rebuttal (R) indicating circumstances in which the general authority of the warrant would have to be set aside. To mark these further distinctions, we may write the qualifier (Q) immediately beside the conclusion which it qualifies (C), and the exceptional conditions which might be capable of defeating or rebutting the warranted conclusion (R) immediately below the qualifier.

To illustrate: our claim that Harry is a British subject may normally be defended by appeal to the information that he was born in Bermuda, for this datum lends support to our conclusion on account of the warrants implicit in the British Nationality Acts; but the argument is not by itself conclusive in the absence of assurances about his parentage and about his not having changed his nationality since birth. What our information does do is to establish that the conclusion holds good 'presumably', and subject to the appropriate provisos. The argument now assumes the form:

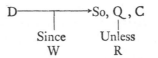

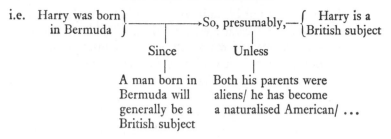

We must remark, in addition, on two further distinctions. The first is that between a statement of a warrant, and statements about its applicability—between 'A man born in Bermuda will be British', and 'This presumption holds good provided his parents were not both aliens, etc.' The distinction is relevant not only to the law of the land, but also for an understanding of scientific laws or 'laws of nature': it is important, indeed, in all cases where the application of a law may be subject to exceptions, or where a warrant can be supported by pointing to a general correlation only, and not to an absolutely invariable one. We can distinguish also two purposes which may be served by the production of additional facts: these can serve as further data, or they can be cited to confirm or rebut the applicability of a warrant. Thus, the fact that Harry was born in Bermuda and the fact that his parents were not aliens are both of them directly relevant to the question of his present nationality; but they are relevant in different ways. The one fact is a datum, which by itself establishes a presumption of British nationality; the other fact, by setting aside one possible rebuttal, tends to confirm the presumption thereby created.

One particular problem about applicability we shall have to discuss more fully later: when we set out a piece of applied mathematics, in which some system of mathematical relations is used to throw light on a question of (say) physics, the correctness of the calculations will be one thing, their appropriateness to the problem in hand may be quite another. So the question 'Is this calculation mathematically impeccable?' may be a very different one from the question 'Is this the relevant calculation?' Here too, the applicability of a particular warrant is one question: the result we shall get from applying the warrant is another matter, and in asking about the *correctness* of the result we may have to inquire into both these things independently.

THE PATTERN OF AN ARGUMENT: BACKING OUR WARRANTS

One last distinction, which we have already touched on in passing, must be discussed at some length. In addition to the question whether or on what conditions a warrant is applicable in a *particular* case, we may be asked why *in general* this warrant should be accepted as having authority. In defending a claim, that is, we may produce our data, our warrant, and the relevant qualifications and conditions, and yet find that we have still not satisfied our challenger; for he may be dubious not only about this particular argument but about the more general question whether the warrant (W) is acceptable at all. Presuming the general acceptability of this warrant (he may allow) our argument would no doubt be impeccable—if D-ish facts really do suffice as backing for C-ish claims, all well and good. But does not that warrant in its turn rest on something else? Challenging a particular claim may in this way lead on to challenging, more generally, the legitimacy of a whole range of arguments. 'You presume that a man born in Bermuda can be taken to be a British subject,' he may say, 'but why do you think that?' Standing behind our warrants, as this example reminds us, there will normally be other assurances, without which the warrants themselves would possess neither authority nor currency—these other things we may refer to as the *backing* (B) of the warrants. This 'backing' of our warrants is something which we shall have to scrutinise very carefully: its precise relations to our data, claims, warrants and conditions of rebuttal deserve some clarification, for confusion at this point can lead to trouble later.

We shall have to notice particularly how the sort of backing called for by our warrants varies from one field of argument to another. The *form* of argument we employ in different fields

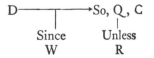

need not vary very much as between fields. 'A whale will be a mammal', 'A Bermudan will be a Briton', 'A Saudi Arabian will be a Muslim': here are three different warrants to which we might appeal in the course of a practical argument, each of which can justify the same sort of straightforward step from a datum to a conclusion. We might add for variety examples of even more diverse sorts, taken from moral, mathematical or psychological fields. But the moment we start asking about the *backing* which a warrant relies on in each field, great differences begin to appear: the kind of backing we must point to if we are to establish its authority will change greatly as we move from one field of argument to another. 'A whale will be (i.e. *is classifiable as*) a mammal', 'A Bermudan will be (*in the eyes of the law*) a Briton', 'A Saudi Arabian will be (*found to be*) a Muslim'— the words in parentheses indicate what these differences are. One warrant is defended by relating it to a system of taxonomical classification, another by appealing to the statutes governing the nationality of people born in the British colonies, the third by referring to the statistics which record how religious beliefs are distributed among people of different nationalities. We can for the moment leave open the more contentious question, how we establish our warrants in the fields of morals, mathematics and psychology: for the moment all we are trying to show is the *variability* or *field-dependence* of the backing needed to establish our warrants.

We can make room for this additional element in our argument-pattern by writing it below the bare statement of the warrant for which it serves as backing (B):

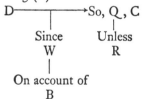

This form may not be final, but it will be complex enough for the purpose of our present discussions. To take a particular example: in support of the claim (C) that Harry is a British subject, we appeal to the datum (D) that he was born in Bermuda, and the warrant can then be stated in the form, 'A man born in Bermuda may be taken to be a British subject': since, however, questions of nationality are always subject to qualifications and conditions, we shall have to insert a qualifying 'presumably' (Q) in front of the conclusion, and note the possibility that our conclusion may be rebutted in case (R) it turns out that both his parents were aliens or he has since become a naturalised American. Finally, in case the warrant itself is challenged, its backing can be put in: this will record the terms and the dates of enactment of the Acts of Parliament and other legal provisions governing the nationality of persons born in the British colonies. The result will be an argument set out as follows:

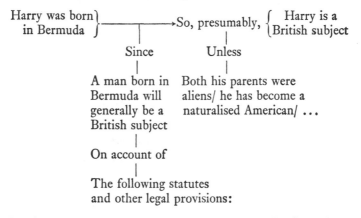

In what ways does the backing of warrants differ from the other elements in our arguments? To begin with the differences between B and W: statements of warrants, we saw, are hypothetical, bridge-like statements, but the backing for warrants can be expressed in the form of categorical statements of fact quite as well as can the data appealed to in direct support of our conclusions. So long as our statements reflect these functional differences explicitly, there is no danger of confusing the backing (B) for a warrant with the warrant itself (W): such confusions arise only when these differences are disguised by our forms of expression. In our present example, at any rate, there need be no difficulty. The fact that the relevant statutes have been validly passed into law, and contain the provisions they do, can be ascertained simply by going to the records of the parliamentary proceedings concerned and to the relevant volumes in the books of statute law: the resulting discovery, that such-and-such a statute enacted on such-and-such a date contains a provision specifying that people born in the British colonies of suitable parentage shall be entitled to British citizenship, is a straightforward statement of fact. On the other hand, the warrant which we apply *in virtue of* the statute containing this provision is logically of a very different character—'*If* a man was born in a British colony, he *may be presumed to be* British.' Though the facts about the statute may

provide all the backing required by this warrant, the explicit statement of the warrant itself is more than a repetition of these facts: it
is a general *moral* of a practical character, about the ways in which
we can safely argue in view of these facts.

We can also distinguish backing (B) from data (D). Though the
data we appeal to in an argument and the backing lending authority
to our warrants may alike be stated as straightforward matters-of-
fact, the roles which these statements play in our argument are
decidedly different. Data of some kind must be produced, if there
is to be an argument there at all: a bare conclusion, without any data
produced in its support, is no argument. But the backing of the
warrants we invoke need not be made explicit—at any rate to begin
with: the warrants may be conceded without challenge, and their
backing left understood. Indeed, if we demanded the credentials of
all warrants at sight and never let one pass unchallenged, argument
could scarcely begin. Jones puts forward an argument invoking
warrant W_1, and Smith challenges that warrant; Jones is obliged,
as a lemma, to produce another argument in the hope of establishing
the acceptability of the first warrant, but in the course of this lemma
employs a second warrant W_2; Smith challenges the credentials of
this second warrant in turn; and so the game goes on. Some warrants
must be accepted provisionally without further challenge, if argument is to be open to us in the field in question: we should not even
know what sort of data were of the slightest relevance to a conclusion,
if we had not at least a provisional idea of the warrants acceptable
in the situation confronting us. The existence of considerations
such as would establish the acceptability of the most reliable
warrants is something we are entitled to take for granted.

Finally, a word about the ways in which B differs from Q and R:
these are too obvious to need expanding upon, since the grounds for
regarding a warrant as generally acceptable are clearly one thing,
the force which the warrant lends to a conclusion another, and the
sorts of exceptional circumstance which may in particular cases
rebut the presumptions the warrant creates a third. They correspond,
in our example, to the three statements, (i) that the statutes about
British nationality *have in fact* been validly passed into law, and
say this:..., (ii) that Harry *may be presumed* to be a British
subject, and (iii) that Harry, having recently become a naturalised
American, *is no longer covered* by these statutes.

One incidental point should be made, about the interpretation to be put upon the symbols in our pattern of argument: this may throw light on a slightly puzzling example which we came across when discussing Kneale's views on probability. Consider the arrow joining D and C. It may seem natural to suggest at first that this arrow should be read as 'so' in one direction and as 'because' in the other. Other interpretations are however possible. As we saw earlier, the step from the information that Jones has Bright's Disease to the conclusion that he cannot be expected to live to eighty does not reverse perfectly: we find it natural enough to say, 'Jones cannot be expected to live to eighty, *because* he has Bright's Disease', but the fuller statement, 'Jones cannot be expected to live to eighty, *because* the probability of his living that long is low, *because* he has Bright's Disease', strikes us as cumbrous and artificial, for it puts in an extra step which is trivial and unnecessary. On the other hand, we do not mind saying, 'Jones has Bright's Disease, *so* the chances of his living to eighty are slight, *so* he cannot be expected to live that long', for the last clause is (so to speak) an *inter alia* clause—it states one of the many particular morals one can draw from the middle clause, which tells us his general expectation of life.

So also in our present case: reading along the arrow from right to left or from left to right we can normally say both 'C, because D' and 'D, so C'. But it may sometimes happen that some more general conclusion than C may be warranted, given D: where this is so, we shall often find it natural to write, not only 'D, so C', but also 'D, so C', so C', C' being the more general conclusion warranted in view of data D, from which in turn we infer *inter alia* that C. Where this is the case, our 'so' and 'because' are no longer reversible: if we now read the argument backwards the statement we get —'C, because C', because D'—is again more cumbrous than the situation really requires.

AMBIGUITIES IN THE SYLLOGISM

The time has come to compare the distinctions we have found of practical importance in the layout and criticism of arguments with those which have traditionally been made in books on the theory of logic: let us start by seeing how our present distinctions apply to the syllogism or syllogistic argument. For the purposes of our present argument we can confine our attention to one of the many forms of syllogism—that represented by the time-honoured example:

Socrates is a man;
All men are mortal;
So Socrates is mortal.

This type of syllogism has certain special features. The first premiss is 'singular' and refers to a particular individual, while the second premiss alone is 'universal'. Aristotle himself was, of course, much concerned with syllogisms in which both the premisses were universal, since to his mind many of the arguments within scientific theory must be expected to be of this sort. But we are interested primarily in arguments by which general propositions are applied to justify particular conclusions about individuals; so this initial limitation will be convenient. Many of the conclusions we reach will, in any case, have an obvious application—*mutatis mutandis*—to syllogisms of other types. We can begin by asking the question 'What corresponds in the syllogism to our distinction between data, warrant, and backing?' If we press this question, we shall find that the apparently innocent forms used in syllogistic arguments turn out to have a hidden complexity. This internal complexity is comparable with that we observed in the case of modally-qualified conclusions: here, as before, we shall be obliged to disentangle two distinct things—the force of universal premisses, when regarded as warrants, and the backing on which they depend for their authority.

In order to bring these points clearly to light, let us keep in view not only the two universal premisses on which logicians normally concentrate—'All A's are B's' and 'No A's are B's'—but also two other forms of statement which we probably have just as much occasion to use in practice—'Almost all A's are B's' and 'Scarcely any A's are B's.' The internal complexity of such statements can be illustrated first, and most clearly, in the latter cases.

Consider, for instance, the statement, 'Scarcely any Swedes are Roman Catholics.' This statement can have two distinct aspects: both of them are liable to be operative at once when the statement figures in an argument, but they can nevertheless be distinguished. To begin with, it may serve as a simple statistical report: in that case, it can equally well be written in the fuller form, 'The proportion of Swedes who are Roman Catholics is less than (say) 2%'—to which we may add a parenthetical reference to the source of our information, '(According to the tables in *Whittaker's Almanac*)'. Alternatively, the same statement may serve as a genuine inference-warrant: in that case, it will be natural to expand it rather differently, so as to obtain the more candid statement, 'A Swede can be taken almost certainly not to be a Roman Catholic.'

So long as we look at the single sentence 'Scarcely any Swedes are Roman Catholics' by itself, this distinction may appear trifling enough: but if we apply it to the analysis of an argument in which this appears as one premiss, we obtain results of some significance. So let us construct an argument of quasi-syllogistic form, in which this statement figures in the position of a 'major premiss'. This argument could be, for instance, the following:

> Petersen is a Swede;
> Scarcely any Swedes are Roman Catholics;
> So, almost certainly, Petersen is not a Roman Catholic.

The conclusion of this argument is only tentative, but in other respects the argument is exactly like a syllogism.

As we have seen, the second of these statements can be expanded in each of two ways, so that it becomes either, 'The proportion of Swedes who are Roman Catholics is less than 2%', or else, 'A Swede can be taken almost certainly not to be a Roman Catholic.' Let us now see what happens if we substitute each of these two expanded versions in turn for the second of our three original statements. In one case we obtain the argument:

> Petersen is a Swede;
> A Swede can be taken almost certainly not to be a Roman Catholic;
> So, almost certainly, Petersen is not a Roman Catholic.

Here the successive lines correspond in our terminology to the statement of a datum (D), a warrant (W), and a conclusion (C). On the other hand, if we make the alternative substitution, we obtain:

> Petersen is a Swede;
> The proportion of Roman Catholic Swedes is less than 2%;
> So, almost certainly, Petersen is not a Roman Catholic.

In this case we again have the same datum and conclusion, but the second line now states the backing (B) for the warrant (W), which is itself left unstated.

For tidiness' sake, we may now be tempted to abbreviate these two expanded versions. If we do so, we can obtain respectively the two arguments:

> (D) Petersen is a Swede;
> (W) A Swede is almost certainly not a Roman Catholic;
> So, (C) Petersen is almost certainly not a Roman Catholic:

and, (D) Petersen is a Swede;
> (B) The proportion of Roman Catholic Swedes is minute;
> So, (C) Petersen is almost certainly not a Roman Catholic.

The relevance of our distinction to the traditional conception of 'formal validity' should already be becoming apparent, and we shall return to the subject shortly.

Turning to the form 'No A's are B's' (e.g. 'No Swedes are Roman Catholics'), we can make a similar distinction. This form of statement also can be employed in two alternative ways, either as a statistical report, or as an inference-warrant. It can serve simply to report a statistician's discovery—say, that the proportion of Roman Catholic Swedes is in fact zero; or alternatively it can serve to justify the drawing of conclusions in argument, becoming equivalent to the explicit statement, 'A Swede can be taken certainly not to be a Roman Catholic.' Corresponding interpretations are again open to us if we look at an argument which includes our sample statement as the universal premiss. Consider the argument:

> Petersen is a Swede;
> No Swedes are Roman Catholics;
> So, certainly, Petersen is not a Roman Catholic.

This can be understood in two ways: we may write it in the form:

> Petersen is a Swede;
> The proportion of Roman Catholic Swedes is zero;
> So, certainly, Petersen is not a Roman Catholic,

or alternatively in the form:

> Petersen is a Swede;
> A Swede is certainly not a Roman Catholic;
> So, certainly, Petersen is not a Roman Catholic.

Here again the first formulation amounts, in our terminology, to putting the argument in the form 'D, B, so C'; while the second formulation is equivalent to putting it in the form 'D, W, so C'. So, whether we are concerned with a 'scarcely any...' argument or a 'no...' argument, the customary form of expression will tend in either case to conceal from us the distinction between an inference-warrant and its backing. The same will be true in the case of 'all' and 'nearly all': there, too, the distinction between saying 'Every, or nearly every single A *has been found* to be a B' and saying 'An A *can be taken*, certainly or almost certainly, to be a B' is concealed by the over-simple form of words 'All A's are B's.' A crucial difference in practical function can in this way pass unmarked and unnoticed.

Our own more complex pattern of analysis, by contrast, avoids this defect. It leaves no room for ambiguity: entirely separate places are left in the pattern for a warrant and for the backing upon which its authority depends. For instance, our 'scarcely any...' argument will have to be set out in the following way:

D (Petersen is————————→So Q (almost   C (Petersen is not a
   a Swede) | certainly)   Roman Catholic)
                   Since
                   W
        (A Swede can be taken to be
         almost certainly not a
            Roman Catholic)
                   |
                Because
                   B
        (The proportion of Roman
         Catholic Swedes is less
              than 2%)

Corresponding transcriptions will be needed for arguments of the other three types.

When we are theorising about the syllogism, in which a central part is played by propositions of the forms 'All A's are B's' and 'No A's are B's', it will accordingly be as well to bear this distinction in mind. The form of statement 'All A's are B's' is as it stands deceptively simple: it may have in use both the force of a warrant and the factual content of its backing, two aspects which we can bring out by expanding it in different ways. Sometimes it may be used, standing alone, in only one of these two ways at once; but often enough, especially in arguments, we make the single statement do both jobs at once and gloss over, for brevity's sake, the transition from backing to warrant—from the factual information we are presupposing to the inference-licence which that information justifies us in employing. The practical economy of this habit may be obvious; but for philosophical purposes it leaves the effective structure of our arguments insufficiently candid.

There is a clear parallel between the complexity of 'all...' statements and that of modal statements. As before, the *force* of the statements is invariant for all fields of argument. When we consider this aspect of the statements, the form 'All A's are B's' may always be replaced by the form 'An A can certainly be taken to be a B': this will be true regardless of the field, holding good equally of 'All Swedes are Roman Catholics', 'All those born in British colonies are entitled to British citizenship', 'All whales are mammals', and 'All lying is reprehensible'—in each case, the general statement will serve as a warrant authorising an argument of precisely the same form, D→C, whether the step goes from 'Harry was born in Bermuda' to 'Harry is a British citizen' or from 'Wilkinson told a lie' to 'Wilkinson acted reprehensibly.' Nor should there be any mystery about the nature of the step from D to C, since the whole *force* of the general statement 'All A's are B's', as so understood, is to authorise just this sort of step.

By contrast, the kind of *grounds* or *backing* supporting a warrant of this form will depend on the field of argument: here the parallel with modal statements is maintained. From this point of view, the important thing is the factual content, not the force of 'all...' statements. Though a warrant of the form 'An A can certainly be taken to be a B' must hold good in any field in virtue of *some* facts, the actual sort of facts in virtue of which any warrant will have currency and authority will vary according to the field of argument within which that warrant operates; so, when we expand the simple form 'All A's are B's' in order to make explicit the nature of the backing it is used to express, the expansion we must make will also depend upon the field with which we are concerned. In one case, the statement will become 'The proportion of A's found to be B's is 100%'; in another, 'A's are ruled by statute to count unconditionally as B's'; in a third, 'The class of B's includes taxonomically the entire class of A's'; and in a fourth, 'The practice of doing A leads to the following intolerable consequences, etc.' Yet, despite the striking differences between them, all these elaborate propositions are expressed on occasion in the compact and simple form 'All A's are B's.'

Similar distinctions can be made in the case of the forms, 'Nearly all A's are B's', 'Scarcely any A's are B's', and 'No A's are B's.' Used to express warrants, these differ from 'All A's are B's' in only one respect, that where before we wrote 'certainly' we must now write 'almost certainly', 'almost certainly not' or 'certainly not'. Likewise, when we are using them to state not warrants but backing: in a statistical case we shall simply have to replace '100%' by (say) 'at least 95%', 'less than 5%' or 'zero'; in the case of a statute replace 'unconditionally' by 'unless exceptional conditions hold', 'only in exceptional circumstances' or 'in no circumstances whatever'; and in a taxonomical case replace 'the entirety of the class of A's' by 'all but a small sub-class...', 'only a small sub-class...' or 'no part of...'. Once we have filled out the skeletal forms 'all...' and 'no...' in this way, the field-dependence of the backing for our warrants is as clear as it could be.

THE NOTION OF 'UNIVERSAL PREMISSES'

The full implications of the distinction between force and backing, as applied to propositions of the form 'All A's are B's', will become clear only after one further distinction has been introduced—that between 'analytic' and 'substantial' arguments. This cannot be done immediately, so for the moment all we can do is to hint at ways in which the traditional way of setting out arguments—in the form of two premisses followed by a conclusion—may be misleading.

Most obviously, this pattern of analysis is liable to create an exaggerated appearance of uniformity as between arguments in different fields, but what is probably as important is its power of disguising also the great differences between the things traditionally classed together as 'premisses'. Consider again examples of our standard type, in which a particular conclusion is justified by appeal to a particular datum about an individual—the singular, minor premiss—taken together with a general piece of information serving as warrant and/or backing—the universal, major premiss. So long as we interpret universal premisses as expressing not warrants but their backing, both major and minor premisses are at any rate categorical and factual: in this respect, the information that not a single Swede is recorded as being a Roman Catholic is on a par with the information that Karl Henrik Petersen is a Swede. Even so, the different roles played in practical argument by one's data and by the backing for one's warrants make it rather unfortunate to label them alike 'premisses'. But supposing we adopt the alternative interpretation of our major premisses, treating them instead as warrants, the differences between major and minor premisses are even more striking. A 'singular premiss' expresses a piece of information *from* which we are drawing a conclusion, a 'universal premiss' now expresses, not a piece of information at all, but a guarantee *in accordance with* which we can safely take the step from our datum to our conclusion. Such a guarantee, for all its backing, will be neither factual nor categorical but rather hypothetical and permissive. Once again, the two-fold distinction between 'premisses' and 'conclusion' appears insufficiently complex and, to do justice to the situation, one needs to adopt in its place at least the four-fold distinction between 'datum', 'conclusion', 'warrant' and 'backing'.

One way in which the distinction between the various possible interpretations of the 'universal premiss' may prove important to logicians can be illustrated by referring to an old logical puzzle. The question has often been debated, whether the form of statement 'All A's are B's' has or has not any existential implications: whether, that is, its use commits one to the belief that some A's do exist. Statements of the form 'Some A's are B's' have given rise to no such difficulty, for the use of this latter form always implies the existence of some A's, but the form 'All A's are B's' seems to be more ambiguous. It has been argued, for instance, that such a statement as 'All club-footed men have difficulty in walking' need not be taken as implying the existence of any club-footed men: this is a general truth, it is said, which would remain equally true even though, for once in a while, there were no living men having club feet, and it would not suddenly cease to be true that club-footedness made walking difficult just because the last club-footed man had been freed of his deformity by a skilful surgeon. Yet this leaves us uncomfortable: has our assertion then no existential force? Surely, we feel, club-footed men must at any rate *have* existed if we are to be able to make this assertion at all?

This conundrum illustrates very well the weaknesses of the term 'universal premiss'. Suppose that we rely on the traditional mode of analysis of arguments:

> Jack is club-footed;
> All club-footed men have difficulty in walking;
> So, Jack has difficulty in walking.

For so long as we do, the present difficulty will be liable to recur, since this pattern of analysis leaves it unclear whether the general statement 'All...' is to be construed as a permissive inference-warrant or as a factual report of our observations. Is it to be construed as meaning 'A club-footed man will (i.e. may be expected to) have difficulty in walking', or as meaning 'Every club-footed man of whom we have records had (i.e. was found to have) difficulty in walking'? We are not bound, except by long habit, to employ the form 'All A's are B's', with all the ambiguities it involves. We are at liberty to scrap it in favour of forms of expression which are more explicit, even if more cumbersome; and if we make this change, the problem about existential implications will simply no longer trouble us. The statement 'Every club-footed man of whom we have records...' implies, of course, that there have been at any rate *some* club-footed men, since otherwise we should have no records to refer to; while the warrant 'A club-footed man will have difficulty in walking', equally of course, leaves the existential question open. We can truthfully say that club-footedness would be a handicap to any pedestrian, even if we knew that at this moment everyone was lying on his back and nobody was so deformed. We are therefore not compelled to answer as it stands the question whether 'All A's are B's' has existential implications: certainly we can refuse a clear Yes or No. Some of the statements which logicians represent in this rather crude form do have such implications; others do not. No entirely general answer can be given to the question, for what determines whether there are or are not existential implications in any particular case is not the form of statement itself, but rather the practical use to which this form is put on that occasion.

Can we say then that the form 'All A's are B's' has existential implications when used to express the backing of a warrant, but not when used to express the warrant itself? Even this way of putting the point turns out to be too neat. For the other thing which excessive reliance on the form 'All A's are B's' tends to conceal from us is the different sorts of backing which our general beliefs may require, and these differences are relevant here. No doubt the statement that every club-footed man of whom we have any record found his deformity a handicap in walking, which we have here cited as backing, implies that there have been some such people; but we can back the same warrant by appeal to considerations of other kinds as well, e.g. by arguments explaining from anatomical principles in what way club-footedness may be expected to lead to disability—just how this shape of foot will prove a handicap. In these theoretical terms we could discuss the disabilities which would result from any kind of deformity we cared to imagine, including ones which nobody is known ever to have had: this sort of backing accordingly leaves the existential question open.

Again, if we consider warrants of other types, we find plenty of cases in which the backing for a warrant has, as it stands, no existential implication. This may be true, for instance, in the case of warrants backed by statutory provisions: legislation may refer to persons or situations which have yet to be—for instance, to all married women who will reach the age of 70 after 1 January 1984— or alternatively to classes of persons none of whom may ever exist, such as men found guilty on separate occasions of ten different murders. Statutes referring to people of these types can provide backing for inference-warrants entitling us to take all kinds of steps in argument, without either the warrants or their backing implying anything about the existence of such people at all. To sum up: if we pay closer attention to the differences between warrants and backing, and between different sorts of backing for one and the same warrant, and between the backing for warrants of different sorts, and if we refuse to focus our attention hypnotically on the traditional form 'All A's are B's', we can not only come to see *that* sometimes 'All A's are B's' does have existential implications and sometimes not, but furthermore begin to understand *why* this should be so.

Once one has become accustomed to expanding statements of the form 'All A's are B's', and replacing them, as occasion requires, by explicit warrants or explicit statements of backing, one will find it a puzzle that logicians have been wedded to this form of statement for so long. The reasons for this will concern us in a later essay:

for the moment, we may remark that they have done so only at the expense of impoverishing our language and disregarding a large number of clues to the proper solutions of their conundrums. For the form 'All A's are B's' occurs in practical argument much less than one would suppose from logic text-books: indeed, a great deal of effort has to be expended in order to train students in ways of rephrasing in this special form the idiomatic statements to which they are already accustomed, thereby making these idiomatic utterances apparently amenable to traditional syllogistic analysis. There is no need, in complaining of this, to argue that idiom is sacrosanct, or provides by itself understanding of a kind we could not have had before. Nevertheless, in our normal ways of expressing ourselves, one will find many points of idiom which can serve as very definite clues, and are capable in this case of leading us in the right direction.

Where the logician has in the past cramped all general statements into his predetermined form, practical speech has habitually employed a dozen different forms—'Every single A is a B', 'Each A is a B', 'An A will be a B', 'A's are generally B's' and 'The A is a B' being only a selection. By contrasting these idioms, instead of ignoring them or insisting that they all fall into line, logicians would long ago have been led on to the distinctions we have found crucial. The contrast between 'Every A' and 'Not a single A', on the one hand, and 'Any A' or 'An A', on the other, points one immediately towards the distinction between statistical reports and the warrants for which they can be the backing. The differences between warrants in different fields are also reflected in idiom. A biologist would hardly ever utter the words 'All whales are mammals'; though sentences such as 'Whales are mammals' or 'The whale is a mammal' might quite naturally come from his lips or his pen. Warrants are one thing, backing another; backing by enumerative observation is one thing, backing by taxonomic classification another; and our choices of idiom, though perhaps subtle, reflect these differences fairly exactly.

Even in so remote a field as philosophical ethics, some hoary problems have been generated in just this way. Practice forces us to recognise that general ethical truths can aspire at best to hold good in the absence of effective counter-claims: conflicts of duty are an inescapable feature of the moral life. Where logic demands the form '*All* lying is reprehensible' or '*All* promise-keeping is right', idiom therefore replies 'Lying is reprehensible' and 'Promise-keeping is right.' The logician's 'all' imports unfortunate expectations, which in practice are bound on occasion to be disappointed. Even the most general warrants in ethical arguments are yet liable in unusual situations to suffer exceptions, and so at strongest can authorise only presumptive conclusions. If we insist on the 'all', conflicts of duties land us in paradox, and much of moral theory is concerned with getting us out of this morass. Few people insist on trying to put into practice the consequences of insisting on the extra 'all', for to do so one must resort to desperate measures: it can be done only by adopting an eccentric moral position, such as absolute pacifism, in which one principle and one alone is admitted to be genuinely universal, and this principle is defended through thick and thin, in the face of all the conflicts and counter-claims which would normally qualify its application. The road from nice points about logic and idiom to the most difficult problems of conduct is not, after all, such a long one.

THE NOTION OF FORMAL VALIDITY

The chief morals of this study of practical argument will be our concern in the final pair of essays. But there is one topic—the one from which this present essay began—about which we are already in a position to say something: namely, the idea of 'logical form', and the doctrines which attempt to explain the validity of arguments in terms of this notion of form. It is sometimes argued, for instance, that the validity of syllogistic arguments is a consequence of the fact that the conclusions of these arguments are simply 'formal transformations' of their premisses. If the information we start from, as expressed in the major and minor premisses, leads to the conclusion it does by a valid inference, that (it is said) is because the conclusion results simply from shuffling the parts of the premisses and rearranging them in a new pattern. In drawing the inference, we re-order the given elements, and the formal relations between these elements as they appear, first in the premisses and then in the conclusion, somehow or other assure for us the validity of the inference which we make.

How does this doctrine look, if we now make our central distinction between the two aspects of the statement-form 'All A's are B's'? Consider an argument of the form:

> X is an A;
> All A's are B's;
> So X is a B.

If we expand the universal premiss of this argument as a warrant, it becomes 'Any A can certainly be taken to be a B' or, more briefly, 'An A is certainly a B.' Substituting this in the argument, we obtain:

> X is an A;
> An A is certainly a B;
> So X is certainly a B.

When the argument is put in this way, the parts of the conclusion are manifestly the same as the parts of the premisses, and the conclusion can be obtained simply by shuffling the parts of the premisses and rearranging them. If that is what is meant by saying that the argument has the appropriate 'logical form', and that it is valid on account of that fact, then this may be said to be a 'formally valid' argument. Yet one thing must be noticed straight away: provided that the correct warrant is employed, any argument can be expressed in the form 'Data; warrant; so conclusion' and so become formally valid. By suitable choice of phrasing, that is, any such argument can be so expressed that its validity is apparent simply from its form: this is true equally, whatever the field of the argument—it makes no difference if the universal premiss is 'All multiples of 2 are even', 'All lies are reprehensible' or 'All whales are mammals.' Any such premiss can be written as an unconditional warrant, 'An A is certainly a B', and used in a formally valid inference; or, to put the point less misleadingly, can be used in an inference which is so set out that its validity becomes formally manifest.

On the other hand, if we substitute the backing for the warrant, i.e. interpret the universal premiss in the other way, there will no longer be any room for applying the idea of formal validity to our argument. An argument of the form 'Data; backing; so conclusion' may, for practical purposes, be entirely in order. We should accept without hesitation the argument:

> Petersen is a Swede;
> The recorded proportion of Roman Catholic Swedes is zero;
> So, certainly, Petersen is not a Roman Catholic.

But there can no longer be any pretence that the soundness of this argument is a consequence of any formal properties of its constituent expressions. Apart from anything else, the elements of the conclusion and premisses are not the same: the step therefore involves more than shuffling and re-ordering. For that matter, of course, the validity of the (D; W; so C) argument was not really a *consequence* of its formal properties either, but at any rate in that case one could state the argument in a particularly tidy form. Now this can no longer be done: a (D; B; so C) argument will not be formally valid. Once we bring into the open the backing on which (in the last resort) the soundness of our arguments depends, the suggestion that validity is to be explained in terms of 'formal properties', in any geometrical sense, loses its plausibility.

This discussion of formal validity can throw some light on another point of idiom: one in which the customary usage of arguers again parts company with logical tradition. The point arises in the following way. Suppose we contrast what may be called 'warrant-using' arguments with 'warrant-establishing' ones. The first class will include, among others, all those in which a single datum is relied on to establish a conclusion by appeal to some warrant whose acceptability is being taken for granted—examples are 'Harry was born in Bermuda, so presumably (people born in the colonies being entitled to British citizenship) Harry is a British citizen', 'Jack told a lie, so presumably (lying being generally reprehensible) Jack behaved in a reprehensible way', and 'Petersen is a Swede, so presumably (scarcely any Swedes being Roman Catholics) Petersen is not a Roman Catholic.' Warrant-establishing arguments will be, by contrast, such arguments as one might find in a scientific paper, in which the acceptability of a novel warrant is made clear by applying it successively in a number of cases in which both 'data' and 'conclusion' have been independently verified. In this type of argument the warrant, not the conclusion, is novel, and so on trial.

Professor Gilbert Ryle has compared the steps involved in these two types of argument with, respectively, the taking of a journey along a railway already built and the building of a fresh railway: he has argued persuasively that only the first class of arguments should be referred to as 'inferences', on the ground that the essential element of innovation in the latter class cannot be made the subject of rules and that the notion of inference essentially involves the possibility of 'rules of inference'.

The point of idiom to be noticed here is this: that the distinction we have marked by the unwieldy terms 'warrant-using' and 'warrant-establishing' is commonly indicated in practice by the word 'deductive', its affiliates and their opposites. Outside the study the family of words, 'deduce', 'deductive' and 'deduction', is applied to arguments from many fields; all that is required is that these arguments shall be warrant-using ones, applying established warrants to fresh data to derive new conclusions. It makes no difference to the propriety of these terms that the step from D to C will in some cases involve a transition of logical type—that it is, for instance, a step from information about the past to a prediction about the future.

Sherlock Holmes, at any rate, never hesitated to say that he had *deduced*, e.g., that a man was recently in East Sussex from the colour and texture of the fragments of soil he left upon the study carpet; and in this he spoke like a character from real life. An astronomer would say, equally readily, that he had *deduced* when a future eclipse would occur from the present and past positions and motions of the heavenly bodies involved. As Ryle implies, the meaning of the word 'deduce' is effectively the same as that of 'infer'; so that, wherever there are established warrants or set procedures of computation by which to pass from data to a conclusion, there we may properly speak of 'deductions'. A regular prediction, made in accordance with the standard equations of stellar dynamics, is in this sense an unquestionable deduction; and so long as Sherlock Holmes also is capable of producing sound, well-backed warrants to justify his steps, we can allow that he too has been making deductions—unless one has just been reading a text-book of formal logic. The protestations of another sleuth that Sherlock Holmes was in error, in taking for deductions arguments which were really inductive, will strike one as hollow and mistaken.

The other side of this coin is also worth a glance: namely, the way in which the word 'induction' can be used to refer to warrant-establishing arguments. Sir Isaac Newton, for instance, regularly speaks of 'rendering a proposition general by induction': by this he turns out to mean 'using our observations of regularities and correlations as the backing for a novel warrant'. We begin, he explains, by establishing that a particular relation holds in a certain number of cases, and then, 'rendering it general by induction', we continue to apply it to fresh examples for so long as we can successfully do so: if we get into trouble as a result, he says, we are to find ways of rendering the general statement 'liable to exceptions', i.e. to discover the special circumstances in which the presumptions established by the warrant are liable to rebuttal. A general statement in physical theory, as Newton reminds us, must be construed not as a statistical report about the behaviour of a very large number of objects, but rather as an open warrant or principle of computation: it is established by testing it in sample situations where both data and conclusion are independently known, then rendered general by induction, and finally applied as a rule of deduction in fresh situations to derive novel conclusions from our data.

In many treatises on formal logic, on the other hand, the term deduction is reserved for arguments in which the data and backing positively entail the conclusion—in which, that is to say, to state all the data and backing and yet to deny the conclusion would land one in a positive inconsistency or contradiction. This is, of course, an ideal of deduction which no astronomer's prediction could hope to approach; and if that is what formal logicians are going to demand of any 'deduction', it is no wonder they are unwilling to call such computations by that name. Yet the astronomers are unwilling to change their habits: they have been calling their elaborate mathematical demonstrations 'deductions' for a very long time, and they use the term to mark a perfectly genuine and consistent distinction.

What are we to make of this conflict of usage? Ought we to allow any argument to count as a deduction which applies an established warrant, or must we demand in addition that it should be backed by a positive entailment? This question we are not yet ready to determine. All we can do at the moment is register the fact that at this point customary idiom outside the study tends to deviate from the professional usage of logicians. As we shall see, this particular deviation is only one aspect of a larger one, which will concern us throughout a large part of our fourth essay and whose nature will become clearer when we have studied one final distinction. To that distinction, between 'analytic' and 'substantial' arguments, we must now turn.

ANALYTIC AND SUBSTANTIAL ARGUMENTS

This distinction is best approached by way of a preamble. We remarked some way back that an argument expressed in the form 'Datum; warrant; so conclusion' can be set out in a formally valid manner, regardless of the field to which it belongs; but this could never be done, it appeared, for arguments of the form 'Datum; backing for warrant; so conclusion'. To return to our stock example: if we are given information about Harry's birthplace, we may be able to draw a conclusion about his nationality, and defend it with a formally valid argument of the form (D; W; so C). But the warrant we apply in this formally valid argument rests in turn for its authority on facts about the enactment and provisions of certain statutes, and we can therefore write out the argument in the alternative form (D; B; so C), i.e.:

> Harry was born in Bermuda;
> The relevant statutes ($W_1 \ldots$) provide that people born in the colonies of British parents are entitled to British citizenship;
> So, presumably, Harry is a British citizen.

When we choose this form, there is no question of claiming that the validity of the argument is evident simply from the formal relations between the three statements in it. Stating the backing for our warrant in such a case inevitably involves mentioning Acts of Parliament and the like, and these references destroy the formal elegance of the argument. In other fields, too, explicitly mentioning the backing for our warrant—whether this takes the form of statistical reports, appeals to the results of experiments, or references to taxonomical systems—will prevent us from writing the argument so that its validity shall be manifest from its formal properties alone.

As a general rule, therefore, we can set out in a formally valid manner arguments of the form 'D; W; so C' alone: arguments of the form 'D; B; so C' cannot be so expressed. There is, however, one rather special class of arguments which appears at first sight to break this general rule, and these we shall in due course christen *analytic* arguments. As an illustration we may take the following:

> Anne is one of Jack's sisters;
> All Jack's sisters have red hair;
> So, Anne has red hair.

Arguments of this type have had a special place in the history of logic, and we shall have to pay close attention to them: it has not always been recognised how rare, in practice, arguments having their special characteristics are.

As a first move, let us expand this argument as we have already done those of other types. Writing the major premiss as a statement of backing, we obtain:

> Anne is one of Jack's sisters;
> Each one of Jack's sisters has (been checked individually to have) red hair;
> So, Anne has red hair.

Alternatively, writing warrant in place of backing, we have:

> Anne is one of Jack's sisters;
> Any sister of Jack's will (i.e. may be taken to) have red hair;
> So, Anne has red hair.

This argument is exceptional in the following respect. If each one of the girls has been checked individually to have red hair, then Anne's hair-colour has been specifically checked in the process. In this case, accordingly, the backing of our warrant includes explicitly the information which we are presenting as our conclusion: indeed, one might very well replace the word 'so' before the conclusion by the phrase 'in other words', or 'that is to say'. In such a case, to accept the datum and the backing is *thereby* to accept implicitly the conclusion also; if we string datum, backing and conclusion together to form a single sentence, we end up with an actual tautology—'Anne is one of Jack's sisters and each one of Jack's sisters has red hair *and also* Anne has red hair.' So, for once, not only the (D; W; so C) argument but also the (D; B; so C) argument can—it appears —be stated in a formally valid manner.

Most of the arguments we have practical occasion to make use of are, one need hardly say, not of this type. We make claims about the future, and back them by reference to our experience of how things have gone in the past; we make assertions about a man's feelings, or about his legal status, and back them by references to his utterances and gestures, or to his place of birth and to the statutes about nationality; we adopt moral positions, and pass aesthetic judgements, and declare support for scientific theories or political causes, in each case producing as grounds for our conclusion statements of quite other logical types than the conclusion itself. Whenever we do any of these things, there can be no question of the conclusion's being regarded as a mere restatement in other words of something already stated implicitly in the datum and the backing: though the argument may be formally valid when expressed in the form 'Datum; warrant; so conclusion', the step we take in passing to the conclusion from the information we have to rely on—datum and backing together—is a substantial one. In most of our arguments, therefore, the statement obtained by writing 'Datum; backing; *and also* conclusion' will be far from a tautology—obvious it may be, where the legitimacy of the step involved is transparent, but tautological it will not.

In what follows, I shall call arguments of these two types respectively *substantial* and *analytic*. An argument from D to C will be called analytic if and only if the backing for the warrant authorising it includes, explicitly or implicitly, the information conveyed in the conclusion itself. Where this is so, the statement 'D, B, and also C' will, as a rule, be tautological. (This rule is, however, subject to some exceptions which we shall study shortly.) Where the backing for the warrant does not contain the information conveyed in the conclusion, the statement 'D, B, and also C' will never be a tautology, and the argument will be a substantial one.

The need for some distinction of this general sort is obvious enough, and certain aspects of it have forced themselves on the attention of logicians, yet its implications have never been consistently worked out. This task has been neglected for at least two reasons. To begin with, the internal complexity of statements of the form 'All A's are B's' helps to conceal the full difference between analytic and substantial arguments. Unless we go to the trouble of expanding these statements, so that it becomes manifest whether they are to be understood as stating warrants or the backing for warrants, we overlook the great variety of arguments susceptible of presentation in the traditional syllogistic form: we have to bring out the distinction between backing and warrant explicitly in any particular case if we are to be certain what sort of argument we are concerned with on that occasion. In the second place, it has not been recognised how exceptional genuinely analytic arguments are, and how difficult it is to produce an argument which will be analytic past all question: if logicians had recognised these facts, they might have been less ready to treat analytic arguments as a model which other types of argument were to emulate.

Even our chosen example, about the colour of Anne's hair, may easily slip out of the analytic into the substantial class. If the backing for our step from datum, 'Anne is Jack's sister', to conclusion, 'Anne has red hair', is just the information that each of Jack's sisters has *in the past* been observed to have red hair, then—one might argue—the argument is a substantial one even as it stands. After all, dyeing is not unknown. So ought we not to rewrite the argument in such a way as to bring out its substantial character openly? On this interpretation the argument will become:

Datum—Anne is one of Jack's sisters;
Backing—All Jack's sisters have previously been observed to have red hair;
Conclusion—So, presumably, Anne now has red hair.

The warrant relied on, for which the backing is here stated, will be of the form, 'Any sister of Jack's may be taken to have red hair': for the reasons given, this warrant can be regarded as establishing no more than a presumption:

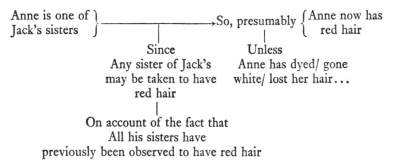

It seems, then, that I can defend my conclusion about Anne's hair with an unquestionably analytic argument only if at this very moment I have all of Jack's sisters in sight, and so can back my warrant with the assurance that every one of Jack's sisters has red hair at this moment. But, in such a situation, what need is there of an *argument* to establish the colour of Anne's hair? And of what relevance is the other sisters' hair-colour? The thing to do now is use one's eyes, not hunt up a chain of reasoning. If the purpose of an argument is to establish conclusions about which we are not entirely confident by relating them back to other information about which we have greater assurance, it begins to be a little doubtful whether any genuine, practical argument could *ever* be properly analytic.

Mathematical arguments alone seem entirely safe: given the assurance that every sequence of six or more integers between 1 and 100 contains at least one prime number, and also the information that none of the numbers from 62 up to 66 is a prime, I can thankfully conclude that the number 67 is a prime; and that is an argument whose validity neither time nor the flux of change can call in question. This unique character of mathematical arguments is significant. Pure mathematics is possibly the only intellectual activity whose problems and solutions are 'above time'. A mathematical problem is not a quandary; its solution has no time-limit; it involves no steps of substance. As a model argument for formal logicians to analyse, it may be seducingly elegant, but it could hardly be less representative.

THE PECULIARITIES OF ANALYTIC ARGUMENTS

For the rest of this essay, two chief tasks remain. First, we must clarify a little further the special characteristics of analytic arguments: after that, we must contrast the distinction between analytic and substantial arguments with three other distinctions whose importance we have already seen:

(i) that between formally valid arguments and those which are not formally valid,

(ii) that between warrant-using and warrant-establishing arguments,

(iii) that between arguments leading to necessary conclusions and those leading only to probable conclusions.

As to the nature of analytic arguments themselves, two things need to be discussed. To begin with we must ask upon what foundation arguments of this type ultimately depend for their validity: after that, we must go on to reconsider the criteria provisionally suggested for distinguishing analytic arguments from others—for the 'tautology test' turns out, after all, to involve unsuspected difficulties.

To see how the first question arises, one should first recall how much less sharply than usual, in the case of analytic arguments, we can distinguish between data and warrant-backing—between the information we argue *from*, and the information which lends authority to the warrants we argue *in accordance with*: so far as it concerns the conclusion that Anne has red hair, the information that Anne is Jack's sister has, at first sight, the same sort of bearing as the information that every one of Jack's sisters has red hair. This similarity may lead us to construe both pieces of information as data, and if we do so the question may be raised, 'What warrant authorises us to pass from these two premisses jointly to the required conclusion?' Surely we cannot get from *any* set of data to a conclusion without *some* warrant; so what warrant can we produce to justify our inference in this case? This is the problem, and we can tackle it in only two ways: either we must accept the question, and produce a warrant, or alternatively we must reject the question in the form in which it stands, and insist on sending it back for rephrasing. (It is arguable, for instance, that we have a perfectly good warrant for passing from the *first* datum to the conclusion, and that the second piece of information is the backing for that warrant.) For the moment, however, let us consider this problem in the form in which it arises here.

The first thing to notice about this problem is the fact that it is completely general. So long as one is arguing only from Anne's being Jack's sister to her having red hair, the question what warrant authorises our inference is a *particular* question, relevant only to this argument and a few others; but if one asks, what warrant authorises us to pass from the information *both* that Anne is Jack's sister *and* that every single one of Jack's sisters has red hair to the conclusion that Anne has red hair, that question is nowhere near so restricted a question, since it can arise in exactly the same form for all arguments of this type, whatever their explicit subject-matter. The answer to be given must therefore be equally general, and stated in such a way as to apply equally to all such arguments. What warrant, then, are we to say does authorise this particular step? The attempts to answer this question satisfactorily have been prolonged and inconclusive, and we cannot follow them through here: several different principles of a wholly general character have been put forward as the implied warrant for steps of this kind—the 'Principle of the Syllogism', the 'Dictum de Omni et Nullo', and others. But, quite apart from the respective merits of their rival answers, philosophers have not even been agreed about *how* such general principles really authorise us to argue as we do. What sort of a statement is (say) the Principle of the Syllogism?—that is the first question needing attention.

There is a temptation to say that any principle validating all syllogisms alike must be understood as a statement about the meanings of our words—an implicit analysis of such pre-eminently logical words as 'all' and 'some'. One consequence of this view, which we shall scrutinise in the next essay, has been the growth of a rather limited doctrine about the nature and scope of logic. If the only principles of inference properly so-called are statements about the meanings of our words, then (some have argued) it is misleading to apply the title of inferring-rules to other sorts of general statement also, which are concerned with matters of substance and not simply with the meanings of our words: as a result, the whole notion of inference-warrants, as set out in this essay, has been pushed aside as confused.

Now we may agree that there is not an exact parallel between the Principle of the Syllogism and those other sorts of argument-governing rules we have given the name of 'warrant', and yet feel that this conclusion goes too far. Without questioning at the moment the need for some Principle of the Syllogism, we may yet object to its being called a statement *about* the meanings of our words: why should we not see in it, rather, a warrant of a kind that holds good *in virtue of* the meanings of our words? This is an improvement on the previous formulation in at least one respect, for it leaves us free to say that other warrants—those we argue in accordance with outside the analytic field—hold good in virtue of other sorts of consideration. Legal principles hold good in virtue of statutory enactments and judicial precedents, the scientist's laws of nature in virtue of the experiments and observations by which they were established, and so on. In all fields, the force of our warrants is to authorise the step from certain types of data to certain types of conclusions, but, after all we have seen about the field-dependence of the criteria we employ in the practical business of argument, it is only natural to expect that inference-warrants in different fields should need establishing by quite different sorts of procedure.

Accordingly, there seems room for an accommodation—for us to accept the Principle of the Syllogism as the warrant of all analytic syllogisms, while retaining other kinds of general statement as warrants for arguments of other types. Yet there remains something paradoxical about admitting the need for a Principle of the Syllogism at all. With arguments of all other kinds, a man who is given the data and the conclusion and who understands perfectly well what he is told may yet need to have explained to him the authority for the step from one to the other. 'I understand what your evidence is, and I understand what conclusion you draw from it,' he may say, 'but I don't see *how* you get there.' The task of the warrant is to meet his need: in order to satisfy him we have to explain what is our warrant, and if necessary show on what backing it depends, and until we have done this it is still open to him to challenge our argument. With analytic arguments, on the other hand, this sort of situation is hardly conceivable: one is tempted to say of analytic arguments (as of analytic statements) that anyone who understands them must acknowledge their legitimacy. If a man does not see the legitimacy of an analytic step in any particular case, we shall not help him much by proffering him any principle so general as the Principle of the Syllogism.

The suggestion that this principle really does a job for us, by serving as the warrant for all syllogistic arguments, is therefore implausible. Certainly, if it *is* to be regarded as a warrant, it is a warrant which requires no backing: this much is conceded by Aristotle in the fourth book of the *Metaphysics*, where he goes out of his way to reject any demand that the law of non-contradiction should be *proved*—he recognises that no backing we could produce would add anything to the strength of the principle, and that all we need do in its defence is to challenge a critic to produce a meaningful objection to it.

Let us therefore try following the alternative course: let us reject the request for a warrant to lend authority to all analytic syllogisms, insisting instead that one premiss of every such syllogism provides all the warrant we need. The information that *every* one of Jack's sisters has red hair, we may say, serves as backing for the warrant that *any* of his sisters may be taken to have hair of that colour, and it is this limited warrant which takes us from our initial information about Anne's being Jack's sister to the conclusion about her hair-colour: 'that's just analytic!' Our task is now to define more carefully what exactly here is 'just analytic', and to work out clearer tests than we have stated so far for recognising whether an argument is an analytic or a substantial one.

Three different tests suggest themselves, and their merits we must now consider. First, there is the *tautology* test: in an analytic syllogism with an 'all' in the major premiss, the data and backing positively entail the conclusion, so that we can write 'D, B, or *in other words* C', confident that in stating the conclusion we shall simply be repeating something already stated in the backing. The question is whether this is true of *all* analytic arguments: I shall argue that it is not. Secondly, there is the *verification* test: must verifying the backing implicitly relied on in an argument *ipso facto* involve checking the truth of the conclusion? This does not universally lead to the same result as the first test, and will prove to be a more satisfactory criterion. Finally, there is the test of *self-evidence*: once a man has had data, backing and conclusion explained to him, can he still raise genuine questions about the validity of the argument? This might at first seem to amount to the same as the first test but, as we shall see, it corresponds in practice more nearly to the second.

One type of example can be mentioned straight away in which the tautology criterion leads to difficulties. This is the 'quasi-syllogism', discussed earlier, in which the universal quantifiers 'all' and 'no' are replaced by the more restrictive ones 'nearly all' and 'scarcely any'. As an instance, we may take the argument:

> Petersen is a Swede;
> Scarcely any Swedes are Roman Catholics;
> So, almost certainly, Petersen is not a Roman Catholic.

This argument differs from the corresponding 'no' argument—

> Petersen is a Swede;
> No Swedes are Roman Catholics;
> So, certainly, Petersen is not a Roman Catholic—

only in relying on a weaker warrant and so ending in a more tentative conclusion. (Written explicitly as warrants the universal premisses are, respectively, 'A Swede can almost certainly be taken not to be a Roman Catholic' and 'A Swede can certainly be taken not to be a Roman Catholic'.)

The validity of the argument is in each case manifest, and by the test of self-evidence both should be classed as analytic arguments. If we imagine a man to challenge the 'scarcely any' argument, and to demand further backing to show its validity, his request will be no more intelligible than it would be in the case of the 'no' argument: he might ask in the first case to have the *conclusion* more firmly grounded, seeing that so long as we know only that scarcely any Swedes are Roman Catholics the possibility of any particular Swede's being of that persuasion is not ruled out past all question, but the *validity* of both arguments is surely not open to doubt. If he fails to see the force of either argument, there is little more we can do for him; and if he presents the same data and warrant-backing in support of the negated conclusion, the result will in either case be not just implausible but incomprehensible:

> Petersen is a Swede;
> The proportion of Roman Catholic Swedes is less than 5%/zero;
> So, almost certainly/certainly, Petersen *is* a Roman Catholic.

By the test of self-evidence, then, the 'scarcely any' and 'nearly all' arguments have as much right to be classed as analytic as have the 'all' and 'no' arguments.

But if we allow this parallel, how far do our other tests for recognising analytic arguments fit? In checking the backing for our warrant, we asked, would we *ipso facto* check the conclusion of our arguments? (This we called the verification test.) Alternatively, if we wrote down our data and backing, and added the words 'and also C'—C being our conclusion—would the result be a tautology? Traditional syllogisms satisfy all our criteria equally well. Checking exhaustively that the proportion of Roman Catholic Swedes is zero of course involves checking what Petersen's religion is; while in addition the statement, 'Petersen is a Swede, and the proportion of Roman Catholic Swedes is zero, and also Petersen is not a Roman Catholic', can reasonably be called tautological. But when we look at quasi-syllogisms, we find the tautology test no longer applicable.

The verification test still fits the new cases, though it applies in a slightly Pickwickian manner: in checking exhaustively that the proportion of Roman Catholic Swedes was (say) less than 5%, we should *ipso facto* check what Petersen's religion was—whether it was actually Roman Catholicism or not. On the other hand, the statement, 'Petersen is a Swede and the proportion of Roman Catholic Swedes is less than 5%, and also Petersen is not a Roman Catholic', is no longer tautological: it is, rather, genuinely informative, since the conclusion locates Petersen definitely in the 95% majority.

Even if we insert the modal qualifier 'almost certainly' in the conclusion, the resulting statement is not tautological either—'Petersen is a Swede, the proportion of Roman Catholic Swedes is less than 5%, and also, almost certainly, Petersen is not a Roman Catholic.'

As a result, when we look for a general criterion to mark off analytic arguments from others, the verification test will enable us to classify quasi-syllogisms along with traditional syllogisms in a way the tautology test will not. We shall therefore class an argument as analytic if, and only if, it satisfies that criterion—if, that is, checking the backing of the warrant involves *ipso facto* checking the truth or falsity of the conclusion—and we shall do this whether a knowledge of the full backing would in fact verify the conclusion or falsify it.

At this point, two comments are needed about Petersen's case. Once we do have access to the complete backing, we shall of course no longer be entitled to rely simply on the bare percentage of the statistician's tables and our original argument will no longer be in place. We must base our argument about the likelihood of Petersen's being a Roman Catholic on *all* the relevant information we can get: if we in fact possess the detailed census returns, the only proper procedure is to look Petersen up by name, and find out the answer for certain. Secondly, the statement, 'Petersen is a Swede and the proportion of Roman Catholic Swedes is very low, and Petersen is almost certainly not a Roman Catholic', *would* be entirely tautological if one could properly *define* 'certainty' and 'probability' directly in terms of proportions and frequency. But to do this, as we saw, would mean ignoring the practical function of the term 'probability' and its cognates as modal qualifiers. It would also lead to paradox: as things stand, a man can say with perfect propriety, 'Petersen is a Swede and the proportion of Roman Catholic Swedes is very low, and yet Petersen is almost certainly a Roman Catholic'—he will be entitled to say this, for instance, if he knows something further about Petersen which places him very probably in the Roman Catholic minority—whereas, if the original statement were a tautology, this new statement would be bound to be a self-contradiction.

One cannot, then, characterise analytic arguments as arguments in which the statement 'D, B and also C' is a tautology: in some cases at least, this criterion fails to serve our purposes. This helps to explain one further philosophical doctrine—that even analytic syllogisms are not valid in virtue of the meanings of words alone, and that failure to understand such an argument is a sign, not of linguistic incompetence, but rather of a 'defect of reason'. Suppose we tell a man that Petersen is a Swede, and that the proportion of Roman Catholic Swedes is either zero or very low; 'so', we conclude, 'Petersen is certainly—or almost certainly—not a Roman Catholic'. He fails to follow us: what then are we to say about him? If the tautology test were adequate, this would show that he did not really understand the meanings of all the words we had employed: if we give up the tautology view, this explanation is no longer open to us. Now we must say, rather, that he is blind to, i.e. fails to see the force of, the argument. Indeed what else can we say? This is not an explanation: it is a bare statement of the fact. He just does not follow the step, and the ability to follow such arguments is, surely, one of the *basic* rational competences.

This observation can throw some light on the true status of the Principle of the Syllogism. That principle, I suggested, enters logic when the second premiss of an analytic syllogism is misinterpreted as stating a datum instead of a warrant or its backing, and the argument is thereupon (apparently) left without any authorising warrant. The Principle of the Syllogism is then held out to us as somehow showing the *ultimate* foundation for the validity of *all* syllogistic arguments.

When considering arguments in other fields, we may again find ourselves going through this same sequence of steps. Suppose we begin by mistaking the backing of our warrant for an additional set of data; having done this, we shall appear to be arguing straight from data to conclusion, without our step's having any authority; and this lack will be found to affect, not just one, but every argument in the field concerned. To fill these fresh gaps, further completely general principles will now need to be invoked: one basic principle to lie behind all scientific predictions, another to lie behind all properly grounded moral judgements, and so on. (This is a topic which we need mention here only in passing, since we shall have to return to it in the last of these essays.) Now, if the ability to follow valid syllogisms and quasi-syllogisms can best be described as a basic rational competence, and is not really explained in terms of linguistic ability or incompetence, perhaps there will be nothing more to be said in other cases either. The ability to follow simple predictive arguments, whose warrants are backed by sufficiently wide and relevant experience, may just have to be recognised as another simple rational skill, which most men possess but which is lacking in some mental defectives; and for other fields, other basic skills. Could this be said for arguments in all fields whatever? Is the ability to follow, and see the force of simple moral arguments (say), also such a skill? Or simple aesthetic arguments? Or simple theological arguments?...At this point we come directly up against the fundamental philosophical issue: whether all fields of argument alike are open to rational discussion, and whether the Court of Reason is competent to adjudicate equally, whatever the type of problem under discussion.

SOME CRUCIAL DISTINCTIONS

One major task remains for us to perform in this essay: we have to distinguish the division of arguments into analytic and substantial from three or four other possible modes of division. The dangers resulting from confusing these distinctions, and still more from running them together, are serious and can be avoided only with care.

To begin with, the division into analytic and substantial arguments does not correspond at all exactly to the division into *formally valid* arguments and others. An argument in any field whatever *may* be expressed in a formally valid manner, provided that the warrant is formulated explicitly as a warrant and authorises precisely the sort of inference in question: this explains how mathematical computations can be formally valid, even when the data argued from are entirely past and present observations and the conclusion argued to is a prediction about the future. On the other hand, an argument may be analytic, and yet not be expressed in a formally valid way: this is the case, for instance, when an analytic argument is written out with the backing of the warrant cited in place of the warrant itself.

Nor does the distinction between analytic and substantial arguments correspond, either, to that between *warrant-using* and *warrant-establishing* arguments. In a very few cases, warrant-establishing arguments can be stated in a form which is formally valid: thus the argument, 'Jack has three sisters; the first has red hair, the second has red hair, the third has red hair; so all Jack's sisters have red hair', might be said to be at once warrant-establishing, formally valid and analytic. But, by and large, these characteristics vary independently. There can be warrant-using and warrant-establishing arguments both in the analytic field, and in other, substantial fields of argument, and one cannot seriously hope to make the two distinctions cut along one and the same line.

Again, it has sometimes been thought that one could mark off a specially 'logical' class of arguments by reference to the *sorts of words* appearing in them. In some arguments, for instance, the words 'all' and 'some' play a crucial part, and such arguments as these deserve separate consideration. But if we do mark them off from others, we must immediately observe that the division which results corresponds no more closely than the previous two to the division between analytic arguments and substantial ones. Not all arguments are analytic in which the word 'all' appears in the major premiss or warrant: this will be so only in cases where the process of establishing the warrant would involve *ipso facto* checking the truth of the conclusion now to be inferred with its aid, and we do not restrict our use of 'all' to such cases. The task of identifying analytic arguments cannot therefore be performed by looking for key words like 'all' and 'some': it can be done only by looking at the nature of the problem under investigation, and the manner in which we establish the warrants relevant to its solution.

These three distinctions can be recognised easily enough. The fourth and last distinction is at once the most contentious and the most important. Dividing arguments into analytic and substantial is not the same, I shall argue, as dividing them into arguments whose conclusions can be inferred *necessarily* or *certainly* and those whose conclusions can be inferred only *possibly* or with *probability*. As we saw when discussing modal qualifiers, there are some arguments in which the warrant authorises the step from D to C unambiguously, and others in which the step is authorised only tentatively, conditionally or with qualifications. This division is marked in practice by the words 'necessary' or 'conclusive' on the one hand, and 'tentative', 'probable', 'provisional' or 'conditional' on the other, and it is quite independent of the division into analytic arguments and substantial ones. Yet often enough logical theorists have attempted to run these two distinctions together, identifying analytic arguments with necessary or conclusive ones, and substantial arguments with tentative, probable or inconclusive ones. The crucial question is whether this conflation can be justified, or whether, rather, we do not have occasion in practice to classify some arguments as at once substantial *and* conclusive, or as both analytic *and* tentative. If we pay attention to the manner in which these categories are employed in the practical business of arguing, we shall discover plenty of occasions for making use of these seeming cross-classifications. For instance, a great many of the warrants in accordance with which we argue in the explanatory sciences authorise us to draw a conclusion unambiguously and unequivocally. The arguments they figure in are, accordingly, both substantial and conclusive, and scientists who make use of such arguments do not hesitate to round them off with the words '...so necessarily C'. Arguments of this kind are commonly met with in applied mathematics, as when, using the methods of geometrical optics, one calculates from the height of a wall and the angle of elevation of the sun how deep a shadow the wall will cast on level ground when the sun is shining directly on to it—if told that the wall is 6 ft. high and the sun at an angle of 30 degrees, a physicist will happily say that the shadow *must* have a depth of ten and a half feet.

In his *Philosophical Essay on Probabilities*, Laplace draws explicit attention to this class of substantial-yet-conclusive arguments: 'In the applications of mathematical analysis to physics,' he says, 'the results have all the certainty of facts,'[1] and he contrasts them with those arguments in which statistics are relied on, and whose conclusions are no more than probable. It is significant that he draws his distinction in just the manner he does. By applying the Newtonian system of mechanics to a problem in stellar dynamics, he reminds us, we are normally led, not to a whole battery of possible predictions each with a greater or lesser expectation of eventual confirmation, but to one single, unambiguous and unequivocal solution. If we are prepared to acknowledge that Newtonian mechanics is sufficiently well established for the purpose of the problem in hand, then we must accept this particular conclusion as following necessarily from our original data.

The point can be put more strongly: given the present standing of the theory, we are entitled to dispute the necessity of the conclusion only if we are prepared to challenge the adequacy or relevance

[1] Ch. III, 'Third Principle'.

of Newtonian dynamics. This means, not just pointing out that arguments in planetary dynamics are substantial ones (so that their soundness can be questioned *without contradiction*), but showing that they are *in fact* unreliable; i.e. attacking Newtonian dynamics on its own ground. Unless we are prepared to carry through this challenge, with all that it involves, the astronomer is entitled to ignore our objections and to claim that, for his purposes, the theory provides a unique and uniquely reliable answer to his questions. An answer obtained by these methods certainly *must* be the answer, he will say, for it is the answer to which a correctly performed calculation in accordance with well-established procedures necessarily leads us.

Nor do we find these substantial-yet-conclusive arguments in the more elaborate and technical sciences alone. When Sherlock Holmes says to Watson, 'So you see, my dear Watson, it *could only* have been Joseph Harrison who stole the Naval Treaty', or 'I concluded that the thief *must* be somebody living in the house', he does not mean that he can produce an analytic argument to establish his conclusion: he means rather that, by other-than-analytic standards and by appeal to other-than-analytic warrants, the evidence admits of this conclusion alone.

How widely this point of view deviates from that of many formal logicians, we shall see in the next essay. For them it is a commonplace that no argument can be both substantial and conclusive: only the conclusions of analytic arguments, they claim, can properly be classified as necessary, and the conclusions of substantial arguments —however well established and securely based the warrants relied on in reaching them—can never be more than highly probable. Why do they embrace this conclusion? Well, they explain, one can always imagine circumstances in which we might be forced to reconsider any substantial warrant: however well established any theory may appear at the moment, it makes sense to talk of future experiences forcing us to revise it, and so long as that remains the case—as in the nature of things it always must do—it will be presumptuous of us to call any conclusion reached in this way a necessary one. We could escape from this quandary only if the idea of our having to reconsider our inference-warrant gave rise to a positive contradiction, and this could never happen except with an analytic argument, whose warrant was backed not by experience but by an entailment.

If we have occasion to recognise in practice a class of arguments which are at once substantial and conclusive, so also do we recognise a class of analytic arguments with tentative or qualified conclusions. Quasi-syllogisms once more provide a good example. As is clear from their very wording, these arguments are not absolutely conclusive: all they entitle us to infer is (say) that Petersen is *almost certainly*, or *probably*, *not* a Roman Catholic. At the same time, we must accept these arguments as analytic for two reasons: they satisfy our primary criterion of analyticity—the backing for the warrant employed including an implicit reference to the fact we are interested in inferring, even though we ourselves do not possess all the detailed backing; and further, the validity of such arguments must be evident as they stand, or not at all—if a man asks about a quasi-syllogism, 'Does it really follow? Is this really a legitimate inference?', we shall be as much at a loss to understand him as we should had he queried a genuine syllogism. One thing alone seems at first to count against calling quasi-syllogistic arguments analytic: the fact that data and backing taken together are, by linguistic standards, consistent with the negation of the conclusion—there is, as we saw, no positive contradiction in the supposition of Petersen's being a Swede, scarcely any Swedes being Roman Catholic, and yet Petersen's being a Roman Catholic. But then, how could one expect any *positive* contradiction here? The whole point of the qualifier 'probably' is to avoid any positive commitments, and this is its understood effect, whether it appears in an isolated statement or in the conclusion of an argument, and whether that argument is substantial or analytic. So here we have a *prima facie* case of an argument which is analytic without being conclusive.

At this point one objection may be pressed, as follows: 'Granted that quasi-syllogistic arguments are analytic, they nevertheless do not provide the example you require. You claim that they are tentative, but you succeed in giving this impression only by suppressing some of the essential data. If you were to state explicitly all the information needed for such arguments as these to be valid, it would become clear that they are not really tentative at all, but are as conclusive as one could ask.' What sort of information might one say was being suppressed? And would it, if brought to light, remove all inconclusiveness from these arguments? Two suggestions must be considered. Quasi-syllogistic arguments, it might be said, are valid only if we can add the datum, (*a*), ' . . . and we know nothing else relevant about Petersen'—given this extra datum, the argument turns into an analytic one, leading necessarily to the conclusion that the likelihood of Petersen's being a Roman Catholic is small. Or alternatively, it may be argued, we must insert the additional datum, (*b*), ' . . . and Petersen is a random Swede'—making this additional datum explicit, we shall see that a quasi-syllogistic argument is really a conclusive argument in disguise.

We cannot meet this objection by a straight denial, but only by restating it in a way which removes its force. It must of course be conceded that quasi-syllogisms can properly be advanced only if the initial data from which we argue state all that we know of relevance to the question at issue: if they represent no more than a part of our relevant knowledge, we shall be required to argue not categorically but hypothetically—'Given only the information that Petersen is a Swede, we might conclude that the chances of his being a Roman Catholic were slight. . .'. But does this mean that the statement, (*a*), was an essential item in our data, which we should never have omitted? Surely this statement is not so much a statement *of* a datum as a statement *about the nature of* our data: it would naturally appear, not as part of our answer to the question, 'What have you got to go on?', but rather as a comment which we might add subsequently, after having stated (say) the solitary fact about Petersen's nationality.

The objection that we have omitted the information, (*b*), that Petersen is a random Swede (or a Swede taken at random) can be turned in a similar way. The information that he was a red-haired Swede, or a dark-complexioned Swede, or a Finnish-speaking Swede, could be called an 'extra fact' about him, and might possibly affect, in one way or another, our expectations about his religious beliefs. But the information that he was a *random* Swede is not like this at all. It is not a further fact about him which might be relevant to our expectations; it is at most a second-order comment on our previous information, indicating that, for all we know, we are entitled to presume about Petersen anything which established generalities about Swedes would suggest. So, once again, the so-called additional datum, (*b*), turns out to be not so much a datum as a passing comment about the applicability to this particular man of a warrant based only on statistical generalities.

The division of arguments into analytic and substantial is, there-fore, entirely distinct from that into conclusive (necessary) and tentative (probable) arguments. Analytic arguments can be con-clusive or tentative, and conclusive ones analytic or substantial. At once, one terminological precaution becomes urgent: we must renounce the common habit of using the adverb 'necessarily' inter-changeably with the adverb 'deductively'—where this is used to mean 'analytically'. For where a substantial argument leads to an unequivocal conclusion, we are entitled to use the form 'D, so necessarily C', despite the fact that the relation between data, backing and conclusion is not analytic; and where an analytic argu-ment leads to a tentative conclusion, we cannot strictly say any longer that the conclusion follows 'necessarily'—only, that it follows analytically. Once we fall into the way of identifying 'analytically' and 'necessarily', we shall end up by having to conclude an argu-ment with the paradoxical words, '...so Petersen is necessarily probably not a Roman Catholic', or even, '...so Petersen is neces-sarily necessarily not a Roman Catholic'. Perhaps, indeed, it would be better to scrap the words 'deductively' and 'necessarily' entirely, and to replace them either by 'analytically' or by 'unequivocally' according to the needs of the example.

THE PERILS OF SIMPLICITY

This essay has been deliberately restricted to prosaic studies of the different sorts of criticism to which our micro-arguments are subject, and to building up a pattern of analysis sufficiently complex to do justice to the most obvious differences between these forms of criticism. Much of this distinction-making would be tedious if we were not looking ahead to a point where the distinctions would prove of philosophical importance. So, in this concluding section, we can afford not only to look back over the ground which we have covered, but also to glance ahead to see the sort of value which these distinctions will have, and which will give a point to these laborious preliminaries.

We began from a question about 'logical form'. This had two aspects: there was the question, what relevance the geometrical tidiness sought in traditional analyses of the syllogism could have for a man trying to tell sound arguments from unsound ones; and there was the further question whether, in any event, the traditional pattern for analysing micro-arguments—'Minor Premiss, Major Premiss, so Conclusion'—was complex enough to reflect all the distinctions forced upon us in the actual practice of argument-assessment. We tackled the latter question first, with an eye to the example of jurisprudence. Philosophers studying the logic of legal arguments have long since been forced to classify their propositions into many more than three types, and, keeping our eyes on the actual practice of argument, we found ourselves obliged to follow them along the same road. There are in practical argument a good half-dozen functions to be performed by different sorts of proposition: once this is recognised, it becomes necessary to distinguish, not just between premisses and conclusions, but between claims, data, warrants, modal qualifiers, conditions of rebuttal, statements about the applicability or inapplicability of warrants, and others.

These distinctions will not be particularly novel to those who have studied explicitly the logic of special types of practical argument: the topic of exceptions or conditions of rebuttal, for instance—which were labelled (R) in our pattern of analysis—has been discussed by Professor H. L. A. Hart under the title of 'defeasibility', and he has shown its relevance not only to the jurisprudential study of contract but also to philosophical theories about free-will and responsibility. (It is probably no accident that he reached these results while working in the borderland between jurisprudence and philosophy.) Traces of the distinction can be discerned even in the writings of some who remain wedded to the traditions of formal logic. Sir David Ross, for example, has discussed the same topic of rebuttals, especially in the field of ethics. He recognises that in practice we are compelled to allow exceptions to all moral rules, if only because any man recognising more than one rule is liable on occasion to find two of his rules pointing in different directions; but, being committed to the traditional pattern of argument-analysis, he has no category of presumptive arguments, or of rebuttals (R), in terms of which to account for this necessity. He gets around this by continuing to construe moral rules of action as major premisses, but criticising the manner in which they are normally phrased. If we are to be logical, he claims, all our moral rules should have the words *prima facie* added to them: in the absence of these words, he can see no strict possibility of admitting any exceptions.

We accordingly found it more natural to look for parallels between logic and jurisprudence than for parallels between logic and geometry: a clearly analysed argument is as much one in which the formalities of rational assessment are clearly set out and which is couched 'in proper form', as one which has been presented in a tidy geometrical shape. Granted, there is a large class of valid arguments which can be expressed in the neat form, 'Data; Warrant; so Conclusion', the warrant serving precisely as the bridge required to make the transition from data to conclusion; but to call such an argument formally valid is to say only something about the manner in which it has been phrased, and tells us nothing about the *reasons for* its validity. These reasons are to be understood only when we turn to consider the *backing* of the warrant invoked.

The traditional pattern of analysis, I suggested, has two serious defects. It is always liable to lead us, as it leads Sir David Ross, to pay too little attention to the differences between the different modes of criticism to which arguments are subject—to the differences, for instance, between warrants (W) and rebuttals (R). Particular premisses commonly express our data; whereas universal premisses may express either warrants or the backing for warrants, and when they are stated in the form 'All A's are B's' it will often be entirely obscure just which function they are to be understood as performing. The consequences of this obscurity can be grave, as we shall see later, particularly when we allow for the other defect of the traditional pattern—the effect it has of obscuring the differences between different fields of argument, and the sorts of warrant and backing appropriate to these different fields.

One central distinction we studied at some length: that between the field of analytic arguments, which in practice are somewhat rare, and those other fields of argument which can be grouped together under the title of substantial arguments. As logicians discovered early on, the field of analytic arguments is particularly simple; certain complexities which inevitably afflict substantial arguments need never trouble one in the case of analytic ones; and when the warrant of an analytic argument is expressed in the form 'All A's are B's', the whole argument can be laid out in the traditional pattern without harm resulting—for once in a while, the distinction between our data and the backing of our warrant ceases to be of serious importance. This simplicity is very attractive, and the theory of analytic arguments with universal major premisses was therefore seized on and developed with enthusiasm by logicians of many generations.

Simplicity, however, has its perils. It is one thing to choose as one's first object of theoretical study the type of argument open to analysis in the simplest terms. But it would be quite another to treat this type of argument as a paradigm and to demand that arguments in other fields should conform to its standards regardless, or to build up from a study of the simplest forms of argument alone a set of categories intended for application to arguments of all sorts: one must at any rate begin by inquiring carefully how far the artificial simplicity of one's chosen model results in these logical categories also being artificially simple. The sorts of risks one runs otherwise are obvious enough. Distinctions which all happen to cut along the same line for the simplest arguments may need to be handled quite separately in the general case; if we forget this, and our new-found logical categories yield paradoxical results when applied to more complex arguments, we may be tempted to put these results down to defects in the arguments instead of in our categories; and we may end up by thinking that, for some regrettable reason hidden deep in the nature of things, only our original, peculiarly simple arguments are capable of attaining to the ideal of validity.

At this point, these perils can be hinted at only in entirely general terms. In the last two essays in this book, I shall make it my business to show more precisely how they have affected the actual results obtained, first by formal logicians, and then by philosophers working in the field of epistemology. The development of logical theory, I shall argue, began historically with the study of a rather special class of arguments—namely, the class of unequivocal, analytic, formally valid arguments with a universal statement as 'major premiss'. Arguments in this class are exceptional in four different ways, which together make them a bad example for general study. To begin with, the use of the form 'All A's are B's' in the major premiss conceals the distinction between an inference-warrant and the statement of its backing. Secondly, with this class of arguments alone, the distinction between our data and our warrant-backing ceases to be of serious importance. (These first two factors between them can lead one to overlook the functional differences between data, warrants, and the backing of warrants; and so to put them on a level and label them all alike as 'premisses'.) In the third place, arguments of this chosen type being analytic, the procedure for verifying the backing in each case involves *ipso facto* verifying the conclusion; while since they are, in the fourth place, unequivocal also, it becomes impossible to accept the data and backing and yet deny the conclusion, without positively contradicting oneself. These special characteristics of their first chosen class of arguments have been interpreted by logicians as signs of special merit; other classes of argument, they have felt, are deficient in so far as they fail to display all the characteristic merits of the paradigm class; and the distinctions which in this first case alone all cut along one and the same line are identified and treated as a single distinction. The divisions of arguments into analytic and substantial, into warrant-using and warrant-establishing, into conclusive and tentative, and into formally valid and not formally valid: these are regimented for purposes of theory into a single distinction, and the pair of terms 'deductive' and 'inductive', which in practice—as we saw—is used to mark only the second of the four distinctions, is attached equally to all four.

This vast initial over-simplification marks the traditional beginning of much in logical theory. Many of the current problems in the logical tradition spring from adopting the analytic paradigm-argument as a standard by comparison with which all other arguments can be criticised. But analyticity is one thing, formal validity is another; and neither of these is a universal criterion of necessity, still less of the soundness of our arguments. Analytic arguments are a special case, and we are laying up trouble for ourselves, both in logic and in epistemology, if we treat them as anything else. That, at any rate, is the claim I hope to make good in the two essays which follow.

IV

WORKING LOGIC AND IDEALISED LOGIC

SO FAR in these essays I have done my best to avoid any explicit
discussion of logical theory. Whenever I have seen any danger of
a collision with formal logicians, I have sheered away, and put aside
the contentious concept—'logical necessity', or whatever it might
be—with a note to reconsider it later. By now the list of items to
be reconsidered has become pretty long; and we have seen plenty
of signs of a divergence between the categories of practical argument-
criticism and those of formal logic. The time has come when the
collision can no longer be avoided: rather, our task will be to ensure
that we meet it head-on, and with our grappling-irons at the ready.

In the first part of this essay, I shall proceed in the manner of
a scientist. I shall begin by stating my hypothesis: namely, that the
categories of formal logic were built up from a study of the analytic
syllogism, that this is an unrepresentative and misleadingly simple
sort of argument, and that many of the paradoxical commonplaces
of formal logic and epistemology spring from the misapplication
of these categories to arguments of other sorts. I shall then explore
the consequences which follow from treating analytic syllogisms as
a paradigm, and especially the paradoxes generated by treating as
identical a number of ways of dividing up arguments which are
genuinely equivalent in the case of analytic syllogisms alone.
The categories we shall be led to build up by proceeding in this way,
and the conclusions we shall be driven to when applying them in the
analysis of arguments in general, will be our next concern: the first
dividends of our inquiry will come when we turn to the books of
contemporary logicians and philosophers, and find in them just those
categories employed and just those conclusions advocated which my
present hypothesis would lead one to expect. The first part of this
essay will conclude, therefore, with the 'verification' of my hypothesis, when we find how widely these categories and conclusions
have been accepted without question.

The second part of the essay will be judicial rather than scientific.
Supposing my hypothesis to have been established, I shall argue

that formal logicians have misconceived their categories, and reached their conclusions only by a series of mistakes and misunderstandings. They seek to justify their paradoxes as the result of thinking and speaking, for once in a while, absolutely *strictly*; whereas the conclusions they present turn out on examination to be, in fact, not so much strict as *beside the point*. So far as formal logicians claim to say anything of relevance to arguments of other than analytic sorts, judgement must therefore be pronounced against them: for the study of other types of argument fresh categories are needed, and current distinctions—especially the crude muddle commonly marked by the terms 'deductive' and 'inductive'—must be set on one side.

In the third section of the essay, I shall attempt to be at once more historical and more explanatory. The over-simplified categories of formal logic have an attraction, not only on account of their simplicity, but also because they fit in nicely with some other influential prejudices. From the time of Aristotle logicians have found the mathematical model enticing, and a logic which modelled itself on jurisprudence rather than geometry could not hope to maintain all the mathematical elegance of their ideal. Unfortunately an idealised logic, such as the mathematical model leads us to, cannot keep in serious contact with its practical application. Rational demonstration is not a suitable subject for a timeless, axiomatic science; and, if that is what we try to make of logic, we are in danger of ending up with a theory whose connection with argument-criticism is as slight as that between the medieval theory of rational fractions and the 'music' from which it took its name.

AN HYPOTHESIS AND ITS CONSEQUENCES

To start with, let me specify the phenomenon which it is our business to explain. This is best indicated, in general terms, as a systematic divergence between two sets of categories: those we find employed in the practical business of argumentation, and the corresponding analyses of them set out in books on formal logic. Where the standards for judging the soundness, validity, cogency or strength of arguments are in practice field-dependent, logical theorists restrict these notions and attempt to define them in field-invariant terms; where possibility, necessity and the like are treated in practice in a field-dependent way, logicians react in the same manner—or at most concede, grudgingly, that there may be other, looser senses of words like 'necessity' which are used in talking about causation, morality and the like; and whereas any warrant-using argument can be spoken of in practice as a deduction, logicians again demur and allow the term to be applied only to analytic arguments. These are only a few instances of the general tendency for critical practice and logical theory to part company, which it is our business now to explain. Any hypothesis to explain this divergence will need to be verified, not just by inferring from it the existence of *a* divergence of this general sort, but by asking precisely what *form* of divergence it will lead us to expect: a satisfactory hypothesis must lead one to foresee the exact form the divergence actually takes.

I suppose, then, that what happened was the following: having started, like Aristotle, by studying syllogistic arguments, and particularly analytic syllogisms, logicians built up the simplest and most compact set of categories which would serve them reasonably in criticising arguments of this first kind. As a result, they were led to neglect the differences between the four or five crucial distinctions which amount to the same thing in the case of the analytic syllogism alone—the distinctions we noted in the last essay. These are, to summarise them briefly:

(i) The distinction between necessary arguments and probable arguments: i.e. between arguments in which the warrant entitles us to argue unequivocally to the conclusion (which can therefore be labelled with the modal qualifier 'necessarily') and arguments in which the warrant entitles us to draw our conclusions only tentatively (qualifying it with a 'probably') subject to possible exceptions ('presumably') or conditionally ('provided that...').

(ii) The distinction between arguments which are formally valid and those which cannot hope to be formally valid: any argument is formally valid which is set out in such a way that its conclusion can be obtained by appropriate shuffling of the terms in the data and warrant. (It has always been one of the attractions of formal logic that its analysis of validity could be made to depend exclusively on matters of form, in this sense.)

(iii) The distinction between those arguments, including ordinary syllogisms, in which a warrant is relied on whose adequacy and applicability have previously been established, and those arguments which are themselves intended to establish the adequacy of a warrant.

(iv) The distinction between arguments expressed in terms of 'logical connectives' or quantifiers and those not so expressed. The acceptable, logical words include 'all', 'some', 'or', and a few others: these are firmly herded away from the non-logical goats, i.e. the generality of nouns, adjectives and the like, and unruly connectives and quantifiers such as 'most', 'few', 'but'. The validity of syllogisms being closely bound up with the proper distribution of logical words within the statements composing them, we again find ourselves putting valid syllogisms into the first of our two classes.

(v) The fundamental distinction between analytic arguments and substantial ones, which can be glossed over only so long as we state our inference-warrants in the traditional form, 'All (or No) A's are B's'.

It is a matter of history, of course, that formal logic did begin from a study of the syllogism, and especially of the analytic syllogism. What follows is supposition, at any rate in part. I suggest, then, that having made this the starting-point of their analysis, logicians allowed themselves to be excessively impressed by the unique character of the analytic syllogism: it is not only analytic, but also formally valid, warrant-using, unequivocal in its consequences, and expressed in terms of 'logical words'. By contrast, other classes of arguments were apparently less tractable—they were less trustworthy and more tentative, involved substantial leaps, fell away from any formal standards of validity, were expressed in terms of vague, unlogical words and in some cases appealed to no established or even recognisable warrant. Under the pressure of motives about which we shall have to speculate afterwards, logicians thereupon conflated our five distinctions into one single distinction, which they made the absolute and essential condition of logical salvation. Validity they would from now on concede only to arguments which passed all the five tests, and the analytic syllogism thereby became a paradigm to which all self-respecting arguments must conform.

This overall, conflated distinction had to be marked by some pair of terms, and a number of different pairs were used at one time or another: 'deductive', 'conclusive' and 'demonstrative' to mark the favoured class of arguments, 'inductive', 'inconclusive', 'non-demonstrative' for the remainder. What terms shall we ourselves employ? We might do best to choose an entirely non-committal neologism, but the result might be ugly; so let us use a term which has been very commonly associated with this conflated distinction, namely 'deductive'. This term, applied in practical arguing to all warrant-using steps, has been extended by many logicians for purposes of theory to mark all these five distinctions at a single stroke, and we can follow them—at least provided we make use of precautionary quotation-marks.

If we deliberately refrain from marking these five distinctions separately, and instead insist on identifying them, what will happen? Suppose we take the analytic or 'deductive' syllogism—a formally valid, unequivocal, analytic, warrant-using sort of argument—as setting a standard to be aimed at by arguments of all kinds. What kind of logical theory shall we build up, and what sort of theoretical categories and doctrines shall we find ourselves forced to accept?

Starting off from this point, we shall meet difficult problems even in our discussion of the orthodox syllogism. The form of words 'All A's are B's' can, as we have seen, be put to a multitude of uses: it may be used to state either an inference-warrant or alternatively the backing for that warrant, and the backing it states may in its turn be of several kinds—e.g. statistical, statutory or taxonomical. If we begin by assuming that the differences between arguments in different fields are inessential and that all arguments ought to be reducible to a single basic type, we shall be in danger of disregarding this multiplicity of function, and of construing syllogistic arguments of all kinds on a single analytic pattern. In this way, we shall be forced to ask ourselves whether the syllogism—being ostensibly analytic—ought really to be capable of yielding substantial results at all. Aristotle the zoologist certainly wanted to couch substantial arguments in syllogistic form; yet, once we have been struck by the apparently superior cogency of analytic arguments and tempted to demand analyticity as a condition of either 'deductiveness' or 'validity', we cannot consistently allow substantial syllogisms to pass without criticism. A valid analytic syllogism *cannot* in its conclusion tell us anything not already included in the data and warrant-backing, so a syllogism which involves a genuinely substantial step can—from our present point of view—be justified only by begging somewhere in the data and backing the very conclusion which we are intending to establish.

Paradox is here generated partly as a result of failing to distinguish between a warrant and its backing. In the analytic syllogism, the conclusion must in the nature of the case repeat in other words something already implicit in the data and backing; but, looking at the substantial syllogism, we are torn between two apparently contradictory conclusions—saying that data and 'universal premiss' (warrant) necessarily imply the conclusion, and saying that data and 'universal premiss' (backing) are between them formally consistent with the opposite conclusion—both of which are in fact true. Any syllogism can be formally valid, but only analytic syllogisms are analytic!

The consequences of our choice of paradigm will, however, be most striking in our handling of the general logical categories, and in particular of modal qualifiers. Once we start applying a single standard of validity to all arguments whatever, regardless of field, we shall go on as a matter of course to adopt also unique criteria of necessity, possibility and impossibility. In the analytic syllogism, a conclusion follows 'necessarily' if and only if its contradictory is formally inconsistent with the data and backing. Thus we can say,

> 'Anne is Jack's sister;
> Every single one of Jack's sisters has red hair;
> So (necessarily) Anne has red hair',

just because, having stated our data and backing in the first two sentences, to add that Anne's hair is not red would be to take away in the conclusion something already stated. Making this the universal test, we shall now think it proper to call a conclusion 'necessary', or to say that it follows 'necessarily' from our data, only if a full entailment is involved. Likewise, in the case of possibility and impossibility, we shall be tempted to elevate the criteria of possibility and impossibility applicable to analytic arguments into positive definitions of the terms: the term *impossible* will now come to mean to us the same as 'inconsistent' or 'contradictory', and the term *possible* the same as 'consistent' and 'not contradictory'.

The divergence between this theoretical usage and our everyday practice cannot fail to strike us before long: ordinarily, conclusions are regarded as necessary, possible or impossible for quite different reasons. Still, this need not perturb us seriously: our present definitions are being introduced for purposes of logical theory, so we can mark them off by the adverb 'logically'. Thus we shall end up with the following definitions:

(i) 'P is logically impossible' means 'P is either self-contradictory, or contradicts the data and backing on the basis of which we are arguing',

(ii) 'P is logically possible' means 'P is not logically impossible (as just defined)', and

(iii) 'P is logically necessary' means 'the denial of P is logically impossible (as just defined)'.

Consistency, contradiction and entailment will now come to seem the only things which, from a logical point of view, can confer validity on arguments or bar them as invalid.

'How can categories defined in such terms as these be applied to substantial arguments at all? After all, in their case the bearing of the data and backing on the conclusion can, *ex hypothesi*, neither amount to entailment nor run the risk of contradiction.' So long as we retain the traditional syllogistic form, the cutting-edge of this problem will remain hidden behind the ambiguity of the sentence-form, 'All A's are B's'; but, once we make explicit the distinction between data, backing and warrants, we can conceal the problem from ourselves no longer. It was David Hume's great glory that he faced this difficulty resolutely, and declined to take refuge in muffling ambiguities, however paradoxical the consequences.

Let us now try to follow these consequences out, and see where we are led. Paradox must not deter us: it will be unavoidable. To begin with, when compared with our new standard of 'deductive' argument, no substantial argument can claim any longer to be 'deductive'; *a fortiori*, no substantial argument can be necessary, using that term in a logical sense, and no substantial conclusion can follow necessarily, or with more than a high degree of probability. Where, in common parlance, the word 'necessarily' is used to qualify the conclusions of substantial arguments, this (we must now say) is only a loose and imprecise *façon de parler*, resulting from sloppiness of thought. Likewise, any conclusion which avoids contradicting our data must now be admitted as possible, however implausible it may be, and only by leading to a flat contradiction will a conclusion become actually impossible. The world of possibilities becomes indefinitely more extended, and the rational elimination of possibilities—at any rate in substantial arguments—becomes infinitely more difficult.

Some may be inclined to stop at this point, but others will see that one can and should go further. If we are going to define some of our logical categories in terms of consistency, contradiction and entailment, ought we not to define all of them in this way? The term 'probable', in particular, is just as much of a modal qualifier as the terms 'necessary' and 'impossible', so can we really be satisfied, for logical purposes, with anything less than a universal definition of that term also, clearly related to our previous definitions of necessity, impossibility and possibility? If we accept this programme, we shall be forced to define 'probability' in terms of entailments: such a statement as that 'the data and backing at our disposal, e, *make it probable* that h' must now be explained as referring only to the meanings of the component statements e and h and the semantic relations between them. Finally, having analysed 'probable' in this way, we shall be under strong pressure to do the same for such notions as 'confirmation' and 'evidential support'. If logic is to be concerned solely with contradiction, entailment and consistency, and the study of confirmation and evidential support is to be put on a logical basis and become part of the science of logic, there will indeed be no alternative: we *must* find some way of defining these notions also in terms of the semantic relations between evidence e and any suggested conclusion h.

If we do this, we increase our difficulties still further. The divergence between theoretical usage and everyday practice becomes more marked, and the consequent paradoxes more extreme. From now on, we shall not only be forced to reject the claim that some substantial arguments are necessary; we shall no longer be able to admit that they can ever, strictly speaking, be even *probable*. For, in the case of genuinely substantial arguments, probability depends on quite other things than semantic relations. The conclusion is inescapable: in substantial arguments, the conclusions cannot follow with logical necessity, and cannot *logically* follow with probability either. Granted, once again, that in common parlance we do talk of such conclusions as more or less probable; this is to use the term 'probable' in another sense, as different from logical probability as are the 'must' and 'may' and 'cannot' of everyday speech from strict logical necessity, possibility and impossibility.

By the time we reach this position, substantial arguments are beginning to look just about irredeemable. None of the categories in the logical theory we have been building up seems to be within the reach of substantial arguments; whichever category we apply to them, they never come up to standard. Unless we are to question our very paradigm, we must interpret this fact as a sign of pervasive weakness in all substantial arguments. Decent logical connections are apparently too much to look for in their case; judged against our 'deductive' standards, they are irreparably loose and lacking in rigour; the necessities and compulsions which they can claim—physical, moral and the rest—are never entirely compulsive or ineluctable in the way logical necessity can be; while their impossibilities are never as utterly adamantine as a good, solid, logical impossibility. Metaphysical rescue-work may patch up substantial arguments sufficiently to justify one using them for practical purposes, but there is no denying the canker at their hearts.

The road to this conclusion from our initial adoption of analytic syllogisms as the ideal sort of 'deductive' argument is a long one, but the conclusion itself is a perfectly natural one; and, even if we shrink from following the consequences of our initial assumption as far as this, it has more immediate consequences which are hardly less drastic. The only arguments we can fairly judge by 'deductive' standards are those held out as and intended to be analytic, necessary and formally valid. All arguments which are confessedly substantial will be 'non-deductive', and by implication not formally valid. But for the analytic syllogism validity can be identified with formal validity, and this is just what the logician wants to be possible universally. It follows at once that for substantial arguments, whose cogency cannot be displayed in a purely formal way, even *validity* is something entirely out of reach and unobtainable.

THE VERIFICATION OF THIS HYPOTHESIS

There is no need to follow out any further the detailed consequences of the hypothesis from which this argument began. I am supposing that logicians have built up their formal theories by taking the analytic syllogism as a paradigm, developing their categories and working out their conclusions with an eye to that ideal. If the definitions and doctrines I have here set out can be illustrated from the writings of logicians and philosophers, that will help to establish the justice of my diagnosis. But with a good hypothesis, there should be no need to go searching about for verificatory observations, since the truth of its consequences will strike one even in the course of working them out. So here, anyone familiar with the standard views of philosophers and logicians working in this field should have recognised them in my definitions and doctrines, and be able to produce for himself ample confirming instances from the literature. All these doctrines can be found without difficulty in current logic-books. Sometimes they are asserted straightforwardly, sometimes as paradoxes which are regrettable but apparently forced on one, and which can be evaded only with ingenuity; some logicians go all the way, others take fright after a certain point and erect conceptual barriers across the line at which they feel bound to dig in their heels; in some expositions the analytic paradigm is embraced openly, but in others it is taken for granted covertly—the word 'deductive' being *defined*, as is proper, in terms of formal validity, but *used* as though it were equivalent also without further explanation to 'analytic', 'unequivocal', 'necessary' and 'expressed in logical words'. I shall content myself here with five quotations, chosen for the points of general interest they raise.

(1) The following passage is taken from Mr William Kneale's book *Probability and Induction*, p. 21:

It is now a commonplace of epistemology that the results achieved in such sciences as physics, chemistry, biology, and sociology are fundamentally different in character from the conclusions of pure mathematics. At one time the difference was not generally recognised either by philosophers or by scientists, as it is now. But it was set beyond all doubt by the British empiricists, Bacon, Locke, Berkeley, and Hume, and, like some other achievements of philosophical analysis, has become so firmly established in our intellectual tradition that we can scarcely understand how intelligent men ever failed to appreciate it. The sciences I have mentioned are called inductive, and their conclusions, unlike those of pure mathematics, are said to have only high probability, since they are not self-evident and cannot be demonstrated by conclusive reasoning. Some of the results of induction, for instance the generalizations of elementary chemistry, are, indeed, so well established that it would be pedantic to use the word 'probably' whenever we mention them, but we can always conceive the possibility of experience which would compel us to revise them.

When a doctrine has become so firmly entrenched in our intellectual tradition as to seem beyond all doubt, it can with advantage be taken out from time to time, and stripped of accretions. So here, we must ask Kneale just *what* has been put beyond all doubt. He will reply: the distinction between deductive arguments and inductive ones. But in which of our five senses? That is not so clear: as we foresaw, the distinction between analytic and substantial arguments is all too easily confused with those between tentative and unequivocal, formal and informal, warrant-using and warrant-establishing; and Kneale can here be found sliding from one to another.

To begin with, Kneale contrasts arguments in pure mathematics and the experimental sciences, the first being analytic, the second substantial. He then goes on at once to treat this distinction as proving that scientific theories, or the explanations we give in terms of them, must all alike be less-than-certain—the conclusions of the experimental sciences 'have only high probability'. At the same time he acknowledges that this view will appear paradoxical to non-logicians, seeing that we normally draw a distinction between scientific conclusions which must be labelled with a cautionary 'probably' and those which do not need to be so qualified. This divergence he puts down to the *pedantry* of logicians, though hardly in a tone that carries conviction. After all, if this remark were meant seriously, it would be nicely calculated to bring him and his fellow-logicians into ridicule and contempt.

For our purposes, the thing to notice is the *reasons* which Kneale gives for rejecting claims to certainty on behalf of the experimental sciences. These sciences, he argues, are inductive (*sc.* not 'deductive') and their conclusions, unlike those of pure mathematics, are neither self-evident nor capable of being demonstrated by conclusive reasoning (*sc.* they are neither themselves logically necessary, nor analytic consequences of logically necessary propositions). This is his first reason for allowing the sciences nothing more than high probability. As an afterthought, he adds the seemingly additional fact that we can 'always conceive the possibility of experiences' which would compel us to revise any scientific theory, and so to reconsider the explanations hitherto given in terms of it. But this turns out to be the same point restated, for it becomes clear from the context that his words, 'We can always conceive the possibility...', are to be read as meaning, 'It is always *logically* possible that we should have ...', or in other words, 'There is never any *contradiction* in supposing us to have to revise them'. He is not claiming that we have *at present* concrete reasons for supposing that every single result of scientific research, including the most well-established, is in genuine danger of reconsideration within the foreseeable future: to say, 'It is always possible that they may have to be revised', is not for him to express an active reservation, but to talk in the realm of logical possibility alone.

To summarise: Kneale first contrasts the results of the experimental sciences and the conclusions of pure mathematics, in order to point the contrast between substantial and analytic arguments; next, invokes criteria of necessity and standards of certainty relevant to analytic arguments alone; then discovers (not surprisingly) that these criteria and standards are inapplicable, in the nature of the case, to substantial arguments; and presents this result in the form of a paradox. This paradox is finally explained away (surely insincerely) as being so innocent as to verge on pedantry. Kneale does not take the further step of allowing probability also to analytic arguments alone.

(2) What Mr P. F. Strawson has to say in his *Introduction to Logical Theory* is of special interest for our purposes: after binding his own hands at the outset, he makes at the end efforts to extricate himself worthy of a Houdini. The string of definitions with which he ropes himself up in his opening chapter links our modal qualifiers rigidly to the notions of consistency, contradiction and entailment, and he even ties the notion of validity in with this group too:

> To say that the steps (in an argument) are valid, that the conclusion follows from the premises, is simply to say that it would be inconsistent to assert the premises and deny the conclusion; that the truth of the premises is inconsistent with the falsity of the conclusion.[1]

To use our own terms, he treats the *criteria* of necessity, impossibility and validity appropriate to analytic arguments as defining the whole meaning of these terms: in this way, the field-dependent character of the notions is concealed, and a preferential status is given to analytic arguments. In due course, he too has to say something about the natural sciences. At this point, he finds himself faced by the question whether the differences between arguments in different fields may not be irreducible, and tries to save scientific

[1] *Introduction to Logical Theory*, ch. 1, sect. 9, p. 13.

conclusions from their seemingly inferior position by claiming for them standards of their own; but 'hardening of the categories' has set in long since, and he cannot make good his escape.

The following crucial passage comes from Strawson's ch. 9, sect. 7, p. 250:

Suppose that a man is brought up to regard formal logic as the study of the science and art of reasoning. He observes that all inductive processes are, by deductive standards, invalid; the premises never entail the conclusions. Now inductive processes are notoriously important in the formation of beliefs and expectations about everything which lies beyond the observation of available witnesses. But an *invalid* argument is an *unsound* argument; an *unsound* argument is one in which *no good reason* is produced for accepting the conclusion. So if inductive processes are invalid, if all the arguments we should produce, if challenged, in support of our beliefs about what lies beyond the observation of available witnesses are unsound, then we have no good reason for any of these beliefs. This conclusion is repugnant. So there arises the demand for a justification, not of this or that particular belief which goes beyond what is entailed by our evidence, but a justification of induction in general. And when the demand arises in this way it is, in effect, the demand that induction shall be shown to be really a kind of deduction; for nothing less will satisfy the doubter when this is the route to his doubts.... The demand is that induction should be shown to be a rational process; and this turns out to be the demand that one kind of reasoning should be shown to be another and different kind.... But of course, inductive arguments are not deductively valid; if they were, they would be deductive arguments. Inductive reasoning must be assessed, for soundness, by inductive standards. Nevertheless, fantastic as the wish for induction to be deduction may seem, it is only in terms of it that we can understand some of the attempts that have been made to justify induction.

In this passage, like Kneale before him, Strawson acknowledges the divergence between the theoretical analysis of our critical categories given by logicians and the manner in which we employ them in practice; and he does greater justice to it than Kneale, in admitting that the conclusions of logicians often strike a non-philosopher not just as pedantic but as repugnant. He accordingly makes more serious efforts to escape from the difficulty and looks for some way of allowing scientific arguments and conclusions to claim a cogency, strength and validity of their own kind.

He begins with a promising move: that of allowing that arguments may be of different kinds, each of them entitled to be judged in its own terms and by its own standards. Yet he is unable to carry his argument through successfully. The reason for this failure is, for our purposes, the thing we must bring to light. Everything might have turned out all right, if he had not already been committed by his own terminology. Like Kneale, he has stated the contrast between scientific and mathematical arguments in terms of the words 'deductive' and 'inductive', and has left it unclear which of the four or five ideas conflated in these terms he is using the words to mark. This very act—of conflating five different distinctions into one and confusing questions about formal validity and necessity with questions about analyticity—is, however, the source of his trouble. This is what makes the demand 'for induction to be deduction', which he regards as fantastic, on the contrary inevitable.

Consider the statement, 'Of course, inductive arguments are not deductively valid; if they were, they would be deductive arguments' —which is the heart of Strawson's *reductio ad absurdum*. If we now substitute for his word 'deductive' each of its possible translations in turn, we shall see how the difficulty is created. Let us begin with 'analytic'. These two key sentences then become: 'Of course, scientific arguments (being substantial) are not analytically valid; if they were, they would be analytic arguments. Scientific reasoning must be assessed, for soundness, by scientific standards.' This statement is wholly in order, and recognising the truth it expresses is the first step towards throwing off the analytic paradigm: the wish for scientific arguments to be analytic, and therefore not substantial, would indeed be fantastic, as Strawson says. But this insight he uses as the sugar-coating for a decidedly bitter pill, since, on three other possible interpretations, what he says is entirely unacceptable. If, for instance, we substitute for his word 'deductive' the phrase 'formally valid', we get, 'Of course, scientific arguments are not formally valid; if they were, they would be formally valid arguments. Scientific reasoning must be assessed, for soundness, by scientific standards.' Here there is a complete lacuna: why should not scientific arguments be formally valid? Newton, Laplace and Sherlock Holmes would all testify that there is nothing fantastic about *this* wish.

Nor does any absurdity ensue if we substitute 'warrant-using' and 'unequivocal' for Strawson's 'deductive'. The desire that some substantial, scientific arguments should be formally valid, warrant-using and unequivocal, and perfectly properly include a 'must' or a 'necessarily' in the conclusion, will appear absurd only so long as we identify this desire with another, manifestly fantastic wish—the wish for scientific arguments to be analytic. This identification, as we have seen, is one effect of the logical theorist's fourfold contrast between 'deduction' and 'induction'. My only wonder is whether anybody (except perhaps Carnap) ever really wishes to embrace the arrant absurdity of treating substantial scientific arguments, not just as deductions, but as *analytic* deductions.

(3) Kneale rejected any claim that scientific conclusions might follow necessarily from the scientists' data, while being prepared to allow that they might follow probably, or even with high probability. Yet some more radical soul, we saw, might wish to define even probability in terms of consistency and entailment. True to form, Professor Rudolf Carnap appears in this guise. Having distinguished between his two senses of the word 'probability', he allots one of them to precisely this task: statements about his 'probability$_1$' are to be about partial entailments—analytic if true, self-contradictory if false. So also, he argues, are statements including any other of those terms and phrases which cluster round the notion of probability, such as 'gives strong support to', 'confirms', 'furnishes a satisfactory explanation for' and 'is a good reason for expecting'. Since statements about probability, in this sense, assert 'logical relations' between sentences or propositions, and logical relations depend for Carnap solely on the meanings of sentences, and the theory of the meanings of expressions in language is semantics, the whole problem of how evidence backs up theories becomes for him a matter of semantics: 'The problem whether and how much [an hypothesis] *h* is confirmed by [evidence] *e* is to be answered merely by a logical analysis of *h* and *e* and their relations.' (This unambiguous statement is taken from page 20 of Professor Carnap's book, *Logical Foundations of Probability*.)

This conclusion is so extreme that we can leave it without comment, but one of his examples is worth quoting. He discusses the statement that, given such-and-such a batch of meteorological observations, the probability that it will rain tomorrow is one-fifth. If this statement is true, he declares, then it is analytic, his explanation being that the statement 'does not ascribe the probability$_1$-value 1/5 to tomorrow's rain but rather to a certain logical (hence semantic) relation:...therefore it is not in need of verification by observations of tomorrow's weather or of any other facts'. The divergence between Carnap's analysis of probability and our practical notions is clear enough. If he will swallow this camel, we need not wonder at his construing on the same model *all* statements about the bearing of a body of evidence on a theory. The view, after all, has one great advantage. It saves him from having to conclude that scientific arguments cannot lend their conclusions any probability, though only at the price of claiming that they are, *pace* Strawson, analytic arguments.

(4) The problems discussed by Kneale, Strawson and Carnap in the quotations we have been studying all arise when one compares the arguments we meet in the experimental sciences with an analytic ideal. But similar problems may arise equally, if not more acutely, when we turn to consider moral rather than scientific arguments. Mr R. M. Hare, for example, devotes a whole chapter of his book *The Language of Morals* to questions about the inferences involved in moral arguments. By what kind of step, he asks, can we pass from D, a particular collection of information about the situation in which we are placed and the probable consequences of acting in one way or another, to C, the moral conclusion that in the light of this information it is incumbent on us to act *thus*? (Such conclusions he regards as a species of imperative.) An argument of this kind can be acceptable, Hare argues, only if we ourselves provide an additional premiss of an imperative character: 'by no form of inference, however loose, can we get an answer to the question "What shall I do?" out of a set of premises which do not contain, at any rate implicitly, an imperative'.[1]

If Hare's additional premisses were intended only to make moral arguments formally valid, there could be no objection to them: certainly every moral argument depends for its soundness upon the appropriate warrant. But from what he goes on to say, one is driven to conclude that he wants his extra premisses to make ethical arguments not just formally valid, but actually analytic. He does not say so in those very words, of course, since he accepts the words 'deductive' and 'premiss' uncritically, so leaving crucial ambiguities in his argument; but there is a certain amount of internal evidence. For example, when he comes to contrast moral arguments with

---

[1] *The Language of Morals*, p. 46.

others which he takes presumably to be analytic—those conforming to the familiar Principle of the Syllogism, for instance—he concludes by entering judgement against the moral arguments. Decent analytic syllogisms hold good in virtue of the meanings of certain logical words, he argues, and the Principle of the Syllogism is 'about the meanings of the words used'. A moral principle, on the other hand, authorises a substantial step in argument, and cannot therefore be thought of as a warrant or rule of inference: it must be regarded as an extra, personal, existentialist 'datum', which we have to add to the facts about our situation before we can be in any position to argue about conduct at all. The extensive parallels between ethical, scientific, geometrical, legal and analytic arguments, which have led us in these studies to envisage the possibility of warrants which hold good in virtue of all sorts of consideration—linguistic consistency, public policy, observed regularities or whatever—make no impression on him. The only genuine rules of inference, in his view, are statements about the meanings of words; and the only acceptable arguments are accordingly analytic ones. The ambiguity of the word 'deductive', with its conflation of the formally valid and the analytic, mercifully shrouds from Hare the restrictive character of his doctrine.

The heart of Hare's position is the thesis which appears also in Professor A. N. Prior's book, *Logic and the Basis of Ethics*. There it is summed up in a magnificently ambiguous sentence (p. 36):

> In our own time the perception that information about our obligations cannot be logically derived from premises in which our obligations are not mentioned has become a commonplace, though perhaps only in philosophical circles.

In reading this passage, one finds oneself quite naturally oscillating between two different interpretations. For the words 'logically derived' are not clear: are they to be read as meaning 'properly drawn from, or justified by appeal to...' or rather as meaning 'inferred analytically from...'? On the latter interpretation, Prior's remark would be trifling enough. A conclusion about a man's obligations cannot be inferred analytically from the facts about his present situation and the probable consequences of his actions alone: this doctrine may well be a commonplace among philosophers, but would it not appear a commonplace to non-philosophers too, if they ever had occasion to address their minds to the question? On the other interpretation, however, Prior's assertion is far from a common-place, and will indeed be grossly repugnant to the non-philosophical. For on this interpretation he appears to be claiming that all arguments of a moral kind are, by a logician's standards, deficient. The doctrine now is that the step from reasons to decisions can never be taken logically, never be taken *properly*; and this has yet to become a commonplace (one hopes) even in philosophical circles. If some philosophers are tempted to entertain this suggestion, that is a consequence of current ambiguities in such terms as 'deduce' and 'derive'. Defending our decisions by appeal to the facts in the light of which they were taken may indeed mean making a logical 'type-jump'; so of course the decisions are not analytically derived from the supporting reasons—how could they be? But such an appeal need involve no offence against *logic*, and the paradox in Prior's remarks lies in his suggestion that it must.

In passing, it is worth remarking on the manner in which Prior characterises our Great Divide, between the formal logician and the practical arguer. Like Kneale and Strawson before him, he recognises that some of his conclusions may be unwelcome to the man-in-the-street: for Prior, however, there is no question of passing the divergence off—with a wry apology for the pedantry of logicians, for instance. The fact of the matter, he implies, just is that the vision of philosophers is clearer, so that a doctrine is perfectly capable of becoming a commonplace among them while yet remaining grossly repugnant to lesser mortals.

(5) As a last illustration, let me choose a classic passage from the end of Book I of David Hume's *Treatise of Human Nature*. This is still the most complete and candid account we have of the divergence between the attitudes of the formal logician and of the average practical man to the categories of rational assessment and the paradoxical commonplaces of philosophers. At the time when he wrote his *Treatise*, Hume was pursuing not only the professional activities of a philosopher, but also the leisure-time occupations of a young man of the world; and he was too candid an observer, too urbane and honest an autobiographer, to gloss over or brush aside the intellectual conflicts to which this double life led. There is here no pretence that they raise questions only for pedants, that they spring from desires which can be shown to be fantastic, or arise from the man-in-the-street's neglect of insights which are by now commonplaces

among philosophers. Instead, while following out relentlessly the conclusions to which—as a philosopher—his logical doctrines lead him, he at the same time shows with great insight and honesty the schizophrenia involved in trying to reconcile these philosophical conclusions with the practice of his everyday life.

The whole section would be worth quoting; but it runs to a dozen pages, and there is room here only for the climax. Hume shows into what bewilderment and scepticism his philosophical principles eventually lead him. On the one hand, he claims, the imagination is subject to illusions, which we can never be certain of detecting; so that we cannot be expected implicitly to trust 'a principle so inconstant and fallacious'. On the other hand, he continues:

If the consideration of these instances makes us take a resolution to reject all the trivial suggestions of the fancy, and adhere to the understanding;... even this resolution, if steadily executed, wou'd be dangerous, and attended with the most fatal consequences. For I have already shewn, that the understanding, when it acts alone, and according to its most general principles, entirely subverts itself, and leaves not the lowest degrees of evidence in any proposition, either in philosophy or in common life.... We have, therefore, no choice left but betwixt a false reason and none at all. For my part, I know not what ought to be done in the present case. I can only observe what is commonly done; which is, that this difficulty is seldom or never thought of; and even where it has once been present to the mind, is quickly forgot, and leaves but a small impression behind it. Very refin'd reflections have little or no influence upon us; and yet we do not, and cannot establish it for a rule, that they ought not to have any influence; which implies a manifest contradiction.

But what have I here said, that reflections very refin'd and metaphysical have little or no influence upon us? This opinion I can scarce forbear retracting, and condemning from my present feeling and experience. The *intense* view of these manifold contradictions and imperfections in human reason has so wrought upon me, and heated my brain, that I am ready to reject all belief and reasoning, and can look upon no opinion as more probable or likely than another. Where am I, or what? From what causes do I derive my existence, and to what condition shall I return? Whose favour shall I court, and whose anger must I dread? What beings surround me? and on whom have I any influence, or who have any influence on me? I am confounded with all these questions, and begin to fancy myself in the most deplorable condition imaginable, inviron'd with the deepest darkness, and utterly depriv'd of the use of every member and faculty.

Most fortunately it happens, that since reason is incapable of dispelling these clouds, nature herself suffices to that purpose, and cures me of this philosophical melancholy and delirium, either by relaxing this bent of mind, or by some avocation, and lively impression of my senses, which obliterate all these chimeras. I dine, I play a game of back-gammon, I converse, and am merry with my friends; and when after three or four hours' amusement, I wou'd return to these speculations, they appear so cold, and strain'd, and ridiculous, that I cannot find in my heart to enter into them any farther.[1]

With Hume's views about the imagination we are not here directly concerned. What he has to say about the understanding, however, is directly relevant to our inquiries. For the argument by which, as he says, 'I have already shown that the understanding when it acts alone...leaves not the lowest degree of evidence in any proposition, either in philosophy or common life', was an argument in which at every step he rejected anything other than analytic criteria and proofs. There is no certainty that a pinch of salt put in water will dissolve. Why? Because, however much evidence I may be able to produce of salt's dissolving in water in the past or present, I may suppose that a pinch dropped in water tomorrow will remain undissolved without contradicting any of this evidence. When two billiard balls lying on a billiard table collide, there is no necessity for the motion of the one to be imparted to the other, however uniformly we have observed this to happen in the past. Why? The answer is as before: because the supposition that the regularity might cease to hold on the next occasion and the ball struck remain still, fails to *contradict*—fails, that is, in the narrowest sense of the term, to conflict 'logically' with—any collection of evidence, however large, about its previous invariability. Throughout the *Treatise* Hume appeals repeatedly to considerations of this kind: the understanding is to admit arguments as acceptable, or 'conformable to reason', if and only if they come up to analytic standards. But, as he soon discovers, all arguments involving a transition of logical type between data and conclusion *must* fail to satisfy these tests: however grotesque the incongruity produced by conjoining the same data with the contradictory of the conclusion, the very presence of a type-jump will prevent the result from being a flat contradiction. And even without a type-jump, an argument *may* be substantial and so fail to reach his standards. Circumscribed in this way, limited to the detection of contradictions and to the recognition of elemen-

[1] *Treatise of Human Nature*, book I, pt. IV, sect. VII.

tary facts about (say) motion and colour, our reason is powerless to reject the most fantastic conclusions: no wonder that for Hume ''tis not contrary to reason to prefer the destruction of the whole world to the scratching of my finger'.

Yet perhaps one should say again, not for Hume, but for Hume *as a philosopher*. He is the first to admit that a good dinner, a game of backgammon, three or four hours in the society of his fellows, are enough to take away his taste for speculation 'so cold and strain'd and ridiculous'. There is something about everyday discussion, and the standards of argument implicit in it, which is completely out of tune with his own epistemological speculation, and which takes away all its plausibility. 'In the common affairs of life,' he explains, 'I find myself absolutely and necessarily determin'd to live, and talk, and act like other people': it is only when he withdraws to the study, and takes on the cloak and criteria of a philosopher, that the sceptical mood returns, and his drastic conclusions take on once more some of their former plausibility.

THE IRRELEVANCE OF ANALYTIC CRITERIA

With all this behind me, I shall feel justified in regarding my hypothesis as established. Logicians have taken analytic arguments as a paradigm; they have built up their system of formal logic entirely on this foundation; and they have felt free to apply to arguments in other fields the categories so constructed. The next question is: supposing the hypothesis established, what judgement are we to pass on the Great Divergence which has resulted? Has the programme which formal logicians have adopted for themselves been a legitimate one, or have they simply missed the point? Can one reasonably hope to build up a system of logical categories whose criteria of application are as field-invariant as is their force? Or will categories of this kind inevitably be disqualified from applying to substantial arguments?

In the first of these studies we examined at length the practical use of one particular class of logical categories, that of modal qualifiers. As a result we saw clearly the field-dependence of the criteria for deciding in practice when any modal qualifier can appropriately be employed—a feature to which formal logicians have paid very little attention. Bearing in mind the proper ambitions with which formal logicians might set out, we must ask: Is this field-dependence unavoidable, or might one find a way of getting round it? In building up their formal systems from the initial, analytic paradigm, logicians have evidently cherished this hope, and in applying the same analytic criteria in all fields of argument regardless, they have been trying to free theoretical logic of the field-dependence which marks all logical practice. But supposing a completely field-invariant logic were attainable, could it be reached by following up this particular track? We are now in a position to show that the differences between the criteria we employ in different fields can be circumvented in this way only at the price of robbing our logical systems of all serious application to substantial arguments.

At the very beginning of our inquiry, we introduced the notion of a *field* of arguments, by referring to the different sorts of problem to which arguments can be addressed. If fields of argument are different, that is because they are addressed to different sorts of problems. A geometrical argument serves us when the problem facing us is geometrical; a moral argument when the problem is moral; an argument with a predictive conclusion when a prediction is what we need to produce; and so on. Since we are unable to prevent life from posing us problems of all these different kinds, there is one sense in which the differences between different fields of argument are of course irreducible—something with which we must just come to terms. There is simply no point in demanding that a predictive argument (say) should be presented in analytic form: the question with which this argument is concerned is, 'Given what we know about the past and present, how can we most reliably answer such-and-such a question about the future?', and the very form of problem rules out the possibility of giving an analytic argument as solution. A man who declines to answer a question of this sort until he has waited to obtain data about the future also—without which no analytic argument could be stated—is refusing to face the problem at issue.

Suppose we ask the question, '*Could* substantial arguments come up to the standards appropriate to analytic arguments?', the answer must therefore be, 'In the nature of the case, *no*'. Apart from anything else, many substantial arguments actually involve type-jumps, arising out of the nature of the problems to which they are relevant. In analytic arguments, no doubt, we are entitled to look for entailments between data and backing on the one hand and conclusion on the other: these entailments will be complete where the argument is also unequivocal, but only partial when the argument (though analytic) is tentative. In the case of substantial arguments, however, there is no question of data and backing taken together entailing the conclusion, or failing to entail it: just because the steps involved are substantial ones, it is no use either looking for entailments or being disappointed if we do not find them. Their absence does not spring from a lamentable weakness in the arguments, but from the nature of the problems with which they are designed to deal. When we have to set about assessing the real merits of any substantial argument, analytic criteria such as entailment are, accordingly, simply irrelevant.

With this point in mind, we can dismiss one more claim which is made on behalf of formal logic. When logicians do remark on the divergence between their theories and the practice of everyday arguers, they frequently claim to be speaking more strictly than the people for whom the logical categories actually do a practical job. 'Scientists no doubt say sometimes that their conclusions *must* be the case, although the steps by which they have reached them are inductive (i.e. substantial); but this is a loose manner of speaking since, to be absolutely accurate, *no* conclusion of an inductive argument *could*, strictly speaking, be entitled to claim necessity.' The time has now come to put a very large question mark against the phrase 'strictly speaking' as so used. To tolerate only arguments in which the conclusion was entailed by the data and backing might be very *particular* or *fussy*, and if this were the sense of strictness intended, well and good; but more is normally implied—logicians are not just claiming to be unusually selective or choosy: they are claiming to have exceptional insight, which leads them to refuse the titles of 'necessary' conclusion, 'conclusive' argument, or 'valid' inference to the arguments and conclusions which working scientists unhesitatingly accept.

This claim to superior insight must be disputed. So long as we allow logicians to use the term 'inductive' in stating their point, there may seem to be something in the claim. Once more explicit substitutions are made, it becomes clear what they are insisting on: that the criteria for assessing analytic arguments should be given a preferential status, and arguments in all fields be judged by these criteria alone. 'Strictly speaking' means, to them, *analytically* speaking; although in the case of substantial arguments to appeal to analytic criteria is not so much strict as beside the point. It is no shortcoming of an argument which issues in, e.g., a prediction that it does not match up to analytic standards; for, if it were to succeed in doing so, it would cease to be a predictive argument, and so cease to be of any use to us in dealing with predictive problems.

LOGICAL MODALITIES

One is tempted, therefore, to enter judgement against the formal logicians outright, on grounds of sheer irrelevance. One thing, however, complicates the situation: for certain purposes, considerations of consistency and contradiction may be relevant, even when the arguments we are discussing are substantial. Before we reach any final conclusions, we must look and see how this comes about, and what relevance the notions of 'logical' possibility, impossibility and necessity do have to the criticism of non-analytic arguments.

Traditionally—in the tradition of logic text-books, that is—any proposition so expressed as to avoid lapsing into incoherence and incomprehensibility is entitled to be called logically possible; and any conclusion which does not contradict the data it is inferred from can be called a logically possible conclusion. Likewise, only a conclusion which positively contradicts the data is called impossible, and only one whose denial contradicts the data is called necessary. This, at any rate, is the orthodox doctrine to accept from the point of view of *logic*. This doctrine, however, is liable to be gravely misleading, for it gives the impression that 'the logical point of view' is a genuine alternative to the points of view of physics, ethics and the like, and that this distinct point of view is somehow more rigorous than those of the practical and explanatory sciences. Only if we can dispel this impression shall we come to see clearly the true relation between logic and these other subjects.

To begin with a counter-exaggeration: the phrases 'logically possible', 'logically necessary' and 'logically impossible', I shall claim, are plain misnomers. To say that a conclusion is possible, impossible or necessary is to say that, bearing in mind the nature of our problem and data, the conclusion must be admitted to consideration, ruled out, or accepted as forced on us. The 'logical' criteria of possibility, impossibility and necessity, on the other hand, do nothing to show us that any conclusion we shall be concerned with in practice is genuinely possible, impossible or necessary—at any rate so long as the problem with which we are concerned involves us in the use of *substantial* arguments. This is why I claim that 'logical' modalities are misnamed.

Glance back at any of the illustrations we gave to show how the notion of possibility is used in practice: if the question arises, 'Is this a possible conclusion?', we need to be assured not just that the proposition put forward successfully avoids contradicting our data, but that it is a genuine candidate-solution whose backing we shall have to investigate and whose acceptability we shall have to evaluate. For these purposes, the mere absence of contradiction takes us no distance—no-one outside the philosopher's study, for example, would ever speak of Dwight D. Eisenhower as a *possible* member of the U.S. Davis Cup team. Practical questions about possibility are concerned with more than consistency; and questions about impossibility and necessity, likewise, call for a study of more than mere intelligibility and meaningfulness.

To go further: logical possibility—if by this we mean meaningfulness—is not so much a sub-species of possibility as a *prerequisite* of either possibility or impossibility; while logical impossibility, inconceivability or meaninglessness, far from being a sub-species of impossibility, *precludes* either possibility or impossibility. Can a proposition expressed in an unintelligible form even be dismissed from consideration as impossible? We must surely eliminate inconsistencies and self-contradictions before we shall have expressed ourselves in an intelligible manner, and until this is done genuine questions about possibility, impossibility or necessity can hardly arise at all. Given the minimum requirement of intelligibility, an *impossible* conclusion will be one which, though it may be consistent with our data so far as language alone goes, we have conclusive reasons for ruling out: an *inconsistent* conclusion never even reaches the stage at which its claim to be possible can be considered. Perhaps in a limited range of problems—analytic arguments and computations—the presence or absence of contradictions does become relevant to an actual assessment; but, this limited class of cases apart, the things that count for necessity, impossibility and so on are considerations of entirely another kind.

The relation between logical possibility and other kinds can be clarified once again by looking at the parallel with law. Suppose that I have an obscure sense of grievance against a neighbour, and decide that I must get my wrongs redressed in the courts: I may go to a lawyer, tell him a tale of woe about what the neighbour has done to me, and end up with the inquiry, 'Have I a possible case?' Now it should be noticed that, at this stage, there can be no reply to my question: as things stand the question cannot be tackled, since the time for asking it has not yet properly been reached. If all I have produced is a chronicle of the man's behaviour towards me over the last few months, without indicating in what respect I feel aggrieved or on what account his conduct might provide grounds for an action, the lawyer may have to ask me quite a number of other questions before the inquiry, whether my case is a possible one, can seriously be faced. Even at this stage I might of course ask the question, 'Is there any *sort* of a case that I could bring against him?', but it has to be decided what sort of case is in question before we can go on to ask whether the case is *possible*. So first I must say what kind of a case I had it in mind to bring, and roughly which of the facts in my chronicle I shall rely on to demonstrate the soundness of my case. Only when, with the help of the lawyer, I have succeeded in working out both the kind of case to be brought and the way in which my evidence supports the case, will the further question arise. The case has, in other words, to be set out first of all *in proper form*. Once it is in proper form, at any rate roughly, the time will have come for asking how far the case is a possible one—i.e. whether it is the sort of case which one should even consider bringing into court.

It may, however, not only be too *early* to ask whether a case is a possible one: it may also be too *late*. This question arises only for so long as the issue has not yet been settled. Suppose that I go to court, and the judge gives a verdict: once this has happened the question whether my case is possible can no longer be asked. If I go back to my lawyer afterwards and ask him again whether I have a possible case, he will be at a loss to answer me. No doubt my case is still stated in proper form and is still free from contradictions, but it has been settled, and the time for asking whether it is *possible* is past.

This legal example has a logical analogue. Consistency and

coherence are prerequisites for rational assessment. A man who purports to make an assertion, but contradicts himself in doing so, will fail even to make himself understood: the question whether what he says is true cannot even be reached. So also, a man who puts forward a series of statements as an argument, but whose final conclusion contradicts certain of his data, fails to make himself understood: until his case is stated in consistent, coherent form, questions about merits of the argument or conclusion cannot yet be asked. Self-contradictory statements, and conclusions inconsistent with our data, are ones which have to be ruled out before we can even get a case stated clearly or in proper form: this incoherence is accordingly a preliminary matter, which compels us to debar them at the very outset.

Statements and arguments free from contradictions are, correspondingly, those against which there is no preliminary objection on grounds of mere incoherence or inconsistency: the mistake is to see in this freedom a *prima facie* case in their favour. As for logically necessary statements and arguments, these are like law cases which have already been decided: in accepting a certain set of data, one is committed in sheer consistency to accepting those other propositions which are entailed by the aggregate of data—so the question whether these other propositions are 'possible' inferences from our data is itself misleadingly weak. 'They were married on a Wednesday, so it is possible that they were married on a weekday': such a conclusion is past being a possible one, for it is in fact forced on us.

Let us at this point return to my initial assertion that the phrase 'logical possibility' and its cognate are misnomers. This may perhaps have been an exaggeration, but it was a pardonable one. Nothing is decided by merely putting a case in proper form, but rather a situation is created in which we can begin to ask rational questions: we are put into a position in which we can use substantial decision-procedures. We do, it is true, have occasion sometimes to rule out suggested propositions or conclusions as impossible on the preliminary ground of sheer inconsistency, or to acknowledge them as being consistent linguistically with those data, or even forced on us by the acceptance of these data; but to say that a conclusion is logically necessary, or logically impossible, is not to say that in the first case the problem has been solved by the discovery of cast-iron arguments or utterly overwhelming evidence, while in the latter case the proposition had to be ruled out for similar reasons. It is to say, rather, that in the latter case the problem never really got under way, since the proposed solution turned out to be one which, for reasons of consistency alone, was ruled out from the start; while in the former case, having accepted the data to begin with, we were no longer in the position of having to assess the strength of any arguments involved—since no arguments were needed.

So long as no more than this is meant by the phrases 'logically possible, impossible and necessary', they are innocuous and acceptable enough: yet the danger remains of confusing logical possibility, impossibility and necessity with other sorts, and of suggesting, e.g., that some conclusion needs taking into consideration, when it has only been shown not to be in actual contradiction with our previous information. How blithely philosophers often take this further step anyone who has read their works will know. Descartes, for instance, suggests that all our sensory experience might *possibly* be a hallucination contrived by an ingenious demon. Bertrand Russell, too, professes doubts and hesitations even about tomorrow's sunrise, suggesting further that, for all we know, the world might *possibly* have been created five minutes ago with fossils and memories all as they are. In each case all that has been established in fact is that the suggestion is not formally out-of-order. The proper reply can be stated in the form of a general motto: 'Logical considerations are no more than formal considerations', that is, they are considerations having to do with the preliminary formalities of argument-stating, and not with the actual merits of any argument or proposition.

Once we leave the preliminary formalities behind, questions of consistency and contradiction remain relevant only to the severely limited class of analytic arguments; and even then they represent at most the *grounds* or *criteria* of possibility and impossibility, and not the whole *meaning* of these terms. In the first of these studies we drove a wedge between the notion of self-contradiction and the notion of mathematical impossibility: even there it was an error to suppose that the contradiction and the impossibility could be identified, or defined one in terms of the other—a mathematically impossible conclusion is, rather, one which has to be ruled out *qua* inconsistent or self-contradictory. The same wedge can now be driven between the notions of impossibility and inconsistency: for the formal logician's purposes, too, it is enough that consistency and contradiction should be taken as criteria of possibility and impossibility, and to try to define one in terms of the other is to over-reach oneself. Apart from anything else, it leaves us without our normal term for ruling contradictory propositions out: once impossibility is identified with contradiction, the question, 'Why has a logically impossible (contradictory) proposition to be ruled out?', becomes—paradoxically and unfortunately—a meaningful one.

The categories of logical possibility, necessity and impossibility cannot therefore be dismissed as positively improper; but we can see that they are normally somewhat confused. As normally defined, for instance, they leave the distinction between spotting a self-contradiction and drawing the appropriate moral quite unmarked. Yet this distinction is as important for logicians as for everyone else: they, like us, do want to mean more by 'impossible' than by 'self-contradictory', and to retain 'impossible' as the natural term for ruling self-contradictions out—they certainly do want, that is, to retain the old everyday implications of the idea of impossibility in their new, technical context.

Similar dangers of confusion lie in much of the common use philosophers make of the very words 'logic' and 'logical': often enough, they want to retain the everyday implications of these terms, even when they have in effect eliminated them as a result of their narrower, professional definitions. Recall our earlier quotation from Professor A. N. Prior. A practical arguer will admit as logical any argument which is properly set out, and so not open to objection merely in respect of the formalities involved: to tell him that an argument is not logical is to suggest to him that the argument is incoherent, as involving positive contradictions, and is therefore one in which the substantial questions cannot even be raised, let alone seriously considered or settled. Prior, on the other hand, declines to call any argument 'logical' unless it satisfies a much more stringent condition: it must now be analytic, and substantial arguments are ruled out as not being logical, simply because they are substantial arguments.

The consequences of restricting the field of the logical in this way are most striking in the field of ethical arguments: the statement 'Ethical arguments are not logical' implies for the practical arguer that all ethical arguments are incoherent, invalid and improper, and so necessarily unsound for procedural reasons; and this is a much

stronger claim than the innocent one Prior wishes to insist on—
namely, that ethical arguments are not, and could not be, analytic.
If no more were involved here than a plain ambiguity, the difficulty
could be cleared up quickly enough. But one does not have to read
far before one sees that for philosophers like Prior the absence of
entailments from ethical arguments is, by comparison with analytic
arguments, a weakness and a falling-short: the fact that such
arguments are 'not logical' is still held against them.

This confusion in the notion of 'logic' and its affiliates has had
one particularly unfortunate consequence. What that is we can see
if we return to the question whether the Court of Reason can adjudicate in all fields of argument, or whether in some fields there is
no possibility of settling or assessing claims by a judicial type of
procedure. For that question is too easily sidetracked and its true
force misrepresented. If one follows Hume, one ends by allowing
the Court of Reason to adjudicate only in cases where analytic
arguments can properly be demanded: ethical and aesthetic arguments, predictive and causal conclusions, statements about other
minds, about material objects, about our memories even, fall in
turn before the philosophers' criticism, and we find the judicial
function of the reason progressively more and more restricted.
Following Hume's track, we are bound to end up in his metaphysical
dilemma.

The question has, however, an alternative interpretation which
lands us in no such difficulty. Without demanding that arguments in
all fields should be analytic, we may still ask—analyticity apart—
in what fields can inter-personal and judicial procedures or assessments be employed? The answer to this question will depend not
on the vain search for entailments which in the context are out of
the question, but on something else. Whatever field we are concerned
with, we can set our arguments out in the form

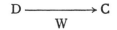

$$D \longrightarrow C$$
$$W$$

Appeal to such an argument carries the implication that the warrant
W not only authorises us to take the step from D to C, but is also
an *established* warrant. Rational discussion in any field accordingly
depends on the possibility of *establishing* inference-warrants in that
field: to the extent that there are common and understood inter-

personal procedures for testing warrants in any particular field, a judicial approach to our problems will be possible. When we ask how far the authority of the Court of Reason extends, therefore, we must put on one side the question how far in any field it is possible for arguments to be analytic: we must focus our attention instead on the rather different question, to what extent there are already established warrants in science, in ethics or morality, in law, art-criticism, character-judging, or whatever it may be; and how far the procedures for deciding what principles are sound, and what warrants are acceptable, are generally understood and agreed. Two people who accept common procedures for testing warrants in any field can begin comparing the merits of arguments in that field: only where this condition is lacking, so that they have no common ground on which to argue, will rational assessment no longer be open to them.

To sum up the results of this section: I have suggested two factors which tend at present to confuse our ideas about the application of logic. These are, first, a failure to recognise that the field-dependence of our logical categories is an *essential* feature, which arises from irreducible differences between the sorts of problem with which arguments are designed to deal; and, secondly, the gross ambiguity of the word 'deductive', as it is commonly used in formal logic. Only once one is clear about the kind of problem involved in any particular case can one determine what warrants, backing, and criteria of necessity and possibility are relevant to this case: there is no justification for applying analytic criteria in all fields of argument indiscriminately, and doing so consistently will lead one (as Hume found) into a state of philosophical delirium. The absence of entailments in the case of substantial arguments is not a sign of weakness but is a consequence of the problems they have to do with— of course there are differences between fields of argument, and the Court of Reason is able to adjudicate not only in the narrow field of analytic arguments.

Behind these two immediate factors there lie other considerations at which we have not yet looked. If philosophers have been tempted to take analytic arguments as their paradigm, their choice has not been haphazard. It is not enough to recognise the fact of this choice, and to trace out the paradoxes to which it inevitably leads: we must now try to *explain* it. At this point we shall have to enter the realm of speculation, but two possible influences will prove at any rate worth discussing:

(i) the ideal of logic as a set of timeless truths, to be expressed for preference in the form of a coherent, mathematical system;

(ii) the idea that, by casting the subject into such a formal system, we shall be able to bring into play a necessity stronger than mere physical necessity and an impossibility harder than mere physical impossibility.

These ideas will occupy us for the rest of the present essay.

LOGIC AS A SYSTEM OF ETERNAL TRUTHS

The ambition to cast logic into a mathematical form is as old as the subject itself. For as long as logic has had any separate existence—since Aristotle, in other words—formal logicians have had a double aim: on the one hand, they have seen themselves as systematising the principles of sound reasoning and theorising about the canons of argument, while on the other hand they have always held out for themselves the ideal of the subject as a formal, deductive, and preferably an axiomatic science. In the opening sentence of Aristotle's *Prior Analytics* we found this double aim already expressed: logic, he says, is concerned with *apodeixis* (i.e. with the way in which conclusions are to be established), and it is also the science (*episteme*) of their establishment—he already takes for granted that one can set the subject out in the form of an *episteme*, i.e. as a deductive theoretical science.

This same double aim remains implicit in the practice of formal logicians down to our own day. Since the seventeenth century the subject has, if anything, tended to become more mathematical rather than less, first in the hands of Leibniz, and subsequently through the work of Boole, Frege and the twentieth-century symbolic logicians. Nowadays, indeed, many logicians probably regard the mathematical ideal of logic as more important than its practical applicability: Strawson, for instance, professes himself content that logicians should restrict their interests to questions about the consistency and inconsistency of arguments and statements, and for this limited purpose a purely formal theory may indeed be sufficient. Yet most logicians still think from time to time that their subject is concerned with the principles of valid reasoning, even if their definition of 'deduction' limits them in practice to the principles of valid analytic reasoning—Carnap, for instance, is prepared to assert, even at the risk of a *non sequitur*, that his analytic theory of probability is applicable to problems about betting, our expectations for the harvest, and whether we should accept a new scientific theory. Yet no one could be more insistent than Carnap that logic, like mathematics, is concerned with timeless truths about its own theoretical entities— in this case, semantic relations.

Let us begin by seeing what is involved in accepting this mathematical ideal for the formulation of logical theory. For the Greeks, the first and most dramatically successful *episteme* was geometry: when they turned to logic, their approach to the subject was taken over from geometry, and their ambition was to expound the principles of logic in the same sort of form as had already proved fruitful in the other field. They were not, however, unanimous in the account they gave of the nature of geometry, and there is a similar ambiguity in the points of view adopted by formal logicians towards their subject. Just as the Greeks were divided over the question, what the propositions of geometry are about—some of them claiming that the mathematical relations discussed in the subject applied directly to the changeable objects of the material world, while others claimed that they referred rather to an independent class of change-free things—so among logicians also one finds two views. Both parties agree in accepting the mathematical model as a legitimate ideal, indeed as *the* legitimate ideal for logic; but they differ in the account they give of their theories, and in the lengths to which they think the idealisation should be carried.

One can distinguish a more extreme view from a less extreme one. The less extreme view corresponds to the first of the two Greek theories of geometry: formal logic is to be the *episteme* of logical relations, and these relations are to be expressed in timeless, tenseless propositions which, if true at any one time, must—like other mathematical propositions—be true at all times whatever; but the units or things between which these logical relations hold need not, like the relations themselves, be change-free or 'out of time'. They may, for instance, be statements of a perfectly familiar sort, whose truth-value can alter with the passage of time—for example, the statement 'Socrates is bald', which can be first inapplicable, then true, then false, then true and finally inapplicable again. All that our mathematical ideal demands, according to this less extreme view, is that the relations directly discussed in logical theory shall be themselves timeless, after the manner of geometrical relations. 'An equiangular triangle is equilateral'—that is true once and for all; and the truth of the principles of formal logic must be equally exempt from temporal change.

The more extreme view corresponds to the second of the Greek accounts of geometry. According to this view, it is not enough that the propositions of formal logic should themselves be timelessly true. The subject will not have reached its ideal, mathematical condition until the units between which these logical relations hold have also been transformed into change-free, time-independent objects. This means that a bare, everyday statement like 'Socrates is bald' is, as it stands, not yet ripe for the formal logician's consideration: it must be processed, transformed, frozen into timelessness before it can be built into the formal structure of logical theory. How is this to be done? One way is to write into our normal statements explicit references to the occasion of their utterance—the resulting form of words being referred to as a 'proposition'. In this technical sense, the 'proposition' corresponding to a particular utterance of the words 'Socrates is bald' will be (say) 'Socrates bald as of 400 B.C.', and that corresponding to the statement 'I am hungry' will be (say) 'Stephen Toulmin hungry as of 4.30 p.m., 6 September 1956'—the verb 'is' or 'was' is here omitted in order to mark the fact that all 'propositions' are *tenseless*: there are obvious dangers in using the word 'is' both as the tenseless copula of expressions within formal logic and as the main verb of statements referring to the present time. On the more extreme view, then, a completely mathematical logic will be composed of timeless formulae expressing unchanging relations between tenseless 'propositions'.

Both these forms of idealisation are, from our point of view, illegitimate. The trouble does not lie within the formal systems themselves: it would be pointless to argue that one *could* not have formal mathematical calculi concerned with the relations between propositions, since everyone knows what elaborate and sophisticated propositional calculi have *in fact* been built up in recent years. The objections turn rather on the question, what application these calculi can have to the practical assessment of arguments—whether the relations so elegantly formalised in these systems are, in fact, the ones which concern us when we ask in practice about the cogency, force and acceptability of arguments.

Let me deal with the more extreme doctrine first. The fundamental objection to both doctrines will prove to be the same, but the very difference between the two doctrines can give us a first clue to its nature. An advocate of the more extreme view, like Professor W. V. Quine, insists on re-phrasing all statements as 'propositions' before admitting them into his system of logic: in the act of doing so, he removes the formulae of his theory one step further from their ostensible application. The data and conclusions of practical arguments are statements, not (speaking technically) propositions. A critic's business is to inquire how far certain statements cited as data support a conclusion or statement of claim; so that a formal logic of propositions will have to be transcribed so as to refer to statements before we can hope to apply its results.

This is not a serious objection in itself. The formulation of logical theory in terms of propositions rather than statements might bring with it important theoretical gains: physicists—to cite an apparent analogy—are justified in using the tensor calculus in relativity physics, despite the fact that one transforms one's theoretical results out of tensor notation into normal algebra before giving them an empirical interpretation in terms of actual observations or measurements. Still, in the case of logic, it is not made clear what the corresponding theoretical gains are, and logicians are divided over the question whether in any case one need confine the application of logical formulae to timeless propositions.

Certainly language as we know it consists, not of timeless propositions, but of utterances dependent in all sorts of ways on the context or occasion on which they are uttered. Statements are made in particular situations, and the interpretation to be put upon them is bound up with their relation to these situations: they are in this respect like fireworks, signals or Very lights. The ways in which statements and utterances require to be criticised and assessed reflect this fact. The questions which arise are, e.g., whether in one given situation a particular statement is an appropriate one to make, or whether in another situation a certain collection of data can properly be put forward as entitling one to predict a subsequent event. Only in pure mathematics can our assessments be entirely context-free.

Criticism of this sort is, in the widest sense of the word, *ethical* criticism: it treats an utterance as an action performed in a given situation, and asks about the merits of this action when looked at in the context of its performance. Propositional logic, on the other hand, approaches language in a manner more akin to *aesthetic* criticism: propositions are treated as the frozen statues of statements, and the merits for which the logician looks are timeless, universal merits like those of the *Winged Victory of Samothrace* or the *David* of Michelangelo. What relation such criticism could have to the time-bound problems of practical arguers is unclear. In any case, as Prior has argued, this particular attitude is not essential for formal logic. There is in fact a sharp contrast between the logic of the last few centuries and medieval logic. Medieval logicians did not insist on replacing statements by propositions before admitting our utterances into their systems of logic: they were content that the expressions of their logical theory should be themselves tenseless, without demanding that the units between which logical relations held must also be eternal and unchanging. So a formal logic of statements is quite possible, and in some ways, as Prior goes on to argue, such a logic can be richer and fuller of potentialities than the more fashionable logic of propositions.

It is intriguing to ask, by the way, about the reasons for this particular historical transition. Why should the medieval logic of statements have been abandoned, and displaced almost entirely by a propositional logic which relates not context-dependent utterances but context-invariant propositions? Had the change-over, perhaps, something to do with the invention of printing? The suggestion is a tempting one: in a largely pre-literate world the transient firework-like character of our utterances would remain overwhelmingly obvious. The conception of the proposition as outlasting the moment of its utterance—like a statue which stands unaltered after the death of the sculptor who fashioned it—would become plausible only after the permanent recorded word had come to play a much larger part in the lives of speculative men.

There is however little evidence that the invention had any direct influence, and a good deal of evidence to point to an alternative explanation. In a number of respects, the seventeenth-century revolution in thought can be characterised as a revival of Platonism and a rejection of Aristotelianism. What I have called the less extreme view, both of logic and of geometry, is an Aristotelian one, and the medieval statement-logic was an integral part of the Aristotelian tradition. The 'new thinkers' of the sixteenth and seventeenth centuries set up in opposition to Aristotle the figures of Pythagoras, Plato and above all Euclid. It was their ambition to employ mathematical methods and models in all speculations, and they can often be found expressing Platonist views about the status of mathematical entities. The idea that logical relations, quite as much as geometrical ones, hold between eternal objects was congenial to their point of view, and we need probably look no further for our explanation. The two explanations are not, however, incompatible: it might be argued that the Platonist revival and the apotheosis of Euclid were themselves an outcome of the spread of the printed page. In that case, the transition from the medieval statement-logic to the more recent propositional-logic would also be an effect of this invention, although only an indirect one.

This is a chapter in the history of ideas which, regretfully, we must refrain from exploring any further, and we must return to our proper subject. So far, we have shown only that the double idealisation involved in the more extreme view of logic is unnecessary. If a formal study of the logical relations between 'propositions' is possible, then the same thing is possible equally for relations holding between statements instead: the real question is, whether it is genuinely possible in either case. Whatever the objects between which logical relations hold, is it in order to idealise even these relations themselves? Can one cast into a timeless mathematical mould the relations upon which the soundness and acceptability of our arguments depend, without distorting them beyond recognition? I shall argue that this cannot be done: by insisting on treating these relations mathematically, one will inevitably end by misrepresenting them, and a divergence must result between the categories of applied logic and those of logical theory of the very sort we have already been forced to recognise. This criticism, if established, would undercut the less and the more extreme views equally, and we must now try to press it home.

It is unnecessary, we argued, to freeze statements into timeless propositions before admitting them into logic: utterances are made at particular times and in particular situations, and they have to be understood and assessed with one eye on this context. The same, we can now argue, is true of the relations holding between statements, at any rate in the majority of practical arguments. The exercise of the rational judgement is itself an activity carried out in a particular context and essentially dependent on it: the arguments we encounter are set out at a given time and in a given situation, and when we come to assess them they have to be judged against this background. So the practical critic of arguments, as of morals, is in no position to adopt the mathematician's Olympian posture.

As a result strength, cogency, evidential support and the like—all the things that Carnap tries to freeze into semantic relations—resist idealisation as much as our utterances themselves. This fact comes out most clearly if we look at the case of predictions. A man who offers a prediction as more than a piece of guesswork can be called upon to support it with an argument: he will be required to produce warrants based on his general knowledge and experience, and also particular evidence (data) about the subjects of his prediction which between them are reliable and accurate enough to make his prediction a trustworthy one, *having regard to the occasion of its utterance*. At the time a prediction is made, this is the only kind of criticism it can be asked to stand up to; and, whether or no the event turns out as predicted, this question can always be revived by asking whether the original prediction was a *proper* or an *improper* one. At the moment it is uttered, of course, we cannot yet ask whether or no it is *mistaken*—the time for that question arrives only with the event itself.

Nevertheless, between the time of the prediction and the event predicted, the question of its soundness may arise again in several ways. Fresh evidence may become available which leads us to modify the prediction without changing our general ideas about the subject concerned; or alternatively, with increasing experience, we may have to change our minds even about the bearing of the original evidence upon the question at issue. As time goes on, that is to say, we may find ourselves not only making a different prediction about this event, but also being forced to withdraw our allegiance from the argument produced in the first place. This happens most drastically if the event itself turns out in a way other than that predicted: unless the prediction was suitably guarded or made subject to exceptions, the argument on which it was based will then be hopelessly comprised. The train of events can, therefore, force us to modify our rational assessments, and an argument quite properly regarded as sound in one situation may later on have to be rejected. Most notably, an argument for a prediction must *of course* be judged by fresh standards, once the event has taken place—when the prediction has become a retrodiction, all our logical attitudes will be transformed.

If, on the other hand, questions about 'logical relations' are to be dealt with timelessly and tenselessly, there will be no room for this progressive revision of our standards. When looked at from a quasi-mathematical point of view, arguments are simply *defined* by stating their conclusions (in this case, the prediction) and the evidence produced in their support: thus, the argument

D: observed positions   C: precise moment at
   of sun, moon and   which next eclipse
   earth up to   ——————————→   of moon after
   6 September 1956 | 6 September 1956
                         | becomes total
          W: current laws of
              planetary dynamics
                  |
         B: totality of experience
            on which the current laws
            are based up to
            6 September 1956

will be regarded as 'one and the same' argument, whether it is put forward on the particular day the prediction is actually made, or at any later or even—*per impossibile*—at any earlier time. If this is a good argument, logicians imply, it must surely be good once and for all: if it is not a good one, then its defects must surely be eternal ones likewise.

Questions about the soundness of predictive arguments can, however, be handled in a time-invariant manner only if we disregard both the context in which a prediction is made and that in which it is now being assessed—if validity is to be a timeless 'logical relation' between the statements alone, facts about their occasion of utterance must be swept aside as irrelevant. The formal logician demands to be shown the statements, all the statements and nothing but the statements: looking down from his Olympian throne, he then sets himself to pronounce about the unchangeable relations between them. But taking this kind of God's-eye-view distracts one completely from the practical problems out of which the question of validity itself springs: whether we ought to accept, trust and rely on the man's prediction, his grounds for it being what they are, or alternatively whether we should reject and disregard it—that is the question we express in practice by the words, 'Is this argument *sound?*', and by divorcing 'logical relations' from all possible contexts we deprive ourselves of the means of asking it. Questions about the acceptability of arguments have in practice to be understood and tackled *in a context* quite as much as questions about the acceptability of individual utterances, and this practical necessity the purely formal logician strikes out of the account before even beginning his work.

Accordingly, in order to get a logic which is lifelike and applicable, it will not be enough for us to replace propositions by statements. We shall also have to replace mathematically-idealised logical relations—timeless context-free relations between either statements or propositions—by relations which in practical fact are no more timeless than the statements they relate. This is not to say that the elaborate mathematical systems which constitute 'symbolic logic' must now be thrown away; but only that people with intellectual capital invested in them should retain no illusions about the extent of their relevance to practical arguments. If logic is to remain mathematical, it will remain *purely* mathematical; and when applied to the establishment of practical conclusions it will be able to concern itself solely with questions of internal consistency. Some logicians may view this prospect with composure and be prepared to pay the price: Strawson for one is content, despite his final excursion into induction and probability, to limit his discussion for most of the time to the notions of consistency and inconsistency. But this means making great changes in Aristotle's original programme, which was concerned in the first place with the ways in which conclusions are to be established (*apodeixis*), and only in the second place with the science (*episteme*) of their establishment. Had Aristotle himself recognised that demonstration was not a suitable subject for a formal science, he would surely have abandoned, not the study of demonstration, but any attempt to cast the theory of demonstration into a wholly mathematical form.

A word is in place here about the title of the present essay, for a peace-loving reader might put forward this suggestion: 'What you say may be all right so far as it goes, but it really has no bearing at all on the things that mathematical logicians like Quine are concerned with. Their business is with logical theory; you are concerned with logical practice; and there need be no real disagreement between you.' This suggestion is tempting, but must be rejected. The title 'Working Logic and Idealised Logic' was selected deliberately and with reason, in preference to the more obvious alternative, 'Logic in Practice and Logic in Theory', since the alternative title begs a crucial question.

If all that the suggestion meant were that, as mathematics, the 'propositional calculus' is as legitimate a subject of study as the other parts of pure mathematics, there could indeed be no disagreement; but the question still needs to be pressed, whether this branch of mathematics is entitled to the name of 'logical theory'. If we give it this name, we imply that the propositional calculus plays a part in the assessment of actual arguments comparable to that played by physical theory in explaining actual physical phenomena. But this is just what we have seen reason to doubt: this branch of mathematics does not form the theoretical part of logic in anything like the way that the physicist's mathematical theories form the theoretical part of physics. By now, mathematical logic has become a frozen calculus, having no functional connection with the canons for assessing the strength and cogency of arguments. This frozen calculus may be connected by an unbroken historical chain with Aristotle's original discussion of the practice of argument-criticism, but the connection is now no more than historical, like that between seven-dimensional geometry and the techniques of surveying. The branch of mathematics known as 'pure geometry' long ago stopped pretending to be the theoretical part of surveying, and 'pure logic' can remain mathematical only by following the same path.

All this is said in no spirit of disrespect for mathematical logic, regarded as an object of intellectual study: all we have to get clear about is the sort of subject it is. Once this is done, we shall no longer want to accept the sort of peace-terms offered by Carnap: he concedes that the methods of assessing practical arguments may form an enthralling and important object of study having no functional connection with the propositional calculus, but goes on to propose, in seeming innocence, that this study should be entitled

'Methodology', so as to distinguish it from 'Logic' which (as everybody knows) is a formal, mathematical subject. There are several reasons why this proposal must be rejected. To put the matter at its lowest, it is an invitation to connive at the fraudulent conversion of endowments. All over the world there are university chairs and departments dedicated to the study of logic: yet how many of these departments and chairs, one may ask, were established with the aim of promoting the study of pure, applicationless mathematics?

No doubt there have been phases in history when logicians were preoccupied with the formal aspects of their subject, but even in the latest and most mathematical period the phrase 'formal logic' has never become a complete tautology. Sometimes disregarded, but always waiting to be considered, there has been another group of questions—neither formal questions, in any mathematical sense, nor questions concerned with the preliminary formalities of argument —and these make up what may be called material, or practical, or applied logic. Yet questions about the strength of arguments, as opposed to their internal consistency, have never been entirely forgotten. Somewhere in the minds of logicians—even if often at the back of them—it has always been assumed that, in sufficiently devious ways, the results of their labours could be used in judging the cogency and strength of actual, everyday arguments. Carnap's consigning all these questions to another subject, methodology, implies that any residual hopes we have of applying the mathematical calculi of logic to the criticism of practical arguments must be abandoned, and this is probably true enough; but he implies also, and this is more questionable, that the monies sunk in endowing departments of logic should be laid out in future for the benefit of pure mathematics alone.

To sum up: Aristotle characterises logic as 'concerned with the way in which conclusions are established, and belonging to the science of their establishment'. It now turns out that the results of logical inquiry cannot be cast into a 'science', at any rate in the narrow sense of the term suggested by the Greek word *episteme*. Demonstration is not a suitable subject for an *episteme*. Looked at from our point of view, this result need not be at all surprising: if logic is a normative subjective, concerned with the *appraisal* of arguments and the recognition of their *merits*, one could hardly expect anything else. For certainly no value-judgements of other sorts can be discussed in purely mathematical terms. Jurisprudence, for instance, elucidates for us the special logic of legal statements, yet it eludes mathematical treatment; nor are ethical and aesthetic problems formulated more effectively by being made the subject for a calculus.

Even in the case of morals, there are no doubt certain peripheral considerations, to do with self-consistency and the like, which lend themselves to formal treatment; so that Professor G. H. von Wright and others have been able to work out a system of 'deontic logic', which displays the formal parallels between the moral notion of obligation and the logician's categories of truth and validity. But the fact that this can be done shows, surely, not that morals too should become a branch of mathematics: does it not show rather that, even when we are concerned with questions of truth and validity, the aspects which we can handle in a purely formal manner are comparatively peripheral? In logic as in morals, the real problem of rational assessment—telling sound arguments from untrustworthy ones, rather than consistent from inconsistent ones—requires experience, insight and judgement, and mathematical calculations (in the form of statistics and the like) can never be more than one tool among others of use in this task.

SYSTEM-BUILDING AND SYSTEMATIC NECESSITY

The main argument of this essay is now complete. We have shown the great divergence which has developed through the history of logic between the critical categories we make use of in practice and the formal analyses logicians have given of them, traced this divergence to its source—the adoption of the analytic type of argument as a universal (though inappropriate) paradigm—and suggested some possible motives which may have led logicians to adopt this paradigm, in particular their time-honoured ambition to cast the truths of logic into a purely mathematical system. The last major item on our agenda will be to trace the consequences of this divergence farther afield into the speculations of epistemologists and general philosophers, and this will be our task in the final essay. But a number of loose ends remain from all that has gone before which can conveniently be tied together in the rest of the present essay. These include:

(i) the special notion of logical necessity,

(ii) the sorts of 'formal' or 'systematic' necessity and impossibility characteristic of the mathematical or theoretical sciences, and

(iii) the idea that, by casting logic into a formal system, we shall be able to make of logical necessity a necessity stronger than any physical necessity, and of logical impossibility a kind of impossibility harder than physical impossibility. (This idea, we suggested, might help to explain why a formal, geometrical system has been thought to provide so desirable a model for logic.)

We can usefully discuss all these three topics at once, and incidentally throw a little more light on the manner in which a system of propositions becomes frozen into an abstract calculus.

In what follows, I shall try to show how a piece of mathematics is born, not by following out any existing branch of the subject, but by taking a novel example and studying it from scratch. This example will have little obvious connection with any of the familiar parts of mathematics or—immediately at any rate—with contentious philosophical questions, and it will be as well at the start to keep clear of the philosophical arena, where the dust of ancient controversies can so easily be kicked up and blind us.

First, however, let me indicate where the example is taken from and hint at the ways in which it may, on examination, prove to illuminate the sources of more deep-seated perplexities. It originated, in fact, on the sports page of a Sunday paper, where there was printed the draw for the annual regatta at Henley, including the following entry:

Visitors' Cup. Heat 1: Jesus, Cambridge v. Christ Church; Heat 2: Oriel v. New College;...Heat 8: Lady Margaret v. winner of Heat 1; ...Heat 26: Winner of Heat 23 v. winner of Heat 24; Final: Winner of Heat 25 v. winner of Heat 26.

A draw of this kind, as used in knock-out competitions, gives rise to a system of propositions which has considerable internal complexity and logical articulation.

Even over so simple a system of propositions, problems of a philosophical kind can arise. Reading the entry here reprinted in Socratic mood, one may find the following dialogue going on in one's mind:

First thought: 'How do they know already which crews the final will be between?'

Second thought, after a moment: 'They don't.'

'But they *say*! It will be between the winner of Heat 25 and the winner of Heat 26'; this remark being accompanied by a nagging feeling that it is a funny kind of regatta in which someone can decide beforehand who will be in the final!

'Ah! But to say that the final will be between the winner of Heat 25 and the winner of Heat 26 implies nothing about the chances of any specific crew you care to name (New College, say) getting into the final.'

'It's not obvious that it doesn't imply just that. After all, the proposition that Heat 8 will be between Lady Margaret and the winner of Heat 1 does imply something very definite about specific crews; namely, that of all the entrants only Lady Margaret, Jesus and Christ Church will have a chance of being in that heat.'

'It is true that the statement that Heat 8 will be between Lady Margaret and the winner of Heat 1 *looks* exactly like the statement that the Final will be between the winner of Heat 25 and the winner of Heat 26, but in the crucial respect they are wholly dissimilar. In fact it is in the nature of a draw—or at any rate of a *fair* draw—that, when you write it out in full like this, the first things you put down shall be completely *specific* as regards named crews, and the last things completely *formal*, having no reference to particular crews. The last things, in fact, say no more about the crews themselves than that the final will be between some two of them, one from each half of the draw; and, since all the entrants must be in one half of the draw or the other, there is—so far as anything written here is concerned—nothing to stop any individual crew you care to name from being in the final. Whether or no they get there depends, accidents apart, only on their own skill.'

The moral of this first dialogue is that one must not be deceived by superficial similarities of expression. The statements 'Heat 8 will be between Lady Margaret and the winner of Heat 1' and 'The Final will be between the winners of Heat 25 and Heat 26' may look alike, but when it comes to the point—in other words, when one comes to the regatta—their implications are entirely different. If it were really decided before the regatta even started which named crews were going to be in the final, one's nagging feeling of injustice would be entirely in place. But provided that there is no implied selection of named crews, the nag is out of place: so in this case. The feeling of injustice arises from one's initial inclination to interpret the statement 'The Final will be between the winners of Heat 25 and Heat 26' as implicitly excluding particular crews from the final, in the way in which 'Heat 8 will be between Lady Margaret and the winner of Heat 1' does exclude all but three crews from Heat 8, and this is a mistake. All the same there is no way of telling, by looking at the propositions alone, whether they have implications about named crews or no. This one can discover only by examining what each proposition means in terms of its application—in terms, that is, of boats, races, trophies, congratulations and so on.

Up to a point, this explanation may seem satisfactory. Yet on reflection one may find oneself still uneasy, at any rate philosophically, and the internal dialogue may continue over a fresh question:

'Clearly, if one were to decide beforehand which named crews were to be in the final, that would be unfair. But if one is not doing this, the only alternative is, apparently, to say no more than this: that the final will be between some two of the entrants. How *can* one say, as is said here, which heat-winners will in fact take part in the Final?'

This is a characteristically philosophical situation. We *do* do something—in this case, say more than can apparently be allowed without inequity—although there seem to be such excellent reasons for insisting that we *cannot* do so. As usual, one must look for ambiguities in the small but key words involved. What is to be understood here, for instance, by such phrases as 'say more'? A phrase of this kind can be a trap, tempting one into asking several questions at once without noticing the fact. In one respect, no doubt, 'The Final will be between Christ Church and Lady Margaret' does *say more* than 'The Final will be between two of the entrants', since it specifies which named crews these two entrants will be: in this respect, the statement 'The Final will be between the winners of Heat 25 and Heat 26' does not say any more than 'The Final will be between two of the entrants'. But in other respects the first of this pair of statements does *say more* than the second: more, however, of a different kind entirely. This more is nothing specific about named crews, but something of a kind which may, without prejudice, be called formal—since it arises from the formal properties of this kind of a draw. If the statement 'The Final will be between the winners of Heat 25 and Heat 26' has implications which the statement 'The Final will be between two of the entrants' does not have, these further implications are in the nature, not of predictions about the eventual outcome of the regatta, but rather of prescriptions for its proper conduct—they have to do, in a word, with *formalities*. Yet these formalities may be important ones: if you are the steward of a regatta, instead of an oarsman, it will matter much more to you that you arrange for the right number of races, in proper sequence, than that the actual crews in these races should come from one particular club or another.

Can one hint at the relevance of this example to philosophical questions, without prejudicing our methodical discussion of the example? Recall the notorious problem of mathematical truth, and in particular the questions, 'Does Pythagoras' theorem say any more than Euclid's axioms? Can it tell us anything not implicitly contained in those axioms? Can deduction be fertile?' Perhaps the intractability of these questions also may spring from ambiguities in the phrases 'say more', 'contained in' and 'fertile'. The analogy works out as follows:

Taken entirely on its own, the assertion that neither of the statements, 'The Final will be between the winners of Heat 25 and Heat 26' and 'The Final will be between two of the entrants', *says any more* than the other is false and paradoxical. It might be acceptable if one had already made it clear that one was talking about named crews (e.g. laying bets on the outcome of the competition) rather than about the conduct of the regatta (e.g. arranging the timetable, for which the names of the crews involved are largely irrelevant), and one can save it from paradox by adding a suitable gloss: 'so far as particular named crews are concerned.' Once the paradox goes, however, the interest of the assertion goes too.

In the case of mathematical truth also: if one asserts, in the air and without the appropriate gloss, that Pythagoras' theorem *tells one no more* than Euclid's axioms, or that it only repeats something already contained in those axioms, one can expect to rouse the ire of conscientious mathematicians like the late Professor Hardy. Unglossed, one's statement will again be gratuitously false and paradoxical, so that a mathematician of Hardy's temperament will want to reply that mathematicians make *discoveries*, that the world of mathematical truths is a real one which lies open to our exploration and contains ever new truths for us to find, and that these truths are certainly not stated in the axioms alone.

Once again, an appropriate gloss will save the situation, but the paradox and apparent originality of one's assertion will evaporate together. Those who say that Pythagoras tells us no more than Euclid mean that his theorem tells us no more, *of a kind* that requires looking and seeing to find out, than Euclid's axioms, since it is a pure deduction from those axioms; and this statement is a good deal less startling than the original one. Even so, such a man as Hardy may not be satisfied: he may protest, 'But mathematicians *do* look and see. They spend their lives looking for and sometimes finding out things they did not already know.' The gloss evidently needs further elucidation; and there will prove to be no resting-place short of the flat conclusion, 'Pythagoras' theorem tells us no more, of a kind that has to be established by looking and seeing, in a sense in which working out deductive relations does not qualify as "looking and seeing", than Euclid's axioms do.' This in turn collapses into a consequence of the truism 'Pythagoras' theorem is *not not* a deduction from Euclid's axioms'—a statement which was unquestioned in the first place.

Questions of the form 'Does A say more than B?', or 'Is the argument by which we get from A to B an infertile or fertile one?', are accordingly liable to lead us into trouble, unless we take good care to counter the ambiguities involved in tricky phrases like *say more than.*

At this point we must study more methodically the way in which a knock-out competition operates, and remark on the different sorts of propositions for which such a draw can be the occasion. As we shall see, practical and formal impossibilities, and procedural improprieties too, are liable in such a case to become closely interlocked, and one must proceed most carefully if one is at all points to keep them clearly distinguished in one's mind. For simplicity's sake, consider a straightforward draw for a knock-out competition between eight crews, and suppose that the draw comes out as follows:

King's ⎫ Lady Margaret⎭	Heat 1⎫		
Jesus ⎫ Christ Church⎭	Heat 2⎭	First semi-final	
Oriel ⎫ New College⎭	Heat 3⎫	Second semi-final	Final
Corpus Christi⎫ Pembroke⎭	Heat 4⎭		

We may have occasion to say a number of different things about this draw, all of which make use of the notion of impossibility. Consider three of these for a start:

(*a*) King's can't get into the final,
(*b*) King's can't get into the second semi-final,
(*c*) King's and Lady Margaret can't both get into the final.

The first of these statements is wholly concerned with the question of *skill* or *ability*. If called upon to justify it, we should appeal to the record of past form as our evidence, saying 'Their stroke is too short', 'Their blade-work is ragged', or 'The other crews in the top half of the draw are too fast for them'. There may be nothing in principle to prevent King's from getting into the final, one might add, but only a brilliant coach could improve their rhythm and ensure that extra punch and speed which alone would give them a chance. If in fact King's did get into the final, we should have to admit to having been mistaken: our assertion having been a clear prediction, this would irremediably falsify it.

Very different considerations are relevant to the other two statements. We are not now concerned with questions about ability: to refer to 'rhythm' or the like would be a sign of misunderstanding, since these impossibilities are not practical ones at all. What kind of impossibility are they, then? Not linguistic ones, either, since we are not concerned here with words or definitions: the denial of these statements would not be meaningless. In one sense the issues are procedural, in another they are formal or systematic.

To begin with, there is no room to say in this case 'It might yet be otherwise': the matter at issue has finally been settled by the draw. One might nevertheless say 'It could *have been* otherwise', for King's and Lady Margaret could have been drawn elsewhere: had the luck of the draw been otherwise, and (say) King's and New College been interchanged, both (*b*) and (*c*) would have been falsified. Where we could have written

The King's crew being as they are, they can't get into the final: could they work up some extra speed, matters might be different,

now one must write

The draw having turned out as it has, King's and Lady Margaret can't both get into the final: matters could have been different only had the draw fallen otherwise.

Are we now to say that in this case also 'cannot' implies 'will not'? One's instinctive answer may be, '*Of course* it does!'; but is this instinct sound? Perhaps it reflects rather the Englishman's admirable habit of taking fair play for granted. The problem can be stated as follows. Having seen the draw for the Visitors' Cup, I utter the three statements printed above. I then turn up at Henley on the day of the races, and find that King's have taken part in the second semi-final and are going on to meet Lady Margaret in the final. Do I now have to say, 'Oh, so I was mistaken', or is there some other conclusion to be drawn?

The answer is that I do not *have* to say this: whether I shall in fact do so will depend upon certain other things, and these I shall be bound to investigate before I shall know quite what to say. Perhaps I was mistaken: maybe the draw was not as I thought, and I got King's and New College exchanged in my mind. On the other hand, I may confirm that the draw was as I thought, and that the subsequent events nevertheless followed as described. What do I say then? Someone may interject, 'There is some inconsistency here!', and indeed there is an inconsistency, but not a self-contradiction. The inconsistency involved is to be sought rather in the conduct of the regatta: I shall wonder, in consequence, what the stewards have been up to while my back was turned, and may protest against this extraordinary lapse in the hope that the contest may be declared null and void. The mere *happening* of the later events in the manner described does not in itself disprove statements (*b*) and (*c*), in the way that events may disprove statement (*a*): rather, it provides grounds for a protest. Nor does the fact that a wife cannot be forced to testify against her husband entail that she will not in fact be so treated: it implies rather that, if she is forced to testify, there are grounds for appeal to a higher court and for public outcry about the conduct of the case. The 'cannot' of (*b*) and (*c*), in other words, is a 'cannot' of procedural propriety, and not one of ability or strength.

Statements (*b*) and (*c*) are accordingly hybrids. There is about them a factual element, which we call the luck of the draw; a procedural element, in which they resemble statements invoking the rules of legal procedure; and finally a formal element. In order to exhibit the formal element in its purity, we must take two more steps: we must eliminate first the luck of the draw, and then the procedural implications.

To begin with, the names of actual crews can be cut out. Statement (*b*) can be expanded into the statement, 'King's have been drawn first, and the first crew in the draw can't get into the second semi-final', and (*c*) into 'King's and Lady Margaret have been drawn first and second, and the first two crews in the draw can't both get into the final'. Dropping the first clause in each case, we obtain:

(*d*) The first crew in the draw can't get into the second semi-final, and

(*e*) The first two crews in the draw can't both get into the final.

How do these propositions compare with the three earlier ones? In these cases, one can no more mention strength, speed or rhythm than one can in the case of (*b*) and (*c*); but now one cannot bring in the luck of the draw either. The chances of the draw do not affect (*d*) and (*e*): they decide only to which named crews the phrases 'first crew in the draw' and 'first two crews in the draw' shall in fact apply, and so of which named crews it will be correct to say '*They* can't get into the second semi-final'. What, then, underlies the impossibilities stated in (*d*) and (*e*)? If skill and chance are both equally irrelevant, what can one point to as their source? All one can reply, it seems, is that the necessity of (*d*) and (*e*) lies *in the very nature* of knock-out competitions, such as a regatta normally comprises.

The question, what would have to be different for (*d*) and (*e*) not to hold, cannot therefore arise, though it can quite properly do so for (*a*), (*b*) and (*c*). Short of changing the very activity in the context of which the terms 'draw', 'heat' and 'final' acquire their meaning, one cannot imagine (*d*) and (*e*) being otherwise; and if one did change this activity, one could fairly be told that one had changed the meaning of these terms also in the process. Furthermore, if anyone were to say, 'But I have known it to happen', one could only reply 'Not at Henley! Not in a properly-conducted regatta!' Supposing he insisted, and turned out not to have in mind (say) the kind of regatta in which the first-round losers are given a second chance (*repêchage*), or an extraordinary case in which all the other crews scratched, one would suspect that he did not even understand what a knock-out competition involved. For surely, if anyone has got the hang of such a competition, he must recognise the necessity of these two statements.

A passing remark at this point may anticipate our discussion of problems in the theory of knowledge. Where we said just now, 'Such a man must *recognise* the necessity of (*d*) and (*e*)', we might instead have said that he must *see* their necessity: so far as English idiom goes, this is a perfectly natural and proper way of speaking, with its counterpart in other languages—'*Je dois vivre: je n'en vois pas la nécessité*'. This idiom is suggestive, but also potentially misleading. It is helpful, as indicating how at this point the notion of 'necessity' begins to shade over into that of a 'need': recognising the necessity of (*d*) and (*e*) goes hand-in-hand with seeing the need of conforming to the rules of procedure they invoke. At the same time, one must avoid the trap-question, with what Inner Eye we do this 'seeing'. Flogging the visual metaphor leads to no more enlightenment in this example than it does with such notorious problem-propositions as 'Seven plus five equals twelve' and 'One ought to keep one's promises'.

In the present case, the facts are surely as follows. Most people in most places who engage in the sort of activity we call 'running regattas' recognise much the same rules as we do. Nevertheless, we might conceivably encounter a people who regularly engaged in activities closely resembling our own, but who yet denied (d) and (e)—and denied them not just from lack of understanding, but because they were prepared to act consistently with this rejection. Despite their running the whole knock-out competition in the way we do, we can imagine their presenting the trophy to the crew which had won the first heat and treating them as the 'Champion Crew' —insisting, when we questioned them, that the first heat *was* the final and so falsifying (e) in a practical manner. No doubt, this would seem to us an odd thing to do, and not just an odd way of *talking*, notably because which crew got the prize and congratulations would now become a matter of chance rather than a matter of skill and speed. In consequence we might well deny to their activity the titles of 'regatta' and 'competition', or say that, if this *is* a regatta, it is a very ill-conducted one. We might prefer to conclude that it was a very odd and different kind of regatta from ours, even perhaps not a regatta at all; certainly 'not what *we* call a regatta'.

Accepting (d) and (e) accordingly goes along with accepting the whole articulated set of practices comprising the running of a regatta. If we acknowledge this as the proper, systematic, methodical way of testing the skill and speed of the competitors, we thereupon commit ourselves to operating with the associated system of concepts for which, in the conditions described, statements (d) and (e) are necessarily true. Bringing out the implications in the two statements, we can accordingly write them:—

Regattas and knock-out competitions being what they are, the first crew in the draw can't get into the second semi-final: to allow that sort of thing to happen would frustrate the whole idea of such competitions.

Clearly we are concerned here with something more than a linguistic, in the sense of a verbal, matter: it is not that we should deny to a sufficiently eccentric activity the mere *name* of 'regatta', but that we should refuse it that *title*. An activity has to earn the title by satisfying certain conditions and fulfilling certain purposes, and is not given it by convention or free choice, as the unit of electric charge was given the name 'Coulomb' by international convention. It is one thing to correct someone on a point of usage, saying, 'That's not what we call a "regatta": the word for that is "raffle".' It is another thing to say, 'That's not a regatta: that's scarcely more than a raffle!' In the first case one is certainly talking about linguistic matters, but the criticism implied in the second case is much more fundamental: one is objecting now not to a matter of usage alone, but to the whole activity which that usage reflects.

So much for (*d*) and (*e*). There may be nothing factual about these statements, but even they are hybrid and combine two different types of impossibility. On the one hand, there is the formal, mechanical mode of operation of knock-out competitions—crews going in two by two, one being excluded each time, the survivors going in two by two, and so on. On the other hand, there is the purpose of this activity, the fact that this procedure is adopted as the fairest way of discovering quickly which of a number of crews is the fastest. Statements such as (*d*) and (*e*) have, correspondingly, a double aspect, reflecting at the same time the formal properties of knock-out competions, and the standards or norms for the conduct of such competitions. Our final task will be to eliminate even this last, procedural element from our example and see what happens when we transform our statements into purely formal ones. This will leave us with something very like mathematics, though nothing at all abstruse: the point of discussing it here will be to establish just *how much* like mathematics it looks—and, indeed, that it not only looks like but *is* mathematics, the hitherto unknown branch of the subject here to be christened the 'calculus of draws'.

For simplicity's sake, let us consider only knock-out competitions in which there are no byes, and in which accordingly the number of entrants is two, four, eight, or some other power of two. Let us call a draw in which there are 2^m entries a draw of rank *m*—a draw with two entries will be of rank 1, a draw with four entries of rank 2, and so on. So as to keep the application to our example clear, let us begin by talking about a draw of rank 3, having eight entries. The crucial step in formalising our discussion is to introduce a symbolism; not because writing the same statements in symbols is meritorious in itself or changes their meaning, but simply because, once we have done so, we shall be in a position to disregard the original application of the calculus—forget about boats, heats, prizes and all—and concentrate on the formal properties of the calculus for their own sake. Let us accordingly allot to each place in the draw a number n, ranging in this case from 1 to 8; and in the same way give each heat, including the final, a number h, ranging from 1 to 7. We shall then have the formal schema:

$$n = \left.\begin{array}{r} 1 \\ 2 \end{array}\right\} \quad h = \left.\begin{array}{r} 1 \\ 2 \end{array}\right\}$$

$$\left.\begin{array}{r} 3 \\ 4 \end{array}\right\} \qquad \left.\begin{array}{r} 5 \\ \end{array}\right\}$$

$$\left.\begin{array}{r} 5 \\ 6 \end{array}\right\} \qquad \left.\begin{array}{r} 3 \\ 4 \end{array}\right\} \qquad \left.\begin{array}{r} 6 \\ \end{array}\right\} \qquad 7$$

$$\left.\begin{array}{r} 7 \\ 8 \end{array}\right\}$$

A number-pair of the form (n, h) can now correspond to crew n being in heat h. In a draw of rank 3, for instance, the expression $(3, 5)$ will signify the third crew in the draw's being in the first semi-final. If a particular combination has formally to be ruled out, this can be expressed by writing an X in front of the corresponding number-pair: so, corresponding to statement (d), we now have the expression

(f) X (1, 6).

Where one possibility excludes another, we can write two corresponding number-pairs with an X between them: so, corresponding to (e), we have the expression

(g) (1, 7) X (2, 7).

Reading these as mathematics: in a draw of rank 3, $n = 1$ excludes or is incompatible with $h = 6$, and the combination $(1, 7)$ excludes or is incompatible with the combination $(2, 7)$.

We have here the beginnings of a calculus, which could no doubt be developed further, and may (for all I know) already have a place in some other form within the corpus of mathematics. One could, for instance, develop a general theory applicable equally to draws of any rank, comprising a set of theorems such as the following:

In a draw of rank m, $(n_1, 2^m - 1) \times (n_2, 2^m - 1)$, for all n_1, n_2 less than 2^{m-1}; where $n_1 \neq n_2$.

This is not, however, the place to follow out these possible elaborations or to go into details about methods of proof, axiomatisation and the like. What matters for our purposes is, first, that all the formal impossibilities implicit in an eight-entry draw can be expressed in the symbolism proposed, and secondly, that such a schema as has here been christened a 'draw of rank three' could be investigated in a purely mathematical manner, with boats, prizes, rules and congratulations all alike forgotten.

What would be involved, we must now ask, in handling this schema in a purely mathematical manner, and treating the calculus of draws as a pure *calculus*? The answer to this question can be given easily enough, but there is a difficulty about it: namely, that one may make the answer sound grotesquely simple—the gist lies less in the answer itself than in the illustrations one gives of its implications. Like Pascal, who remarked that to become a religious believer all one need do was behave as though one already were one, we can say here that, if we treat the calculus of draws in every respect as though it already were a piece of mathematics, nothing else is needed in order for it to become one. There is no halo around symbolic expressions without which they cannot become mathematical ones: it is up to us to give them a mathematical meaning, if we so decide, by treating them in a purely mathematical way. Our question therefore transforms itself into a new form: 'What sign will indicate that the calculus of draws is being treated as mathematics and its propositions as mathematical propositions?' The answer is, roughly speaking, that the criteria by which it is decided to accept or reject propositions must no longer involve procedural or other extraneous considerations, but must lie entirely within the calculus. The propositions must be so treated that their denials are regarded either as the result of slips in the formation of the expressions, or as plain absurdities—absolute and obvious impossibilities—above all, they must not be regarded as signs of something queer outside the calculus itself.

Of course, since the calculus of draws was obtained by abstraction from the procedural schema of a well-conducted regatta, all the resulting theorems will in fact remain *interpretable* in terms of races, prizes, and so on. But in so far as people come to treat the calculus as pure mathematics, this interpretation will cease to interest them. Indeed, it might eventually happen, either that the formal study of the calculus of draws continued even though regattas had fallen entirely into desuetude, or that other applications of the calculus might be discovered and its origin be completely forgotten: it might conceivably be useful in genetical theory, as a way of handling questions about inheritance patterns—in particular, questions of the form, 'From which of his great-great-grandparents did this man get his red hair?' (For that matter, it might be made the basis of a new system for composing atonal music.) In either case, whether the calculus ceased to be applied practically or began to be applied in quite novel ways, the questions what sets of possibilities are allowable, which number-pairs exclude each other and what general theorems hold for all m will remain discussible quite aside from all questions about rowing, and the criteria for judging answers to such questions will lie henceforward in the calculus of draws alone.

Suppose, for instance, that somebody challenges the symbolic expression (g) corresponding to our original statement (e);

$$\text{For } m = 3, \ (1, 7) \ X \ (2, 7).$$

This will now be justified on formal grounds alone. To deny it will be absurd since, in a draw of rank three,

$$(1, 5) \ X \ (2, 5);$$
$$(1, 7) \text{ only if } (1, 5);$$
$$(2, 7) \text{ only if } (2, 5)—$$

all these three statements being axiomatic; and from these it immediately follows that

$$(1, 7) \ X \ (2, 7).$$

This demonstration will represent a straightforward mathematical proof, and never for a moment would a mathematician think of commenting, 'Pretty irregular way of carrying on a regatta to allow both (1, 7) and (2, 7), eh?'

There is an analogy here with the state of geometry before and after Euclid. If a surveyor produces measurements of a field in which a triangle appears to have one of its three sides longer than the other two put together, we may ask him, 'What have you been up to with your theodolite?' But in the mathematics class at school, where we study geometry as a formal science, to talk of a triangle having one side longer than the other two together is ruled out as absurd and inconsistent with Euclid's axioms. A mathematical geometer who came across a triangle ostensibly having this property could say, 'Funny kind of surveying, this!', only as a joke. We would regard his job as being to *prove*, from Euclid's axioms alone, that such a triangle has to be ruled out simply on mathematical grounds. In either branch of mathematics, the propositions studied begin as conditions, norms or standards appealed to in the course of some practical activity—competitive rowing or surveying. In either case, a point is reached where they begin to be treated as necessary truths of a purely formal kind. In this way we passed from (*d*) and (*e*), which are conditions to be satisfied by any well-conducted regatta, to the corresponding symbolic expressions (*f*) and (*g*); and these expressions have no more to do with the conduct of regattas than our school geometry had to do with *geometria* in its original sense of land-measurement.

This is not to say, of course, that we can turn *any* sentence into a mathematical theorem by handling it in a purely mathematical way. The great majority of our statements are of such a kind that the order, 'Treat this statement as pure mathematics!', would make no sense of them. The virtue of our regatta example just is that it provides us with a systematic set of propositions capable of being treated mathematically, in a way in which one could never treat statements like 'It's an ill wind that blows nobody any good' and 'I don't like eating raw beetroot'. The notions of a 'draw', 'heat', and the rest are already articulated in a near-mathematical way, and all we need do to base a calculus on them is concentrate on the formal aspects of their inter-relations. Statements about draws and heats and crews are, as most of our statements are not, potential starting-points for calculi.

One last touch can be put to this already lengthy example, which will help to show the differences between a calculus tailor-made to fit a particular application and one being applied in a context other than that with which it was developed to deal.

As things stand, every proposition within the calculus of draws can be given a direct interpretation in terms of races, prizes and so on; the calculus was, after all, obtained simply by formalising propositions about regattas which can alternatively be written in ordinary English. Formally, however, we can imagine a slightly different calculus, similar in almost every respect to the calculus of draws but including certain possibilities ruled out in our present calculus. Thus, in the calculus of draws of rank m, the possible values of h (numbers of heats) are $1, 2 \ldots 2^m - 1$: i.e. in a draw of rank 3, seven in all. As a result, all number-pairs (n, h) are ruled out for which the value of h is greater than $2^m - 1$. (We may conveniently refer to this form of calculus as a 'limited-h' calculus.) The application of the calculus alone provides the reason why we must place this limitation on the values of h: mathematically speaking, it need have no particular significance, and we could build up a modified, unlimited-h calculus, in which no limit was placed on the values of h, and number-pairs were admitted in which h took the values 2^m, $2^m + 1, \ldots$ or as large as one liked. Forgetting for a moment the application to regattas, one might argue that since the calculus was an eliminative one, and no more elimination was possible when only one n was left, it was self-evident that, if $(r, 2^m - 1)$, then also $(r, 2^m)$, $(r, 2^m + 1)$ and so on.

Let us suppose, now, that this unlimited-h calculus had existed and become familiar before knock-out competitions had begun: it would then have been natural enough, when the time came, to apply it to draws also. In making this fresh application, however, we should find it possible to give a serious interpretation only to those expressions within the calculus in which h took values less than or equal to $2^m - 1$. We might perhaps give a whimsical interpretation to others and say (for instance) in the case of a competition between eight crews, 'Lady Margaret have reached the eighth heat', meaning 'Lady Margaret are the victors'—as golfers may be said to be 'at the nineteenth hole', meaning that they have finished their round and are in the clubhouse bar. But of course, the fact that we can give a whimsical interpretation to these propositions underlines the point that no serious interpretation is open to us: number-pairs for which h is equal to or greater than 2^m may be *mathematically* possible, but they have no *practical* significance.

With this in mind, what shall we say if somebody starts talking to us about the 'ninety-fifth heat'? We shall certainly want in this case to rule out references to 'heat 95', and to lay it down as a principle that a straightforward knock-out competition between eight crews can comprise no more than seven heats. The problem is, what status we are to allot to this principle. In terms of our original, limited-h calculus, we could still regard this as the consequence of a theorem within the calculus, even if one of a specially fundamental and axiomatic kind—the principle would then state a particularly obvious mathematical impossibility. Using the unlimited-h calculus, however, we shall no longer be in a position to call this a mathematical impossibility. For this application, we are using only the part of the calculus covering values of h up to 7 and giving no application (apart from whimsical ones) to values of h greater than 7. Nevertheless, the rest of the calculus will be there, though dormant, in the background: expressions like (5, 95) will seem to make sense mathematically, even though they have now no application to the particular practical activity in question—they will have a 'mathematical sense' in spite of having no practical meaning.

The principle to which we are now appealing, i.e. 'A knock-out competition between p entrants contains only $p - 1$ heats', evidently legislates against a flat, absolute impossibility, quite as much as our earlier statements (d) and (e); but within the unlimited-h calculus this will not be a *mathematical* impossibility at all. If challenged to explain, our response may now be to say that, though conceivable from a mathematical point of view, it is *theoretically* impossible for a knock-out competition between eight crews to include more than seven heats. To make the source of this particular impossibility clear, we have to study not the formal properties of the calculus alone, but also the manner in which calculus and practical application are put into connection. The unlimited-h calculus has a greater degree of complexity than our present application is going to make use of: if we now rule out expressions such as (5, 95), this will be because, in connecting the principles of regatta-procedure with the unlimited-h calculus, no meaning is given to expressions for which the value of h is 2^m or greater. And a similar situation will be found to hold in many cases in which we talk of an impossibility as being a theoretical rather than a practical one.

The philosophical relevance of this last point arises as follows. In thinking about necessities and impossibilities which mix formal considerations with those of other kinds, we tend too often to restrict our attention to tailor-made calculi, i.e. those calculi which, like our original calculus of draws, have come into existence by abstraction from their most familiar and natural applications: two natural examples to quote are Euclidean geometry and the arithmetic of natural numbers. In the case of tailor-made calculi, it is particularly difficult to sort out the purely formal necessities and impossibilities from those with which they are allied, since the origins of the calculus conspire to conceal the differences between them. We tend accordingly to forget that there is any need to create a connection between a calculus and its application, and to read the purely formal properties of the calculus as possessing themselves the sort of force which belongs properly only to the other considerations with which they here go hand-in-hand. This leads to trouble whenever a new application of a previously-existing calculus does not exploit its full possible scope: for instance, when we introduce the notion of an 'absolute zero' of temperature, or speculate about the beginning of time itself—thereby leaving uninterpreted all numbers which, mathematically speaking, lie beyond our origin. It can lead to trouble also in the interpretation of formal logic: there, too, the relations between the formal, systematic necessities and impossibilities of our logical calculi and necessities and impossibilities of other kinds can easily become obscured. To this problem we must now return.

The morals of this whole example reinforce those we stated earlier. After examining the philosopher's notions of 'logical' necessity, possibility and impossibility, we concluded that the scope and relevance of the notions were too often exaggerated. Analytic arguments apart—and they form a very small class in practice— the absence from any argument of positive contradictions is something which we should check simply as a preliminary matter, in order to ensure the bare meaningfulness of the argument, before we ever turn to the substantial question whether the argument is a sound or acceptable one. 'Logical considerations', so understood, are concerned only with preliminary formalities, not with the actual merits of any argument, proposition or case: once we turn to discuss the genuine merits of an argument, questions about 'logical' possibility, impossibility and necessity are no longer to the point; and to suggest that 'logical necessity' and 'logical impossibility' are somehow tougher or more ineluctable than 'mere physical necessity' or 'so-called moral impossibility' is the result of a misunderstanding.

Where a formal calculus is involved, the risk of these misunderstandings is that much the greater. It is bad enough if one is told that to allow the first crew in the draw to race in the second semifinal is a gross procedural blunder; but if, bringing in the calculus of draws, we are told in addition that it is a flat mathematical impossibility, a new and ineluctable barrier seems to have been erected. Yet what is in fact added by this gloss? The systematic necessities and impossibilities of formal calculi can, surely, only re-express in a formal symbolism necessities and impossibilities of other kinds. If all formally admissible expressions in a calculus correspond to genuine possibilities, and all formally inconsistent expressions correspond to genuine impossibilities, this is a sign only that we are employing an *appropriate* calculus—i.e. one in which the rules for the formation of symbolic expressions correspond exactly to the criteria for recognising true statements in the application of the calculus.

Why are we tempted, then, to think that formal necessities can somehow be stronger than necessities of other kinds and actually reinforce them? This probably happens because, within a calculus, improperly formed expressions are treated as completely absurd. In a draw of rank 3, for instance, the invitation to accept both the expressions (1, 7) and (2, 7) would be sheerly unintelligible: there is a striking contrast with the corresponding applied statement, 'Both the first two crews got into the final', which might provoke amazement or indignation but is certainly not unintelligible. This very feature of formal necessities and impossibilities is, however, one which cannot be carried over into their application, and so cannot genuinely reinforce the necessities and impossibilities of practical life. We are at liberty, for instance, to change our ideas and practices about competitive sport, and mathematics cannot stop us. Suppose we do so, the systematic necessities and impossibilities of the calculus of draws will remain what they are: what was unintelligible before will not now become intelligible. What will happen, rather, is that the calculus will cease to be applicable in the way it originally was: a sufficiently eccentric regatta will cease to be an occasion for applying the straightforward calculus of draws. To put the moral in a sentence: systematic necessities serve not to impose but only to *express* conceptual truths, and they can do so only for so long as we do not modify our working concepts in some vital respect.

In conclusion, let me touch briefly on three points at which this moral bears on our previous discussion of the nature and function of logical theory. To begin with, I suggested that one motive for attempting to cast the principles of logic into the form of a mathematical system was the hope that by doing so one could bring into play in the logical field more potent varieties of necessity and impossibility. Once logical necessity and logical impossibility had been enthroned as the most rigorous and inescapable varieties of their species, logicians came to think it sloppy-minded to put up with anything less. Phrases like 'causal necessity' had, they conceded, a certain current usage, but we should not deceive ourselves: when it was seen how easily our views on causal necessity might be over-thrown by a perfectly conceivable change in the facts of the world, any philosopher in his senses must prefer the only A1, stainless guarantee, and hold out for logical necessity alone.

This conception, as we can now see, will not stand up to criticism. The necessities and impossibilities which are at home within the formal system of a calculus can be no stronger or more ineluctable than the everyday necessities and impossibilities which they re-express in symbols. Of course causal necessities are not the same as logical necessities, but they are not for that reason any the weaker. One might indeed ask, what place there was in this context for comparisons of strength—and, for that matter, what sense it made to ask about the 'strength' of a logical or systematic necessity at all. In the case of genuine practical necessities and impossibilities, whether physical, moral or whatever, there is room for talking about 'stronger' and 'weaker'. The action of some causes can be more easily deflected than that of others; the rigour of some laws can be more easily evaded; the force of some moral obligations yields more readily to counter-claims; and so on. But 'logical necessities' and 'logical impossibilities' are not like this at all: they concern not external obstacles which we have to take into greater or lesser account in planning our lives and our actions, but the formal preliminaries involved in setting out our arguments and statements in consistent, intelligible language. So far as they constrain us, they are within our own power: as they are self-imposed, we must either respect them or else resolve to remove them. Only so long as we keep our

concepts or our calculi unmodified do we bind ourselves to acknowledge any particular set of logical necessities and impossibilities,
and any change in either will alter in addition the conditions of
consistency and intelligibility. Strength and weakness, on the other
hand, are characteristics of *external* constraints: in the logical field,
to talk of either is out of place.

Certainly, to go to the extreme, it would be out of place to *lament*
about logical matters: imagine our meeting the captain of the King's
College boat and his explaining as the reason why he looked down-
cast, 'It's a beastly shame, we've been drawn first, so we can't get
into the second semi-final'. This might indeed matter if the luck of
the draw were to deprive one completely even of one's *procedural*
chance of getting through to the final; or if the contest had been so
arranged that the prize went automatically to the winner of the
second semi-final instead of to the winner of the final. Then gloom
might be justifiable. Or again, imagine a mathematician cast down
into the depths of depression because he'd found out that (1, 6) was
not a possibility in draws of rank 3. It is not as though discovering
a mathematical impossibility were like having the doctor reveal that
he could not hope to live six months. In another kind of draw this
will be a perfectly good mathematical possibility: let him study that
calculus instead.

Of course, if the mathematician has backed his professional
reputation on this number-pair's being a possibility; if, that is, the
mathematical impossibility has for him become linked adventitiously
with some other impossibility, like the impossibility of retaining his
present professional reputation; then the case will be altered. In
the same way, mathematical necessities in physical theory may
acquire a practical strength from the observed causal necessities
with which they are associated in application. But this is the way
the relation goes: it is the practical necessities which lend their
strength to the systematic necessities they underlie; not the systematic necessities which reinforce the practical. There is no sense in
calling logical and systematic necessities ineluctable, or logical and
systematic impossibilities insuperable: such language is appropriate
only in the case of the most extreme physical obstacles, the most
rigorous laws, or the most binding obligations. If in some cases
the connection between (say) causal and systematic necessity seems
stronger than it is, that is because the branch of mathematics con-

cerned was made to measure to suit this particular application and
so fits perfectly without trimming; with the result that we overlook
the element of choice by which we associated just this calculus with
just that application. In these cases most of all, the built-in articulation of our own systematic construction may present itself to us
in the guise of an arbitrary imposition from outside.

The last two points can be made more briefly. The first is this:
the moment a calculus sets up shop on its own and begins to be
treated as pure mathematics, without regard to its original application,
one will need to re-consider its right to the title which originally
belonged to it without question. For an Englishman, the word
'geometry' is a term of mathematical art, and no longer carries with
it the suggestion, implicit in the original Greek, that it is the science
of land-surveying. On the other hand, though rational fractions may
first have been of interest because of their use in explaining the
vibrations of musical strings, to call the arithmetic of fractions by
its medieval name of 'music' would be both misleading and perplexing; and to retain the name 'probability-calculus' for the mathematical theory not of practical probabilities but of partial entailments
really does prove misleading.

Warned by these examples, we must be careful before we allow
any formal calculus to assume the title of 'logic'. There may be
room to treat a limited range of problems mathematically in logic,
as in physics; and handling this mathematical side has certainly
proved in both fields so technical and elaborate a matter as to
become a profession in itself. Symbolic logic may accordingly claim
to be a part of logic—though not so large a part—as mathematical
physics is of physics. But can it claim to be more?

It is no reflection on mathematical physics to point out that some
physical problems are a matter for the cyclotron rather than for the
calculator, and that, divorced from all possible application to
experiment, mathematical calculations would cease to be a part of
physics at all. Suppose, for instance, that mathematical physicists
became entirely absorbed in axiomatising their theories; no longer
bothered to keep in touch with their colleagues in the laboratory;
fell into the habit of talking about all the various axiomatic systems
they developed as different 'physics' (construing the noun as a
grammatical plural), in the way mathematicians now talk about
different 'geometries'; and ended up by mocking the experimenters

for continuing to speak of their humble occupation, in the singular, as 'physics'. Would one not feel, if this happened, that the mathematical physicists had somehow overlooked a vitally important aspect of their work—that, almost by an oversight, they had become pure mathematicians and ceased to be physicists any longer? And can logic hope, any more than physics, to set up as a completely pure and formal discipline, without similarly losing its character? The main aim of the present essay has been to make the answer an obvious 'No'.

We can close on a point which looks forward to the next essay, as well as backwards over this present one. Studied for their own sake, as pure mathematics, the arguments within our systematic calculi are analytic: all the mathematician asks of them is that they should avoid self-contradictions, and come up to his standards of consistency and proof in all their internal relations. But as soon as calculi are put to work in the service of practical argument, our requirements are altered. Arguments in applied mathematics, though formally identical with arguments in pure mathematics, are none the less substantial rather than analytic, the step from data to conclusion frequently involving an actual type-jump. We can ensure the *formal* adequacy of our arguments by expressing them either in the form (D; W; so C)—a warrant being in effect a substitution-rule, authorising the simplest of all mathematical steps—or alternatively in the form of a mathematical argument taken from the appropriate calculus. In either case, we can properly call the resulting argument a *deductive* one, as physicists and astronomers have long been accustomed to doing—despite the fact that the conclusion differs substantially in force from data and backing taken together, and that the step from one to the other involves more than verbal transformation. Micro-physiologically, our arguments may thus remain mathematical in structure. But at the larger anatomical level, they can yet be substantial arguments, by which we make genuine and even far-reaching steps, passing from our original data and warrant-backing to conclusions at once fresh and of quite different types.

V

THE ORIGINS OF
EPISTEMOLOGICAL THEORY

THE STATUS of epistemology has always been somewhat ambiguous. Philosophers' questions about our claims to knowledge have often appeared to be of one kind, while the methods employed in answering them were of another. About the questions, there has been a strong flavour of psychology, the epistemologist's object of study being described as the 'understanding', the 'intellect', or the 'human reason': on the other hand, if we take psychology to be an experimental science, the methods used by philosophers in tackling these questions have only rarely been psychological ones—until recent years, when Piaget began to study methodically the manner and order in which children acquire their intellectual capacities, the development of the human understanding had been the object of little deliberate experimental inquiry. Instead of conducting elaborate scientific investigations and building up their picture of the human understanding *a posteriori*, philosophers had proceeded quite otherwise: namely, by considering the arguments upon which claims to knowledge can be based, and judging them against *a priori* standards. Epistemology, in short, has comprised a set of logical-looking answers to psychological-looking questions.

To say this is not to condemn the way in which philosophers have attacked the subject. There are, it is true, some people who talk as though no serious questions whatever could be answered *a priori*; and who would advocate the massive collection of factual observations and experimental readings as a necessary preliminary to any intellectual inquiry. If the problems of epistemology were clearly of a psychological character, there might be something to be said for this point of view in the present case also: then one might indeed argue that the solutions of epistemological problems must await the progressive uncovering of the relevant factual material. But our very difficulty lies in this, that the problems of epistemology, if psychological at all, are pretty clearly not psychological questions of any ordinary sort.

If on the other hand epistemology—or the theory of knowledge—
is more properly thought of as a branch of comparative applied logic,
then the philosophers' general method of tackling them will become,
not only understandable, but acceptable. In that case also, the
results of our earlier essays, in which we scrutinised the categories
of applied logic, will have a bearing on the nature and solution of
epistemological problems which they would otherwise lack. As a
first task, therefore, we must try to clear up this initial ambiguity, so
that, in the body of the essay, the relevance to epistemology of our
earlier discoveries can be made entirely clear.

Up to a point, as we shall see, the ambiguity about the status of
epistemology is inevitable. Considered as psychology, the subject is
concerned with intellectual or 'cognitive' *processes*, with our intellectual equipments and endowments, with 'cognition' and its
mechanism: considered as a branch of general logic, it is concerned
with intellectual or rational *procedures*, with methods of argument,
and with the rational justification of claims to knowledge. At the
abstract level, these might appear to be entirely separate topics, but
in practice they are far from separable. Rather, in the two sorts of
discussion the same activities are regarded, first from an empirical,
and then from a critical point of view. A child doing a sum, a
counsel presenting a case, an astronomer predicting an eclipse: all
their activities can be looked at either psychologically, as involving
'cognitive processes', or instead critically, as involving the employment or misemployment of rational procedures. Rational procedures
and methods do not exist in the air, apart from actual reasoners: they
are things which are learned, employed, sometimes modified, on
occasion even abandoned, by the people doing the reasoning, and
to this extent the field of logic is inevitably open on one side to the
field of psychology. On the other hand, psychologists cannot afford
to talk as though 'cognitive processes' were purely natural phenomena, which spring into existence in individual human beings for
reasons known only to God (or natural selection) and which can
accordingly be studied in a purely empirical, *a posteriori* manner.
The boundary between psychology and logic is open in both directions, and psychologists ought to recognise how far rational procedures are human artefacts rather than natural phenomena.

In the seventeenth century, when the picture of epistemology as
a study of the 'human understanding' grew up, there was a

special reason for this ambiguity about the subject. For one of the questions with which philosophers were at that time preoccupied looked even more like a question in psychology than usual. This was the problem of 'innate ideas'. The question philosophers were asking was, in part at any rate, whether every concept an intelligent adult operates with is acquired at some specifiable period during his upbringing, and whether every truth about which we have reason to be confident must have come to our knowledge at some time in the course of our lives. Some philosophers wanted to answer both these questions with a strong affirmative: nothing, they argued, could be pointed to 'in our intellects' which had not come to them during our lifetimes 'by way of the senses'. (*Nihil est in intellectu quod non prius fuerit in sensu.*) But other philosophers could envisage no way in which certain of our fundamental concepts could possibly be built up within our lifetimes, by learning processes whose authenticity they were prepared to acknowledge; they therefore concluded that some ideas were innate. Like some non-intellectual habits and skills, certain intellectual habits and skills must be thought of as instinctive: the infant, it was suggested, has neither to learn to suck at the breast nor (perhaps) to build up from scratch an idea of God.

It can be argued, however, that the controversy about innate ideas was never an essential part of epistemology. So long as philosophers operated with an over-simple picture of the senses and the intellect, it seemed impossible (no doubt) for them to evade the problem. Treating the senses as a sort of ante-chamber to the intellect, through which all concepts and truths must pass in order to reach the seat of our reason, or alternatively as a kind of duct down which sensory material had to be channelled in order to impinge and impress itself on the intellectual target at the far end, they were pressed with difficulties which might have been avoided, had they accepted a more active picture of our intellectual equipment, and one less exactly copied from the physiology of the sense-organs. But there is no reason why we should do the same: in all that follows, while acknowledging that in the last resort one cannot set the psychological and logical aspects of epistemology utterly and completely apart, I shall concentrate on the latter. It may not be realistic in any actual situation to try and keep epistemological questions completely apart from psychological ones, but for our present purposes we can concentrate on the logical questions to which such 'epistemological situations' give rise. These situations we must now attempt to characterise and understand.

Recall the points made in the second essay about the nature of claims to knowledge: in particular, about the true force of the question, 'How do you know that p?' If a man claims to know something-or-other, saying, 'I know the times of the trains to Oxford (the name of the President of Ecuador, that Queen Anne is dead, how to make butterscotch)', he does not necessarily tell us anything autobiographical about the process by which he came to be in a position to speak about or do these things, nor anything about his current psychological activity or state of mind. Rather, as Professor J. L. Austin made clear to us, he puts forward in each case a claim to speak with authority, an assurance that in this case his word is especially reliable. Whereas the forms of words 'I believe...', 'I am confident...' and 'I am sure...' introduce assertions uttered for one's own part, with an implied 'take it or leave it', to say 'I know so-and-so' is to issue one's assertion as-it-were *under seal*. It is to commit oneself, to make oneself answerable in certain ways for the reliability of one's assertion. Likewise, when we say of someone else 'He knows', we claim for him a position of authority, or endorse a claim he may himself have made. This is not to say, of course, that *we* can be regarded as pledging *his* credit, for we may sometimes say 'He knows' where he himself would hesitate to say 'I know': we cannot stake his claim to be an authority, any more than we can make his promises or sneeze his sneezes. But we do thereby stake our own reputations on his opinion's proving reliable; and, if we are not prepared to commit ourselves as to his reliability, still more if we have any reason to doubt it in this case, we do right to say only 'He believes (is confident, is sure)..., e.g. that the Tories will win the next General Election', and this, even though he himself may go so far as to claim that he knows.

These things must be remembered when we turn to such questions as 'How do you know?' and 'How does he know?'; for the purpose of such questions is to elicit the grounds, qualifications or credentials of a man on whose behalf a claim to knowledge has been made, not to bring to light the hidden mechanism of a mental activity called 'cognising'. With this in mind, we can explain both why such questions, as normally employed, require the kinds of answers they do, and why they are not paralleled by any straightforward first-person question, 'How do *I* know?'

About the question 'How do I know?': it is true that we sometimes use it to echo the challenge 'How do you know?' when we set about establishing our credentials—'How do I know? *This* is how I know: ...'. But the occasions on which we find it necessary to establish to ourselves either our own credentials, or the reliability of something about which we are already quite certain, are comparatively few and specialised. It is therefore no wonder if we have less use for the question 'How do I know?' than for the questions 'How do you know?' and 'How does he know?', whereas if these questions were questions about observable mental processes of cognising they should all be on a par.

As for the question 'How do you know?': this calls for different kinds of answer on different occasions. Sometimes, where the question is how we know that something is the case, e.g. that there are no trains to Dingwall on Sunday afternoons, that there are no prime numbers between 320 and 330, or that aluminium is a super-conductor at $1°$ A, the question may be a *logical* one. In such cases we must produce grounds (evidence, proof, justification) for whatever we assert. But on other occasions, when the question is equivalent to the question 'How have you come to be in a position to speak about this?', the proper answer is a *biographical* one: 'I know there are no trains to Dingwall on Sunday afternoons, because I was looking at *Bradshaw* this morning', 'I know how to make toffee because my mother taught me'.

Which kind of answer is appropriate depends on the context, and it is not always clear in which sense the question is to be taken: indeed, it is sometimes of no practical consequence which way we take it. When a scientist publishes an account of experiments which have led him to a novel conclusion, e.g. that aluminium is a super-conductor at $1°$ A, his report gives one both kinds of answer in one. In it he is required to justify his conclusion by setting out fully his experimental grounds for asserting what he does; but his report can often be read equally as an autobiographical account of the sequence of events which put him into a position to make this assertion, and it will in fact normally be expressed in the past indicative: 'I took a cryolite crucible of cylindrical cross-section, etc.' For philosophical purposes, however, the ambiguity of the question 'How do you know?' is a crucial one, and logic not biography will be our concern. Though this form of question calls sometimes for supporting grounds and sometimes for personal back-history, according as the matter at issue is the *justification* of our opinions or the *history* of how we came to hold them, we shall be concentrating here on the justificatory use.

About the question 'How does he know?', only this needs pointing out here: that the question almost always requires the biographical type of answer. The reason is not hard to see. Just as it is for each of us to make his own promises, since *my* word will be held to bind *you* only if you have given me power of attorney or appointed me as your delegate for certain purposes, so it is for each of us to justify his own assertions. If I myself assert on my own account that aluminium is a super-conductor at $1°$ A, I am at liberty to quote a scientist's paper among my grounds: he likewise can cite the results of his experiments as evidence for his own assertion. But if I am talking about the scientist, anything I quote from his paper will be understood as biography. Only if 'How does he know?' were taken as elliptical for 'If he were to set about justifying his assertion, how would he do it?', could we talk of producing grounds in reply—and these would not be 'our' grounds for 'his' assertion, but our conjecture as to his grounds for saying what he does. Even so, this question seems to be better expressed in the words 'Why does he believe that...?', rather than 'How does he know that...?'; for, if we can quote all his grounds and really think he *knows* (i.e. if we really believe that his conclusion is a trustworthy one), we are in a position to make and justify the assertion on our own accounts.

Epistemological situations give rise, therefore, to questions of a number of different kinds. Whenever a man makes a claim to knowledge he lays himself open to the challenge that he should make his claim good, justify it. In this respect, a claim to knowledge functions simply as an assertion carrying special emphasis and expressed with special authority. To meet this challenge, he must produce whatever grounds or argument he considers sufficient to establish the justice of his claim. When this is done, we can settle down and criticise his argument, using whichever categories of applied logic are called for in the nature of the situation. The trains of questioning and criticism into which we are led need not in themselves have anything psychological or sociological about them.

The question now will not be whether people usually think like this, or what in their childhood or education results in their thinking like this: it will solely be whether this particular argument is up to standard, whether it deserves our respectful acceptance or our reasoned rejection.

At this point, the question what sorts of standards we should apply in the practical criticism of arguments in different fields becomes highly relevant, and from now on this will again be our principal topic. But we should not turn finally to the consideration of this question without remarking once more how, in the event, questions of this type spring up out of the very same situations as questions in child psychology and in the sociology of education. 'How do we know the things that we know?': if one asks how in the course of children's lives they come to pick up the concepts and facts they do, or by what educational devices particular rational techniques and procedures are inculcated, one will of course have to proceed *a posteriori*, using methods drawn from psychology and sociology, and the final answer may very likely be that different children and different educational systems proceed in different ways. If, on the other hand, one asks whether the sorts of grounds we have for believing the things we do in some field of study are up to standard, the question ceases to be a psychological one and becomes a critical one: inductive *a posteriori* procedures are no longer in place, and the issue becomes one for the philosopher or applied logician.

FURTHER CONSEQUENCES OF OUR HYPOTHESIS

From this point on, therefore, we must interpret the questions 'How do we know that...?' and 'Do we ever really know that...?' in a logical sense. We shall not be asking directly 'How does our cognitive mechanism work?' and 'Does our cognitive mechanism ever function really successfully?', for to do so might lead us into irrelevant psychological investigations: instead our questions will be 'What adequate grounds do we ever have for the claims to knowledge that we make?' and 'Are the grounds on which we base our claims to knowledge ever really up to standard?' (One might even perhaps argue that to talk about 'cognitive mechanism' and its effectiveness was itself really to talk in a disguised way about our arguments and their merits, but this suggestion must not detain us now: if there were anything in it, that would only confirm us in thinking that the logical questions are the more candid ones, and must be considered first.)

The logical criticism of claims to knowledge is, as we saw, a special case of practical argument-criticism—namely, its most stringent form. A man who puts forward some proposition, with a claim to *know* that it is true, implies that the grounds which he could produce in support of the proposition are of the highest relevance and cogency: without the assurance of such grounds, he has no right to make any claim to knowledge. The question, when if ever the grounds on which we base our claims to knowledge are really adequate, may therefore be read as meaning, 'Can the arguments by which we would back up our assertions ever reach the highest relevant standards?'; and the general problem for comparative applied logic will be to decide what, in any particular field of argument, the highest relevant standards will be.

Now there are two questions here. There is the question, what standards are the most rigorous, stringent or exacting; and there is the question, what standards we can take as relevant when judging arguments in any particular field. In the last essay, we saw how often formal logicians have concentrated on the first question at the expense of the second. Instead of building up a set of logical categories designed to fit the special problems in each field—categories for which the criteria of application are in theory, as they are in practice, *field-dependent*—they have seen in the analytic type of argument an ideal to which alone they will allow theoretical validity, and treated the criteria of analytic validity, necessity and possibility as universal, *field-invariant* standards of validity, necessity and possibility. The same idealisation of analytic arguments, we shall now see, lies at the bottom of much epistemological theory, as it has developed from Descartes to the present day. The respects in which substantial arguments differ—and must in the nature of the case differ—from analytic ones have been interpreted as deficiencies to be remedied, gulfs to be bridged. As a result, the central question of epistemology has become, not 'What are the highest relevant standards to which our substantially-backed claims to knowledge can aspire?', but rather 'Can we screw substantial arguments up to the level of analytic ones?'.

For the moment, therefore, do not let us i   ch on the

matter of relevance. Instead let us assume once again that all arguments can be judged by the same analytic standards, and spend a little time spinning out further consequences from this hypothesis. Clearly, if philosophers have the slightest tendency to regard the standards of judgement appropriate to analytic arguments as superior to the standards we employ in practice in judging arguments from other fields, on the grounds of their being more rigorous, then, when these same philosophers turn to consider questions in the theory of knowledge, they will have an obvious motive for insisting on analyticity of argument as a prime condition of true knowledge. For claims to knowledge involve claims to reach the highest standards; and what standards, they may ask, could be higher than the standards we insist on in the case of analytic arguments? On this view, claims to knowledge will be seriously justifiable only when supporting information can be produced entailing the truth of the proposition claimed as known: the epistemologists' task will then be to discover under what circumstances our claims can properly be so backed.

As soon as we get down to examples, serious difficulties become apparent, especially in those cases where our argument involves a logical type-jump. In many situations, the propositions we put forward as known are of one logical type, but the data and warrant-backing which we produce in their support are of other types. We make assertions about the future, and back them by reference to data about the present and past; we make assertions about the remote past, and back them by data about the present and recent past; we make general assertions about nature, and back them by the results of particular observations and experiments; we claim to know what other people are thinking and feeling, and justify these claims by citing the things that they have written, said and done; and we put forward confident ethical claims, and back them by statements about our situation, about foreseeable consequences, and about the feelings and scruples of the other people concerned. We often find ourselves in the sorts of situation of which these are samples, and already the central difficulty should be apparent. For, if we are going to accept claims to knowledge as 'justifiable' only where the data and backing between them can entail the proposition claimed as known, it is open to question whether any of these sample claims to knowledge are going to prove 'justifiable'.

Consider the confident predictions of astronomers. What grounds have they for making them? A vast collection of records of telescopic observations and dynamical theories tested, refined and found reliable over the last 250 years. This answer may sound impressive, and indeed, from the practical point of view, it should do so; but the moment a philosopher begins to demand entailments, the situation changes. For, in the nature of the case, the astronomers' records can be no more up-to-date than the present hour; and, as for their theories, these will be worth no more to the epistemologist than the experiments and observations used to test their adequacy— experiments and observations which, needless to say, will also have been made in the past.

We may accordingly produce the astronomers' calculations, pointing out how, by apparently cast-iron arguments, they use these theories to pass from data about the earlier positions of the heavenly bodies concerned to predictions about the positions they will occupy at future times. But this will not save us from the philosopher's severity: if we accept the theories, he will allow, no doubt we can construct arguments from the past to the future which are by *formal* standards satisfactory enough, but the problem is whether our trust in the theories is itself justifiable. A theory, once accepted, may provide us with a warrant to argue from the past to the future, but the philosopher will go on to inquire about the backing for the warrants the theory gives us and, once analytic arguments are left behind, there is no longer any question of data and warrant-backing together entailing conclusions. All the information the astronomer can hope to multiply will remain information about the present and past. This may for practical purposes be of some use to him, but in the eyes of the consistent epistemologist it will avail him nothing. His assertion is about the future, his data and backing are about the present and past, and that is that: the type-jump itself is the source of difficulty and, so long as nothing is done to get over it, claims to knowledge of the future must all of them alike appear in jeopardy.

Similar troubles afflict us in other cases, as soon as we allow the philosopher loose on our arguments. Suppose an archaeologist tells us about life in England in 100 B.C., and a historian in his turn discusses the foreign policy of Charles II or puts forward confident assertions about events in London in A.D. 1850. So long as we remain within sight of Hume's backgammon table, we may be prepared to accept their arguments as being sufficiently cogent and conclusive for practical purposes. 'But are they really cogent, really conclusive?', the philosopher can now ask. Surely all the archaeologist has to go on is a lot of humps and bumps on the ground, a few bits of broken pot and some rusty iron; while the historian's conclusions, even about events in 1850, rest in the last resort upon a mass of written and printed documents whose authenticity there is no longer any question of proving past the possibility of contradiction. Even here, when we appeal to data from the present and the immediate past to back up claims about the remoter past, entailment must in the nature of the case elude us. The caution with which we very properly receive the more tentative claims of archaeology must be extended, we are accordingly told, to matters about which we had previously experienced no serious doubt—e.g. to the belief that in 1850 Palmerston was Foreign Secretary. The apparently superior cogency of the historian's arguments about A.D. 1850 over those of archaeologists about 100 B.C. strikes the philosopher as a mere matter of degree since, however much more documentary evidence about the nineteenth century we may accumulate, it will still be so much paper existing in the present, and the ambition of entailing truths about the past will remain as far off as ever.

General claims, psychological claims, moral claims: these in turn fall under blows from the same hammer. General claims have the defects both of claims about the future and of claims about the past, in addition to some further defects of their own: even in the present, they involve us implicitly in assertions about objects we have never inspected, over and above those observed when assembling our data and warrant-backing—so in this case entailment is trebly hard to achieve. Claims to know what other people are thinking and feeling are in hardly better a position. An athlete who has just won a race smiles, shows every sign of cheerfulness, and utters words of happiness: surely, one might think, we are entitled to say with confidence that we know him to be happy. No, the philosopher replies, you may find it difficult to believe that the athlete is in fact hiding a disappointment, concealing a broken heart, playing a part; but there is no contradiction in supposing this to be so, for all that we can point to in the way of gestures, grimaces or tones of voice. Whatever we point to as evidence of the genuineness of his feelings may equally, without contradiction, be pointed to as evidence of the consummateness of his pretence. Insistence on analytic standards, it seems, is bound to land us here too in the same difficulty. Likewise with ethical, aesthetic and theological claims: the facts we point to, whether as the particular grounds of our present conclusion or as the backing for warrants invoked in our argument, will be (ostensibly at any rate) of a different logical type from the conclusion itself. In each case, therefore, the philosopher will be able to raise the same central difficulty—that, however large our collection of data and backing may be, no contradiction will be involved in setting it alongside the negated conclusion. Analyticity will not have been achieved.

Once we are securely embarked on this inquiry, there is no holding us. For the difficulty which arises for the philosopher most acutely in the case of predictions can be raised equally with regard to any substantial argument whatever; and just how rare completely analytic arguments are we have seen in earlier essays. Our doubts were awakened first about the astronomer's remote predictions and the archaeologist's remote retrodictions, but they are now liable to spread almost without limit. No collection of statements, however large, about the present condition and contents of ostensibly nineteenth-century documents can entail any statement about Palmerston and 1850; no collection of statements about our present situation, the consequences of our actions, or the moral scruples of our contemporaries and fellow-citizens can entail a conclusion about our obligations; no amount of information about a man's gestures, grimaces, utterances and reactions can entail a conclusion about his feelings; no analysis, however exhaustive, of the distribution of pigment and varnish over the different parts of a piece of canvas can entail a conclusion about the beauty of the picture which they compose; any more than our astronomical observations and physical experiments in the present and past can ever put us into a position to predict, without the possibility of mistake being even meaningful, the position at some time in the future of any celestial object whatsoever.

But worse is to come. The difficulties which afflict claims to knowledge about the past or about the future may be raised next about the present also, when the objects concerned are for the moment out of sight or out of earshot. We saw earlier that the argument:

Anne is Jack's sister;
All Jack's sisters have red hair;
So Anne has red hair,

will be a genuinely analytic argument only if Anne is at present visible to us, since only in this case will the second premiss be interpretable as meaning 'Every one of Jack's sisters has (we observe) red hair at this moment'—so providing analytic backing for a warrant leading to the conclusion 'So Anne has red hair at this moment'. If this condition is not fulfilled, and Anne is at the moment out of sight, the suggestion that she may since we last saw her either have lost her hair or dyed it cannot be ruled out past the possibility of contradiction.

We may next begin to feel a little shaky even about things at present in sight or within earshot. After all, if we really ask what we have to go on when we make claims to knowledge about these things too, we can point only to the way things *look* to us and *sound* to us at this moment, and all the traditional arguments leading to scepticism about the senses can immediately be brought to bear on us: no collection of data, however large, about how things *seem* to us now can entail the truth of a conclusion about how they in fact *are*. Statements about seemings are of one logical type: statements about the actual state of things in the world around us are of another, and entailments can no more be hoped for between statements of these two types than they can in any other case where an argument involves a type-jump.

If we are going to hold out for analyticity, therefore, we shall find a general problem arising over all fields of argument other than analytic ones. Claims to knowledge, however well-founded they may appear in practice, are never going to come up to the philosopher's ideal standard. Once we have accepted this ideal, there seems no hope of salvaging our everyday claims to knowledge—pure mathematics apart—without resorting to philosophical rescue-work of a drastic kind. What this might be is our next question.

CAN SUBSTANTIAL ARGUMENTS BE REDEEMED?

I: TRANSCENDENTALISM

When we turn to consider how claims to knowledge outside the analytic field might be justified, three sorts of theory present themselves as possibilities. These three possibilities spring immediately from the form of the general problem which here faces us. In each example, our claim to knowledge has involved putting forward some proposition as a confident and authoritative assertion: this corresponds, in our analysis, to the conclusion C. When we are asked to supply the rest of the argument of which this is the conclusion, we first produce data D of a different logical type from the conclusion C, and a warrant W authorising us to pass from D to C; but, under pressure, are forced to concede that the warrant itself rests upon backing B which is also of a different logical type from C. Our quandary about claims to knowledge arises directly from the fact that, however exhaustive the evidence provided by D and B together, the step from these to the conclusion C is not an analytic one. The transition of logical type involved in passing from D and B on the one hand to C on the other presents itself to us as a *logical gulf*: the epistemological question is what can be done about this gulf. Can we bridge it? Need we bridge it? Or must we learn to get along without bridging it?

These three questions are the starting-points of three lines of exploration which are now open to us. Can the logical gulf be bridged? Suppose our supporting information (D and B) were not as complete as it seemed, this might yet prove possible: if all substantial arguments really involve suppressed premisses, and we make explicit the additional data they express (or take for granted), may we not be able to judge the resulting arguments by analytic standards after all? Alternatively, is there really a gulf there to bridge? Supposing that the conclusions (C) of our argument were not as different from the supporting information as they seemed, even this might be doubtful. We might now be able to establish that the type-jump involved in the passage from D and B to C is only apparent: having proved the apparent type-jump illusory, we should then hope that a sufficiently exhaustive set of data and backing could yet entail the required conclusion. Finally—the last resort, in case the type-jump proves obstinately real and extra gulf-bridging data cannot be found—shall we be any the worse if the gulf remains unbridged? Perhaps our claims to knowledge were always premature, and the logical gulf in substantial arguments is something which we can, and must, learn to recognise and tolerate.

These are the three most tempting routes along which we may try to make good our escape from the quandary in which we find ourselves. But we can do so in each case only at the cost of unwelcome paradox. Let us take each theory in turn, develop it, and see how it leads to difficulties.

Suppose, for a start, that we try to get out of our quandary by invoking extra premisses of a new, gulf-bridging sort: there are bound to be awkward questions, both about the genuineness of the data these premisses express, and about their precise logical status. It is one thing to wave airily in the general direction of 'extra data', and quite another to establish that these really do exist and will do the job required of them. We can take once more the example of predictive arguments: on some occasions, it will now be suggested, our familiarity with the processes leading towards some future event is so exhaustive and intimate that we have the wholly new experience of 'seeing the future in advance'. This novel experience provides the analytic guarantee we hitherto lacked. Or, it may be said, by immersing ourselves in the natural processes going on in the world around us and familiarising ourselves with them, we may reach a point at which we grasp directly—past reach of subsequent disproof —some general character of things which in turn entails the truth of our prediction.

When the historian's statements about the past are called in question, we may again find ourselves attracted towards the idea of extra data, in the form either of directly-grasped general truths or, more simply, of *ad hoc* experiences. A historian who studies the material relics and records of an epoch sufficiently deeply and for sufficiently long can eventually (on this view) get himself inside the skin of the people he is interested in, and so 'read the mind' of William the Silent or whoever it may be. A faculty of 'empathy' will now be an important part of any historian's equipment, for without it he will be unable to be confident of 'getting back into the past', and he will be dependent on it for any authentic historical knowledge.

A similar faculty may be called in to get over our difficulties about 'knowledge of other minds'. Perhaps, after all, when we make claims about the feelings, thoughts and states of mind of our friends and acquaintances, we do really have more to go on than their behaviour and utterances: perhaps we sometimes manage to 'put ourselves in their place' in a more-than-figurative sense, and accordingly 'have their feelings for ourselves'. If sometimes we were able, not only to sympathise with their feelings, but positively to

share ('empathise') them, then our logical gulf might again appear
to have been bridged, and our epistemological quandary resolved.
Likewise in other fields: we need only invoke a sufficient range of
extra faculties and abilities, and we can—if this line of argument is
acceptable—obtain all the extra data we need to bridge the gulfs
there too. Given the evidence of our moral, intellectual or religious
senses, claims to knowledge about material objects in the external
world, about beauty or goodness or the existence of God, will all
appear to be rescued from the threat of scepticism.

Theories of this general type undoubtedly have a certain plausibility. We do in many cases speak of people having exceptional
faculties or skills, because they regularly make assertions—about
the states of mind of other people, about the future, about the past,
or whatever—which prove well-founded, though the evidence they
originally had appeared very thin. Some people are exceptionally
sensitive to the feelings of others, some have an unusual eye for the
merits of paintings, some have an uncanny flair for spotting the
faults in a defective machine, some have a gift beyond the ordinary
for reconstructing a past era and discerning the motives of the
historical figures involved. In each case, where most of us can only
stumble and guess, they reach confident, unambiguous conclusions
—saying, for instance, 'There must be a blockage in the inlet
manifold', or 'William the Silent's intention must have been to lull
the Spaniards into a false confidence'. And provided people of this
kind do, in the light of later discoveries, regularly prove to have been
right in their assertions, one may feel that they are entitled to the
confidence they display.

The question for us is, however, whether there is any *logical*
difference between these exceptional people and other mortals.
When they say so confidently, 'It must be the case that p', does
this mean that a claim for knowledge which we could back only by
a substantial argument is one which they can establish analytically?
Does the flair, prescience, aesthetic sense, intuition or sympathy in
which they excel us provide them with a logical bridge over the gulf
which afflicts the rest of us, or is it simply that they are rather better
at getting across the gulf without a bridge than the rest of us are?

It is not hard to show that, while extraordinary skills such as these
are of great advantage to their possessors, they can do nothing to
get us out of our common epistemological quandary. This quandary,

after all, is inherent in the situation in which we all find ourselves, and which in each case defines the nature of the problem that is our concern. It is Jones who is resentful, and Smith whose remarks show his sympathetic recognition of this fact: however infallible Smith's sympathy proves in practice, the extra datum, 'Smith is convinced that Jones is feeling resentful', takes us no nearer to an analytic proof of the fact in question. Even if Smith's feats of sympathetic intuition are so striking as to be positively 'telepathic', the data they yield us can do nothing to *entail* conclusions about Jones' actual feelings, though they may in the event encourage us to take the substantial step from signs and symptoms to feelings with less timidity than we otherwise should. Similarly with the astronomer or the historian: predictive ability or historical empathy, even amounting to near-clairvoyance, leaves their predictions and retrodictions unentailed. So marked may the abilities of a few people be that we are tempted to say that for them it is *as though* the past (or the future) were the present; but there is no getting away from the crucial 'as though', or of treating phrases like 'seeing the future in advance' or 'getting inside William the Silent's skin' as any more than *façons de parler*.

The same conclusion awaits us if we attempt to bridge the 'logical gulf' between data and conclusion in a substantial argument not by introducing particular *ad hoc* extra data, but by invoking general logical (or epistemological) principles. It might, for instance, be argued that one could establish analytically such a prediction as:

'Tomorrow midnight Jupiter's position *will be* (so-and-so)'

by appealing to a combination of the facts already available to us:

'The planetary positions up to date *have been* (...)' and 'The position predicted for Jupiter tomorrow midnight, calculated in accordance with the theories reliable up to now, *is* (so-and-so)'

together with one further general principle, whose soundness we have to assume for the purposes of any astronomical argument, to the effect that:

'The theories of planetary dynamics which have proved reliable in the past *will continue* to prove reliable in this case.'

As a purely formal exercise, the making of this last assumption may be all very well, but it does nothing to get us out of our quandary. For making this assumption is not like assuming the truth of some current matter of fact of which we have no direct evidence. This general principle is something of whose truth we could have a positive assurance only when the occasion for making our current prediction was past. After the event, we can indeed put forward an analytic argument of the form:

'The planetary positions up to three days ago *were* (...)';
'The position for Jupiter at midnight last night calculated from the data available three days ago in accordance with the standard theories *was* (so-and-so)';
'Our theories *proved* reliable in the event';
So 'Jupiter's position at midnight last night *was* (so-and-so).'

This argument is certainly analytic. We could not consistently assert that our theories proved reliable in the event, as the third premiss here says, unless the conclusion to which those theories led us was borne out by the events. A man who accepted these three premisses after the event and yet denied the conclusion would accordingly be contradicting himself. But this is no longer our original, predictive argument. By formal standards alone, it may appear to be the same: the three 'facts' stated by the three 'premisses' are—from the formal logician's point of view—the same in each of the two arguments. But there remains this crucial difference, that in the first case the premisses were uttered before the event, and in the second case after it: so that the second argument is better considered, not as a repetition of the first, but as a post-mortem upon it. Our epistemological quandary springs directly from the fact that, on the first occasion of utterance, the argument is a predictive one, and it remains untouched: no additional premiss which can be established only by waiting until the argument is no longer predictive can help us to escape from the consequences of that fact.

So much for the first attempted avenue of escape—what may be called, following Professor John Wisdom, the 'transcendentalist' or 'intuitionist' type of theory. Wherever we depend upon genuinely substantial arguments in order to establish our conclusions, the situation will be the same: neither the discovery of 'extra data' nor the assumption of additional general truths can serve to render our arguments analytic. Even if intuition could be thought of as a source of extra data—and I shall argue later that this view rests on a misunderstanding—such fresh data would leave our arguments as substantial as ever: and though, by assuming additional general truths, we may be able to transform our substantial arguments formally into analytic ones, epistemologically we shall be no better off, since in practice these assumptions not only *do* not have the backing they require, but *could* not have it without changing the nature of our problem.

CAN SUBSTANTIAL ARGUMENTS BE REDEEMED?

II: PHENOMENALISM AND SCEPTICISM

At this point the second line of argument becomes attractive: this may be called the 'phenomenalist' or 'reductionist' type of theory. Once it is recognised that extra premisses, expressing either intuitive data or general assumptions, are useless as ways of bridging the logical gulf in substantial arguments, it becomes difficult to see how substantial conclusions can ever be (analytically) justified, or claims to knowledge ever be (by analytic standards) made good. If we are not to be driven to the sceptical conclusion that almost all claims to knowledge are without proper justification, there appears only one possibility left open to us—to argue that the substantial appearance of the arguments concerned is misleading, since (at bottom) the conclusions of substantial arguments are, despite appearances, of the same logical type as the data and backing on which they rest. If we can talk away the apparent type-jump involved in so many substantial arguments, perhaps we shall succeed in talking away our quandary also, for now, it may be argued, a sufficient accumulation of data and backing may be capable of entailing our conclusion after all.

Let us see where this new suggestion leads us. To begin with, we have to argue that claims about the future, or the feelings of others, or the merits of actions, or objects in the external world, are not really as different as ordinary men think them to be from data about the present and past, or gestures and utterances, or scruples and consequences, or the way things look to us. So long as statements about the table in the next room are taken to be radically different in type from statements about visual or tactile sensations, we shall naturally see no hope of data and backing of the latter sort entailing conclusions of the former. But supposing this type-difference were illusory? If statements about tables were, fundamentally, of the same logical type as statements about sensations, then the goal of entailment might not be so completely unattainable. Multiply the sensory experiences which make up our evidence—past, present and future, our own and other people's—and our ostensibly substantial argument might turn out nevertheless to be analytic. With the type-difference out of the way, we can argue that a conclusion about tables is 'logically constructible', by analytic transformations, out of data about sensations; and this is what the phenomenalist's answer to the problem of material objects has always been.

Similar proposals, of varying plausibility, have been made in order to rescue other substantial arguments. In a few fields, the reductionist type of solution has been accepted almost universally by philosophers: for instance, the doctrine that statements about logical impossibility or possibility are of a type with statements about the presence or absence of contradictions. In other cases, reductionism has had distinguished advocates but has failed to sweep the field: one might cite the behaviourist doctrine that claims about feelings and states of mind are really on a par with claims about actual or possible gestures, motions and utterances, or alternatively the ethical theories which treat statements about merit or value as of a type with statements about consequences, scruples or interests. In certain fields, finally, the position has always demanded a good deal of hardihood: it takes a professional paradoxologist to assert either that the astronomer's statements about the future are really disguised statements about the present and past (and so entailable by our existing data), or that the historian's statements about the past are in reality statements about confirmatory experiences yet to come.

The weaknesses of the reductionist approach are most obvious in the case of astronomy and history, but they are in fact general. One has, in fact, to be decidedly sophisticated and shut oneself in the study—far from Hume's dining and backgammon tables—if one is to be attracted by it at all. For when we make assertions about the future, or the past, or the feelings of others, or the merits of actions or pictures, the type-differences between our assertions and the information with which we support them spring from the very nature of our problems, and cannot be talked away. Suppose we give an astronomer a collection of data about the present and past, and ask him a question about the future: if his answer, though grammatically in the future tense, turns out to have been intended only as yet another statement about the present or past, then he has simply failed to answer our question—what we asked for was a genuine prediction, not a disguised retrodiction. Such extra plausibility as attaches to the phenomenalist account of material objects and the behaviourist account of feelings and mental states comes from the references they include to future and possible sensations and actions, in addition to past and present actual ones; for these references covertly reintroduce, at least in part, the type-jump which the phenomenalist first claimed to be talking away. Where a reductionist theory genuinely denies the type-jump from our data and backing to our conclusion, its effect is not to solve our epistemological problems, but to shirk them.

Having got this far, we shall find that one course alone remains open to us—only one course, that is, short of abandoning the analytic ideal of argument. Claims to knowledge about matters of astronomy or history, about the minds of others, about the merits and values of actions, persons and works of art, even about the material objects which surround us: these have turned out, in succession, to rest upon data and backing of logical types other than those of the conclusions put forward as 'known'. The transcendentalist solution has failed: no extra data or assumptions could be found capable of lending our conclusions a genuinely analytic authority. The phenomenalist solution has failed: type-differences between data and backing on the one hand, and conclusions on the other, are the undeniable consequences of the natures of the problems concerned. There is a logical gulf, and we have no means of bridging it: the only conclusion, it seems, is that the gulf cannot be bridged. In all these cases, the arguments on which our claims to knowledge rest prove radically defective when measured against the analytic ideal. If a genuine claim to knowledge must be backed by an analytic argument, then there can be no authentic claim to knowledge in such fields as these. The future, the past, other minds, ethics, even material objects: about all these we ought, strictly speaking, to admit that we *know* nothing. Scepticism alone remains as a solution for us, and the only problem is on what terms we reconcile ourselves to the existence of these unbridgeable logical gulfs.

We may perhaps follow Hume and argue that, though in principle scepticism is unassailable and unavoidable, nature will protect us where reason cannot help us, so that outside the study we shall find all sorts of habits of mind *natural* which by strictly rational standards are completely unjustifiable. Alternatively we may go on and argue that outside the analytic field claims to knowledge were always presumptuous and dispensable. Provided our methods of argument are sufficiently good for practical purposes, we shall be none the worse off in ordinary life for leaving this purely logical gulf unbridged: there is no necessity to claim actual knowledge in any of these fields, so long as we have in practice the means for avoiding actual catastrophe. From scepticism, in other words, it is only a short step to pragmatism.

SUBSTANTIAL ARGUMENTS DO NOT NEED REDEEMING

The train of argument followed out in the last three sections has all, however, been hypothetical. We asked what would happen to claims to knowledge in fields where we are dependent upon substantial arguments, supposing that we insisted on measuring these arguments against analytic standards alone, and rejected claims to knowledge wherever our arguments fell short of entailing their conclusions. Some of the theories which we were driven to consider bear obvious resemblances to the theories of actual philosophers, but I have made no attempt to compare them in detail with any specific theories from recent philosophical history. Yet it is, surely, not accidental that in so many fields of philosophy we should find a three-fold sequence of theories being put forward: first the transcendentalist, then the phenomenalist, and finally the sceptical theory. The transcendentalist Locke is answered by the phenomenalist Berkeley, only for the conclusions of both to be swept aside by the sceptic Hume. For all three, the logical gulf between 'impressions' or 'ideas' and material objects is the source of difficulty: Berkeley will have nothing to do with Locke's unobservable 'substratum', and offers phenomenalism as a way of doing without it, but Hume counters with the sceptical view—at any rate on the plane of theory. In moral philosophy, again, G. E. Moore rescues ethical conclusions, which are based at first sight on entirely non-ethical data, by treating them as underwritten by intuitions of 'non-natural' ethical qualities; I. A. Richards and C. L. Stevenson offer a phenomenalist reply, analysing ethical statements in terms of non-ethical ideas alone, so that the gulf between feelings and values is disregarded; while A. J. Ayer, in turn, plays Hume to Stevenson's Berkeley and Moore's Locke, and so avoids or evades the problem which had been facing his predecessors.

So one might go on; illustrating in each non-analytic field of argument the three different sorts of device by which philosophers try to remedy (or reconcile themselves to) the apparent deficiencies in substantial arguments. Yet all three shifts are equally ineffective and all are equally unnecessary—if only we are prepared to give up the analytic ideal. Extra data will not help us, the type-jump is undeniable, and even in theory we cannot be content to deny every claim to knowledge in every non-analytic field. Nor can we, for that matter, be content to say, like modest unassuming pragmatists, that claims to knowledge were in any case more than we needed to make, since in practice we can carry on perfectly well on less; for, as we saw in an earlier essay, if we leave the analytic ideal itself uncriticised, it is not only claims to knowledge which we shall be forced to abandon. We shall not, if we are consistent, even be able to claim any 'probability' for our beliefs, or say that we have any adequate 'reasons' for them, still less that the arguments in their support are or could ever be 'conclusive'.... All our logical words alike will (strictly speaking) be applicable to analytic arguments alone—so long, that is, as we accept the analytic ideal. One thing alone tends to conceal from us the destination to which epistemological arguments are leading. That is our perennial habit of thinking that, if one only hit on a happy word, the results of a prolonged epistemological discussion could be summed up in a single lucid sentence. In fact this hope is delusive: the consistent ambiguity of all our logical terms will frustrate it equally whichever word we pick on.

Every logical word has, on the one hand, its extra-philosophical use, in which it is applied with an eye to field-dependent criteria; and, on the other hand, its intra-philosophical use, in which the criteria for its application refer solely to entailments, contradictions and consistency. Have I been arguing here that deductive arguments and inductive arguments require to be judged by reference to different standards? Yes, and yet no: only in the technician's sense are 'deductive' and 'inductive' arguments necessarily opposed. Have

I been arguing that only analytic arguments can be conclusive?
Certainly analytic arguments alone are analytic—and so, in the
professional logician's sense, 'conclusive'; but in other fields also a
time comes when we have produced in support of our conclusions
data and warrants full and strong enough, in the context, for further
investigation to be unnecessary—so in this sense non-analytic
arguments also can be conclusive. At any rate, then, have I not been
arguing that positive *proof* can and should be asked for only in the
realm of mathematics? Even now one must reply, 'What is proof?'
—and respond in the same way whatever fresh logical term is introduced, even if it means looking like Jesting Pilate. After several
centuries of use, this double set of standards for logical criticism
has become so embedded in our philosophical terminology that we
have been forced in these essays, as an essential first step towards
clarity, to put the existing terms on one side and introduce fresh
terms of our own. That is why our key distinction has been, not that
between induction and deduction, nor that between proof and
evidence, between demonstrative and non-demonstrative arguments,
between necessary and probable inference, or between conclusive
and inconclusive reasoning. Our key distinction has been the distinction between *analytic* and *substantial* arguments; and this
distinction has to be made, and insisted on, before the habitual
ambiguities underlying most epistemological debates can be dis-
entangled.

The only real way out of these epistemological difficulties is (I say)
giving up the analytic ideal. Analytic criteria, whether of conclusiveness, demonstrativeness, necessity, certainty, validity, or justification,
are beside the point when we are dealing with substantial arguments.
At this point the question of relevance, which we put aside earlier,
is inescapable. Certainly substantial arguments often involve type-
transitions in the passage from data and backing to conclusion: all
this means is that we must judge each field of substantial arguments
by its own relevant standards. The fundamental error in epistemology
is to treat this type-jump as a logical *gulf*. The demand that all claims
to knowledge should be justified analytically, and the rejection of all
those which cannot be so justified, are the first temptations to which
this error leads: the next step is to set out, in the hope of remedying
the situation, on the weary trail which leads by way of transcenden-
talism and phenomenalism either to scepticism or to pragmatism.

Give up the idea that a substantial step in argument represents a logical gulf, and both logic and theory of knowledge can then turn to more fruitful problems.

THE JUSTIFICATION OF INDUCTION

Before we return and ask, in conclusion, what these more fruitful problems might be, there are two topics we can afford to look at a little more closely, both of them familiar from recent epistemological discussions: induction and intuition. These topics deserve a section each.

Where the criteria appropriate in judging an argument depend upon the moment in time at which the argument is put forward, the temptation to misapply analytic criteria is particularly acute. As an illustration, we may consider the course of the long dispute over the justification of inductive arguments: i.e. those designed either to establish scientific laws and theories or to make predictions with their aid. For here an entirely general superstition comes into play: namely, the idea that arguments should be judged as valid or invalid, sound or unsound, regardless of their occasion of utterance—'from outside time'. This idea may remain attractive even if one gives up thinking that analytic criteria are of universal applicability; and its effect is to make the problem of justifying induction doubly difficult —by running together the question whether theories and predictions are ever soundly based when made, and the question whether, at some sufficiently far distant time, they may not prove mistaken.

It is worth seeing how the threads get crossed in this dispute, for it represents a nice example of the way in which epistemological problems arise. The standard opening gambit is designed to produce either scepticism, or that fear of scepticism which drives philosophers into even odder paradoxes: it consists in drawing attention to those occasional predictions which in the event prove mistaken, even though at the time of utterance we had every reason to regard them as quite trustworthy. 'If in these cases you proved mistaken,' it is said, 'then it is surely inconsistent of you to say that they were justified.' But if they were not justified, then—slurring over the difference between eventual mistakenness, and initial untrustworthiness or impropriety —they should never have been accepted as trustworthy. For, in the nature of the case, there was at the time of utterance no procedure for telling these predictions from any other of our predictions, however well-grounded: if any such procedure had existed, we should have employed it in the course of deciding that these particular predictions were as trustworthy as possible. So we have (it is argued), and until the event itself can have, no conclusive reasons for accepting any prediction as fully trustworthy. All are equally suspect, and there is nothing to be done about it. We are as powerless to help ourselves as a man who is persuaded that he has an invisible bomb under his bed.

Now this argument is hard to counter just because of its Olympian detachment, its timelessness. The demand for a Gods'-eye-view, a justification which is good for all time, looks at first sight a perfectly good one. We overlook the need, if the question of justification is to be determinate at all, to specify whether our claim to know what is going to happen is being considered as originally made, or in the light of events; and we shift uneasily from one interpretation to the other. Having been enticed into this predicament, we see only three ways of proceeding, other than going out the way we came in, and all of them lead to paradox:

(a) we may accept the sceptical conclusion, that we necessarily cannot, and so strictly speaking never do in fact, know what is going to happen;

(b) we may reject the sceptical conclusion, and account for the fact that sometimes we can say we know what is going to happen, despite the force of the sceptic's argument, in terms of a transcendental cognitive faculty which enables us to become, even now, 'eye-witnesses of the future'; or

(c) we may resort to neither of these expedients, insisting instead that initial propriety is all that really matters about claims to knowledge—that these are, after all, only relative, so that even when a claim has proved mistaken one should be allowed to go on saying that one had 'known what was going to happen', provided only that the mistaken claim was made with reason in the first place. (This view makes knowledge a relation comparable to Kneale's 'probabilification'.)

If we will only retrace our steps, however, we shall see that our predicament itself is illusory, since the original demand that induction be justified *sub specie aeternitatis* lands us in an inconsistency. To recognise this, we need to recall the reasons why we hesitate, when a well-founded prediction has proved mistaken, to say that the author of it 'didn't know', and prefer to say that he 'thought he knew, and with reason'. To say 'He didn't know' instead of 'He thought he knew' is, as we saw earlier, to attack the *backing* of his claim: it suggests that something more could have been done at the time which would in fact have led to 'knowledge' and, since we are assuming his claim to have been a well-founded one, we are not entitled to suggest this. In practice, of course, more can often be done at the time—additional data can be collected, for instance—as a result of which we can claim to 'know better' or 'know more exactly' what will happen. But the demand for a Gods'-eye justification is not met by such additional data: however much we collected, this demand could still recur. Only when the implied argument had become analytic would it no longer arise, and by that time the event itself would be upon us.

Justification-for-good-and-all requires either personal observation or eye-witness accounts of the event itself. Nothing less will allow us to identify the criteria by which we judge a claim to knowledge before the event, and those by which we judge it after the event. But this 'additional evidence' is ruled out by the nature of the case: to say that a prediction is being judged before the event *implies* that eye-witness accounts of the event predicted are not available as evidence—implies not merely that they are not in fact available as evidence (though how nice it would be if they were), but that it is nonsense in this context even to talk of them as 'evidence'. It is one thing to judge a prediction beforehand, when eye-witness accounts cannot properly be spoken of as 'evidence', and another to assess it retrospectively once the outcome of the prediction can be ascertained: a God's-eye justification will involve judging our predictions beforehand by standards which can meaningfully be applied to them only retrospectively, and this is a sheer inconsistency.

This point is easier to see in outline than to state accurately. Professor J. L. Austin, for example, in explaining how it is that some of our perfectly proper claims to knowledge may subsequently prove mistaken, calls this fact a 'liability' of which we should be 'candidly aware'; and accounts for it by saying that 'the human intellect and senses are *inherently* fallible and delusive, but not by any means *inveterately* so'.[1] But this last comment is most misleading: the

---

[1] 'Other Minds' in *Logic and Language*, 2nd series, p. 142.

human intellect and senses have nothing to do with the case. No doubt, if our senses and intellects were sharper, less of our predictions would *in fact* prove mistaken; but however much sharper they became, we should be as far as ever from getting over the 'liability' in question. Let our intellectual and sensory equipments be perfect, the future will remain the future and the present the present—only in a timeless universe would there be no *possibility* of reconsidering our judgements in the light of later events.

It is understandable that we should so easily get into this predicament over induction. We are certainly not all candidly aware of the times when, having claimed for the best possible reasons to 'know that p', we had after the event to say 'I thought I knew, but I was mistaken'; and do not gladly contemplate the thought of this happening again, despite our best endeavours. The situation becomes especially puzzling if we suppose that, in saying originally 'I know that p' and later remarking 'I thought that p, but I was mistaken', we are first asserting and then denying the same thing about ourselves: namely, that we were or were not at the moment of the prediction in-the-relation-of-knowledge-towards the future event 'p'—that we did or did not accurately 'cognise' it.

However, knowing is in this respect quite unlike believing or hoping. Suppose I first say 'I hope (or believe) that p', but after the event say 'I told you at the time that I hoped (believed) that p, but it was a lie: even then I secretly hoped (suspected) that it would not happen'. In that case I *contradict* myself. With this model before one's mind we may accept over-hastily the suggestion that a claim to knowledge which proves mistaken must have been an improper claim: it is easy to overlook the evidence to the contrary, such as the fact that we do not after the event say 'I didn't know' on grounds of mistakenness alone. To say first 'I know that p' and later 'I thought that p, but I was mistaken' is (one had better say) first to *utter* a prediction with all one's authority, and later to *correct* it.

Even after we have seen the latent inconsistency in demanding a justification of inductions good for all time, we may still feel that it is eccentric to judge a prediction by one set of standards at one time and by a different set of standards at another. Even after recognising the facts about our actual ideas, that is, we may still find those ideas odd or asymmetrical, and wonder whether they should not be abandoned. Would it not be more precise to use the word 'know' as philosophers have thought we intended to do? Then we could safely treat knowledge as 'cognising', after the model of hoping and believing, and decline to say 'I know that p' or 'He knows that p' except where I believe (or he believes) and it is actually confirmed, for good and all, that p.

In order to counter this suggestion we must, first, dispel the idea that there is any oddity or asymmetry here; and secondly, remind ourselves that the logical features characteristic of words like 'know' and 'probably' could be changed only to our loss. So to counteract the misleading model of hoping and believing, let us ask whether there is any inconsistency, oddity or asymmetry in the following sets of facts:

(i) When I win a pheasant in a raffle, I say 'How lucky I am!', but when later I contract food-poisoning from it, I say 'How unlucky I really was, had I but known!'—this can be compared with 'I know' and 'I was mistaken';

(ii) The two hands of a clock are of different lengths and move at different speeds—these differences are no more unnatural than the difference in backing required for a prediction before, and after, the event;

(iii) A clock has two hands but a barometer only one—and logically, 'believing' is a simpler notion than 'knowing'.

We must also remind ourselves of that nucleus of *force*, unaffected by changes in tense and in field of argument, which shows what we really mean by the verb 'to know', and recognise how this would be affected if we *did* make the proposed change in our ideas. As things stand we can say, indifferently of tense, such things as the following:

'If you know that he $\left\{\begin{array}{l}\text{has murdered}\\ \text{is murdering}\\ \text{is going to murder}\end{array}\right\}$ her, why don't you *do* something about it?'

The philosophical amendment would, however, drive us into saying:

'If you *know* that he $\left\{\begin{array}{l}\text{has murdered}\\ \text{is murdering}\end{array}\right\}$ her, or (alternatively) if you *wonk* that he is going to murder her, why...etc.'

In the case of predictions, that is, we shall now have to introduce a new verb—say, 'wonk'—to do in the future tense what the verb 'know' would no longer be allowed to do under the new regime.

If this is the end-result of 'lining up' the standards by which we judge predictions before and after the event so as to make 'know' function in a manner parallel to 'hope' or 'believe', it is certainly unattractive. The superstition that the truth or falsity, validity or justification of all our statements and arguments should be entirely independent of the circumstances in which they are uttered, may be deeply rooted; but away from the timeless conclusions and analytic arguments of pure mathematics the expectations to which it leads are bound to be disappointed. The concept of knowledge is not like that, and philosophers are asking for trouble if they treat it as though it were.

INTUITION AND THE MECHANISM OF COGNITION

In this essay, I have argued that epistemology should comprise the comparative logic of arguments in different practical fields. The soundness of our claims to knowledge turns on the adequacy of the arguments by which we back them, and our standards of adequacy are, naturally, field-dependent. Seen from this point of view, many traditional modes of epistemological theorising lose their initial plausibility, for they have acquired it largely through our thinking of the subject as an extension of psychology.

This comes out clearly if one looks at the philosophical uses of the term 'intuition'. Many philosophers have seen themselves as concerned with a 'process of cognition', which they have believed to be involved in all knowing; and they have run into special difficulties when discussing how we know such things as moral principles (e.g. that we ought to help those in need) and the elementary propositions of arithmetic (e.g. that two and two make four). These difficulties have led them to introduce into their discussion references to a 'moral sense' or 'intuition', and to use these terms not just as non-committal *façons de parler* but in all seriousness, even to the length of describing these senses in such a phrase as 'rational faculties of immediate apprehension'.

All such references are unnecessary: they result from a series of misconceptions which we are now in a position to unravel. This is worth doing, because these same misconceptions have distracted the attention of philosophers from the really effective questions of epistemology: namely the questions, what sorts of thing one can relevantly take into account when facing actual problems in different fields—arithmetical, astronomical, moral or whatever. The status of the fundamental truths of morals and mathematics, in particular, has been seriously misunderstood as the result of this quasi-psychological preoccupation with the 'mechanism of cognition'.

It is true, of course, that phrases such as 'mathematical intuition', 'a moral sense', 'a sense of what is fitting', and 'a woman's sixth sense' have a perfectly good and familiar currency, divorced from all recondite considerations of philosophical theory. But there is a significant difference between the situations in which this non-philosophical notion of intuition is in place, and those for which philosophers designed the term. It will be worth exploring this contrast a little.

Mr P. G. Wodehouse, that fountain of colloquialisms, writes as follows in his story *The Code of the Woosters*:

> I saw that there would have to be a few preliminary *pourparlers* before I got down to the nub. When relations between a bloke and another bloke are of a strained nature, the second bloke can't charge straight into the topic of wanting to marry the first bloke's niece. Not, that is to say, if he has *a nice sense of what is fitting*, as the Woosters have.

Such a usage lands us in no difficulties. No subtle problems arise, and we understand exactly what is meant. It is transparently obvious that two things are *not* meant: Bertie Wooster is not saying that his relatives are endowed with any physiological or psychological equipment of a kind which it requires abstruse analysis to fathom or elaborate neologisms to describe—the phrase 'rational faculty of immediate apprehension' would cause his jaw to drop a mile—nor that any knowledge which their 'sense of what is fitting' delivers is such as to make them erudite or well-informed: knowing what one ought to do is not so much learning or information as *savoir-faire*, the mark of the well-behaved or considerate, of the man of principle, not the expert.

The contrast between the philosophical and non-philosophical uses of the term 'intuition' can be brought out by returning to the notion of 'grounds': i.e. to those things which have to be specified in reply to the question, 'How do you know?', before an assertion need be accepted as justified. The important thing to notice is this: although very often someone's claim to know that so-and-so must be rejected if he can produce no grounds, there are two distinct classes of situation in which this is not the case, and the demand for grounds may have to be withdrawn. If one fails to draw the necessary distinction between these two classes of situation the result can be an unlimited proliferation of faculties, senses and intuitions. The cardinal difference between them is this: in one class (A) it makes sense to talk of producing grounds in justification of one's assertion, but we do not necessarily dismiss someone's claim as unjustified if he is unable to; but in the other (B) it does not even make sense to talk of producing grounds for one's assertion—the demand that grounds be produced is quite out-of-place. In the first class, re-ferences to 'intuition' are entirely natural and familiar: in the second, they appear quite misconceived. We can look at each class in turn.

(A) Over many questions in everyday life, different people are differently placed; so that we are prepared to trust one man's judgement without demanding grounds for his opinions, where another man would have to produce solid grounds before we should take any notice of him. Sometimes we do not press a man for grounds because we are so sure that he could produce good grounds if we were to ask for them; but in other cases—the ones which here concern us—it does not even matter if he is unable to produce any definite grounds when challenged. I myself, for instance, should be justified in saying that a certain Mr Blenkinsop, a comparative stranger, was exceptionally tired when he went home last night, only if I were able to produce definite and relevant reasons—e.g. if I could describe what a busy day he had yesterday, and what he said as he left the office. But his wife is in a different position. She may know just how he is feeling the moment he enters the house, may run upstairs for his slippers and resolve not to bother him till later about the broken pane in the scullery window. 'How did she know?' asks Mr B. She can't say: she just *knew*. 'But there,' he reflects, as he sinks into the armchair, 'that's the way with wives: they seem to have some kind of a sixth sense—female intuition, I suppose you might call it.'

Mr Blenkinsop is right. This is just the kind of case where phrases like 'a woman's sixth sense' and 'female intuition' do a real job.

Other people would not be able to tell how tired he was: indeed one would not believe them if they were to say that they knew, unless they could produce grounds and so explain how they knew. But Mrs Blenkinsop is unique. One can trust her when she says she knows, even though she cannot say how she knows—cannot produce grounds, in other words. Unlike the others, from whom one would demand grounds, she *just knows*.

For our purposes one fact is crucial: phrases like 'female intuition' are in place only in reports about the justification of assertions. In talking about Mrs Blenkinsop's intuition we beg no biographical questions, about the process by which she came to know what she does. Maybe on looking into the matter we shall decide that what gave her the clue was something about the dead sound of his feet on the stairs or the set of his shoulders as he hung up his coat, something so slight that she cannot herself be sure what it was. But, whether or no we can find out what it was, the justice of talking about her sixth sense is unaffected, for the phrase 'sixth sense' is not used to refer to a channel of perception in competition with the five ordinary senses. The statement, 'She sensed that he was tired', is compatible with any or no biographical explanation such as, 'It was the set of his shoulders that gave it to her': whereas, if references to sensing or intuition hinted at a process by which she came to know, these would be alternative explanations, of which we should ask, 'Did she *sense*, or did she *see*, that he was tired?'

In cases where biography rather than justification is called for, references to intuition, senses or other faculties are clearly out of place. If I am asked what my own brother's name is, and reply truthfully that it is Roger, I shall not expect to be asked *how* I know that it is; and if it is suggested that I must have some basis for my knowledge, or that there must be some faculty in virtue of which I know his name, I can only shrug my shoulders. Having once learnt my brother's name, I need no grounds or premises in order to continue knowing it: I only have not to forget it. As for the faculty with the help of which I originally came to know the name, I picked it up so long ago that I am most unlikely to remember how I did so. With comparative strangers, I may be able to explain how I know their names, and the explanation will involve references to the five ordinary senses, not to any extraordinary ones—he gave the name George over the telephone, answered to it when his wife addressed him, or wrote it down in the visitors' book which we subsequently signed ourselves. The same is presumably the case also with people familiar to one, though the original learning took place so far in the past that one cannot any longer recall it. I may not be able to say now how I know what their names are, but this is because I remember them, not because I intuit them, and is a mark of good memory rather than of good rational apprehension.

'Intuition' and 'sixth sense' accordingly act not as biographical, but as post-mortem phrases or achievement-terms. This explains one further fact which might otherwise be wholly mysterious: the fact that we have a double set of verbs for the five normal senses, but not for our 'sixth sense'. We not only talk of seeing and hearing, but can also give orders in the words, 'Look at this!', 'Listen to that!' and 'Hark!' On the other hand, we never say 'Intuit this!', 'Sixth-sense that!' or 'Sense!'—such instructions are without meaning. And though we say, 'She sensed that he was tired', we do not say, 'From what her sixth-sense told her, she *concluded* that he was tired': there is little temptation to theorise about 'sixth-sense data'.

(B) The other assertions for which we do not demand grounds are very different. Here we are all on the same footing: none need produce grounds for these assertions, because there is now no place for grounds or justification. The simplest mathematical statements provide a natural example. If I say such a thing as, 'The number $(2^{256} - 1)$ is a prime', it always makes sense to ask me how I know; and my proper answer is to set out a proof, consisting of steps none of which is more complex than those we learn to make in arithmetic lessons at school—such as '5 times 7 is 35' and '9 and 7 make 16: 6 and carry 1.' But once this has been completely done, there is no more room for bringing grounds. If I am further challenged with the question, 'And "5 times 7 is 35"—how do you know that?', it will no longer be clear what is wanted. To break the proof down into yet smaller steps would be only a formality, for how can one be confident that a man who questions '5 times 7 is 35' will accept '1 and 1 make 2'? Ordinarily, when this stage is reached, there is no more room for 'proof' or 'grounds'.

This is borne out by the fact that, if the question 'How do you know?' is pressed upon us remorselessly, its natural effect will be to exasperate: 'What do you mean by asking how I know? I've been to school and learnt arithmetic, haven't I?' Where there is no place for a justificatory answer, we can only switch our answers on to the biographical plane. All that we now have left to us as answers to this question are biographical platitudes: the demand for 'grounds' no longer means anything to us.

At this point it is possible to indicate the first of the tangles we must unravel in order to get clear about the notion of 'intuition'. If we are both looking at a railway timetable, and you ask me how I know that there are no trains to Dingwall on a Sunday afternoon, the natural reply is 'I just use my *eyes*.' When, on the other hand, you ask me how I know that five sevens are thirty-five, the answer is 'I've learnt arithmetic', not 'I just use my intuition.' Now, by analogy with 'I use my eyes', it might seem that this last is what I ought to reply, and that by harking back to my schooldays and so giving a biographical answer I am giving an answer of the wrong kind. But to draw this conclusion is to misunderstand the kind of answer actually being given when one says 'I use my eyes.' That answer also is, in effect, a biographical rather than a physiological one: a blind man has eyes but they are of no use to him, and 'I've got eyes' is a proper answer to 'How do you know?' only if it is understood as implying the statement 'I've learnt to read.'

A simple ambiguity is involved here. There are certain sensory abilities which we associate as a matter of experience with particular bodily organs. The ability to tell the colours of objects, for instance, can be classed with the ability to recognise shapes at a distance, the ability to find one's way across a busy street unaided, the ability to draw a landscape, and the ability to point out the Pole Star, as being based on a single sense—the sense of sight—for we find that anyone who has a bandage tied across his eyes loses all these abilities together. As a result we are inclined to use the word 'eye' sometimes to mean 'the organ in virtue of which we do all these things', instead of to refer to a specific, anatomically-identifiable part of the body. Of course it is conceivable (i.e. 'logically possible') that we might encounter a man who lost his normal visual skills only when his ears were stopped, and his auditory ones only when his eyes were covered; such a man we might describe as one whose 'eyes' were really ears and whose 'ears' were really eyes. This ambiguity can be philosophically misleading. The proposition 'Sight observes colour, hearing sound' may be a tautology, but the proposition 'The eye cannot judge of harmony nor the ear of colour' has quite a different logical status, according as we identify the eye and the ear anatomically or by reference to their associated skills.

Despite appearances, therefore, none of the answers we give in everyday life to the question 'How do you know?' ever refers directly to the *mechanism* of perception: this is a technical matter for physiologists, about which most people have only the sketchiest ideas. Our practical answers to questions of this form are concerned either with the justification of claims to know (i.e. with grounds) or with the sequence of events by which we came to be qualified to speak about the issue concerned (i.e. with biographical matters of fact). Philosophical questions about the 'process of cognition' come to life if we confuse the two.

Yet how very different these two things are—as different as the senses in which Mrs Blenkinsop *just knows* that Mr Blenkinsop is tired, and that in which we all *just know* that five sevens are thirty-five; and how misleading it is to carry over into the latter case words such as intuition, faculty and sense, which are at home rather in the former. For when we speak of Mrs Blenkinsop's sixth sense, we do so precisely in order to contrast her with those other less-favourably-placed mortals who would have to say how they knew that her husband was tired before we should accept their claim to know; and when we speak of Fermat's mathematical intuition, we do so precisely to contrast him with the less-talented majority, whose conjectures about complex mathematical questions could never be trusted to prove well-founded. It is only because grounds *could* be produced, but we dispense with them when dealing with Mrs Blenkinsop and Fermat, that there is a point in talking of them as having intuition at all. So if, when we turn (e.g.) to 'Twice two are four', it does not make sense to talk either of grounds or of dispensing with grounds, wherein lies the intuition of those who never *do* produce grounds? It would be very queer if they did!

When philosophers have overlooked the radical differences between the two sorts of 'just knowing' here distinguished, they have tended to regard the *meaninglessness* of demanding grounds in some contexts as equivalent to an *absence* of grounds. This done, they have interpreted the absence as a *chasm* which only 'intuition' will bridge. Every appeal to the multiplication-tables, they have suggested, involves a 're-cognition of their truth': we can produce no grounds for elementary arithmetical truths only because we rely, as Mrs Blenkinsop does, on some obscure signs which we grasp intuitively and cannot describe. Once this conclusion is reached, the impeccable arguments which drive us down the garden path to 'intuition' and 'immediate apprehension' are well under way.

Why should this confusion be so easy to make? The answer perhaps lies in one of the unexamined axioms of modern philosophy, namely, the doctrine that 'All our knowledge is either immediate or inferential.' For this axiom is ambiguous. On one interpretation, a logical one, it is a truism: 'All claims to know that p must be justified, either by producing such grounds as are in the context relevant to the truth of p (including, in suitable cases, none) or by showing that p can be inferred, by some sound mode of inference, from premisses for which any relevant grounds (including, it may be, none) can be produced.' This is a truism, in that it simply states something we all know about the meaning of the term 'justified': the possibility that the grounds appropriate may be *none* has to be mentioned, to cover cases of 'just knowing'—whether of type A or of type B. Furthermore the axiom, so interpreted, implies nothing about the 'mechanism of cognition' or 'process of cognising': it is concerned not with ways of getting to conclusions but with the procedure for justifying them when one has got them.

The interpretation which has been philosophically influential has, however, been a very different one, expressed, not in logical terms at all, but in psychological fancy-dress: 'Whenever we are knowing (cognising) anything, we are either knowing (cognising) it immediately, or inferring it from premisses which we are knowing (cognising) immediately.' This interpretation appears intelligible only so long as the verb 'to know' is thought of as denoting a mental activity ('cognising') or a relation, and as capable of appearing in the form 'I am knowing that...': about this idea Professor Austin has given us good reasons to be sceptical. Yet it is on this interpretation alone that one finds oneself forced to talk of 'immediate apprehension' and the rest. For suppose that, when we say e.g. 'I know that aluminium is a super-conductor at 1° A', we regard our grounds for saying this as *intervening* between us (the 'knower') and that which we assert (the 'known'), and appear to give a substance to this activity or relation which it hitherto lacked; so now, in cases where there are no grounds to appeal to and so nothing can 'come between' us and the truth, it must seem to stand to reason that we are *in direct touch* with it. Accepting at its face-value the fact that no grounds are needed for, e.g., arithmetical axioms, now appears to mean denying that one is after all 'in touch with' (or 'knowing') the thing 'known': to talk of 'just knowing' will now seem legitimate only on the supposition that in all such cases one is, so to speak, directly touching and laying hold of that which one is claiming that one just knows—or, to say the same thing in philosophical dog-Latin, 'im-mediately ap-prehending' it. Banish the false idea that the verb 'to know' is such a verb, and the whole card-castle tumbles to the ground.

THE IRRELEVANCE OF THE ANALYTIC IDEAL

This is the place to sum up the result of our two final essays. In each essay we have traced out the influence on some branch of philosophy of the same, analytic ideal of argument. In Essay IV it was logical theory we considered; and we saw how the categories developed by logicians with an eye to this ideal were bound to diverge from those we employ when we criticise arguments in practical life. In this present essay, we have seen how the effects of adopting the analytic ideal have spread beyond the boundaries of logical theory into general philosophy. Since questions about 'the nature of the human understanding' so often consist of logic masquerading as psychology, confusions within logic have only too easily led to misconceptions in the theory of knowledge also. In this way the desire to achieve analyticity even where it is out of the question— in substantial arguments—has led either to scepticism or, through the fear of scepticism, to equally drastic avoiding action. Only when one removes the initial logical confusions does it become clear that the proper course for epistemology is neither to embrace nor to armour oneself against scepticism, but to moderate one's ambitions —demanding of arguments and claims to knowledge in any field not that they shall measure up against analytic standards but, more realistically, that they shall achieve whatever sort of cogency or well-foundedness can relevantly be asked for in that field.

Within formal logic, it appeared, the analytic ideal has derived its attractiveness largely from the prestige of mathematics. The history of philosophy has been so much bound up with the history of mathematics, both in Classical Athens and at the time of the Scientific Revolution, that this effect is perhaps understandable. It need not surprise us that Plato, the organiser and director of a notable school of geometers, should have found in geometrical proof a worthy ideal for all the sciences; nor that Descartes, the originator of that important branch of mathematics still known as 'Cartesian Geometry' —one that has had an immeasurable influence on the development of modern physics—should have been attracted by the idea of establishing in a quasi-geometrical manner all the fundamental truths of natural science and theology. So too, we can understand how Leibniz, the inventor of our modern differential calculus, should have welcomed the prospect of making philosophy as 'real and demonstrative' as mathematics.

One should not, I say, find these things surprising. But that does not mean that we should be led away by the same ideal ourselves. Indeed, we must rather be on our guard against it, and be quick to recognise at what points its influence is malign. In general, of course, there is nothing original in this observation: but one has to keep all the necessary logical distinctions firmly and clearly in mind if the full consequences of abandoning the analytic ideal are to become apparent. William Whewell, for instance, recognised a century ago the distorting effect on the philosophy of Plato of his predilection for the methods and logic of geometry: an understanding of the 'deductive sciences' alone, he argued in his lecture *On the Influence of the History of Science upon Intellectual Education*, gives one an unbalanced idea of the nature of reasoning. Geometry and jurisprudence, the traditional models for the sciences, have been displaced in recent centuries from their earlier pre-eminence, and one must acquire an understanding also of the methods of thought characteristic of physics, biology and the other natural—or 'inductive'—sciences. Nevertheless, apart from his important insight into the necessity for what he called 'colligating concepts', an insight in which he went far beyond his contemporary J. S. Mill, Whewell left the traditional distinction between deduction and induction largely uncriticised.

It is only when one builds up a more complex, field-dependent set of logical categories that the detailed sources of our epistemological problems come to light. Ever since Descartes, for example, philosophers have been teased by the problems he raised about the fallibility of our senses: in particular by the possibility—the *logical* possibility, of course—that all our sensory experiences might be artfully contrived by an ingenious Demon set on deceiving us into holding the beliefs we do about the existence and properties of objects in the world around us.

No problem could, at first sight, more gravely challenge our self-esteem or our claims to genuine knowledge. Yet it is only the false expectation that arguments from how things look to how they are *could* ideally achieve analytic validity that creates a problem here. All Descartes draws attention to is a 'logical possibility', and this 'logical possibility' (i.e. absence of self-contradiction) is a necessary feature of the case. On the other hand, what we demand in such a field of argument in practice are conclusions for which the presumptions are so strong as to be for practical purposes unrebuttable. So we can reply to Descartes that no collection of statements about our sensory experiences could or need entail any conclusion about the world around us—where we use the word 'entail' to mean 'imply analytically'. The question we ask in such a case, whether any collection of sensory data *justifies* us in claiming knowledge about the world, does not call for entailments at all: the question is rather whether the evidence of our senses is always in fact rebuttable—whether the presumptions it creates are always in fact open to serious dispute—and to this question the answer is surely 'No'. These presumptions are very frequently of the strongest so that, as has well been said, 'Some things it is more unreasonable to doubt than to believe.'

In Descartes, as in Plato, the geometrical connections of the analytic ideal are clear enough. The idea that substantial arguments contain 'logical gulfs', with its implied suspicion of all type-jumps, is a natural consequence of measuring these arguments by yardsticks designed for pure mathematics. Yet type-jumps and field-differences are what we start with, and we can never properly get away from them: type-transitions between our conclusions and their supporting information are not gulfs or deficiencies, but character-istic features of our very fields of argument. The absence of entail-ments from substantial arguments, the fact that they do not conform to analytic criteria: this is nothing to regret, or to apologise for, or to try and *change*.

One need not even say, in a pragmatically-minded way, that analytic guarantees are too much to ask for in such cases—that an assurance that a warrant *has worked* is all we can reasonably demand, and that we must accept this *in default of* entailments. Even this point of view, modest though it may sound (and not wholly unlike the position we have reached in these essays), is misleading. For this is no place to use the words 'in default of': there is once more an implicit apology in them which the situation does not warrant.

It may be helpful to close this discussion with an image: one which will do something to counteract the effects of the rival image enshrined in the phrase 'logical gulf'. We need some way of picturing a trans-type inference which does not bring in the distracting associations of that phrase. Various possibilities suggest themselves: is the passage from information of one logical type to a conclusion of another to be thought of as a change of 'level' rather than as a step across a 'gulf'; or as a change in 'direction'; or as a change of *posture*? Perhaps the last analogy is the most helpful. For changes of posture can be ill-timed, hasty, premature; or alternatively appropriate, justified, timely—judged by the relevant standards. Indeed, there is a point at which postures shade over without any sharp division into signals or gestures, and become positively linguistic: so that a difference in logical type between two utterances just *is*, in this extended sense, a difference between two types of signalling-posture.

A man may look ahead from his car and see that the road is clear, then signal to the car behind him to pass. Seeing the road is clear provides a reason for signalling in this way: the first is the justification of the second. But though to see is one thing, to signal another, there is no 'gulf' between the seeing and the doing—only a difference. To justify our signalling we need only point to the state of the road ahead: we do not have also to provide further principles for crossing the gap between the vision and the act. The practical question now is not 'Can signalling ever itself be tantamount to seeing, or seeing to signalling?', but 'In what cases does seeing something justify the (entirely distinct) activity of signalling?'

On this analogy, we can compare surveying the information we have about (say) the present and past positions of the planets with looking ahead down the road, and uttering a prediction with signalling or gesturing—this time, however, into the future rather than along the highway. Here too, the change in logical type from data and backing to conclusion represents a change in the posture of the arguer, not the leaping of a problematic crevasse. No doubt the presence of a temporal gulf or 'lapse of time' in the case of predictions has done much to foster the idea that foretelling the future involves gulf-crossing; and this helps to explain why the general problem of type-transitions, which in fact lies at the base of all epistemology, has so often been felt to arise first and most acutely over inductions and predictions. But a temporal gulf is one thing, a logical gulf another; and to make a prediction is not so much to cross a yawning chasm as to take up a (justified or groundless) forward-looking attitude.

Was I justified in shaking my fist at him? Or in waving him past? Or in betting on at least one tail coming up? Or in declaring that I knew the answer to his question? These four questions are more alike than we had realised hitherto; and epistemologists need see no more gulfs—and no more problems—in the latter two cases than are present in the former.

CONCLUSION

THE FIRST, indispensable steps in any philosophical inquiry are liable to seem entirely negative, both in intention and in effect. Distinctions are made, objections are pressed, accepted doctrines are found wanting, and such appearance of order as there was in the field is destroyed; and what, asks a critic, can be the use of that?

In immediate effect, the philosopher's initial moves do certainly tend to break down rather than build up analogies and connections. But this is inevitable. The late Ludwig Wittgenstein used to compare the re-ordering of our ideas accomplished in philosophy with the re-ordering of the books on the shelves of a library. The first thing one must do is to separate books which, though at present adjacent, have no real connection, and put them on the floor in different places: so to begin with the appearance of chaos in and around the bookcase inevitably increases, and only after a time does the new and improved order of things begin to be manifest—though, by that time, replacing the books in their new and proper positions will have become a matter of comparative routine. Initially, therefore, the librarian's and the philosopher's activities alike are bound to appear negative, confusing, destructive: both men must rely on their critics exercising a little charity, and looking past the initial chaos to the longer-term intention.

In these present inquiries, for instance, we may seem to have been preoccupied entirely with negative questions: what form logical theory should not take, what problems in theory of knowledge are mare's nests, what is wrong with the traditional notion of deduction, and so on. But, if this has been so, it is not from any love of distinctions and objections for their own sakes. If all were well (and clearly well) in philosophical logic, there would be no point in embarking on these investigations: our excuse lies in the conviction that a radical re-ordering of logical theory is needed in order to bring it more nearly into line with critical practice, and our justification will come only if the distinctions and objections insisted on here bring such a re-ordering nearer.

Still, something can usefully be said in conclusion to indicate what more positive steps are required, both in logic and in theory of knowledge, so as to follow up the critical inquiries which have been our chief concern here. Having thrown out the old 'logic' and 'epistemology' sections from the catalogue of our intellectual library, how are we to set about replacing the scattered volumes in a new and more practical arrangement? The full answer would be a very long affair; but some general remarks can be made here about the principles which will govern any re-ordering. Three things especially need remarking on:

(i) the need for a *rapprochement* between logic and epistemology, which will become not two subjects but one only;

(ii) the importance in logic of the comparative method—treating arguments in all fields as of equal interest and propriety, and so comparing and contrasting their structures without any suggestion that arguments in one field are 'superior' to those in another; and

(iii) the reintroduction of historical, empirical and even—in a sense—anthropological considerations into the subject which philosophers had prided themselves on purifying, more than all other branches of philosophy, of any but *a priori* arguments.

(1) To begin with, then, it will be necessary to give up any sharp distinction between logic on the one hand, and theory of knowledge on the other. The psychological tone and flavour of epistemological questions is (as we saw) misleading. The question, 'How does our cognitive equipment (our understanding) function?', must be treated for philosophical purposes as equivalent to the question, 'What sorts of arguments could be produced for the things we claim to know?'—so leaving aside the associated psychological and physiological questions, which are irrelevant to the philosopher's inquiries —and this question is one for logic. Whether an argument is put forward in support of a bare assertion, or of a claim to knowledge, in either case its adequacy will be a logical question: the fact that in the second case the assertion is made under cover of a claim to authority and reliability ('I know that...') makes no serious difference to the standards for judging the argument in its support.

So long as epistemology was thought of as including both psychological questions about the innate abilities of the new-born and physiological questions about the development of cerebro-physiological structure, as well as questions of a logical kind, it seemed to be an entirely autonomous branch of 'mental philosophy': the human understanding, its genesis and development, was quite another subject from the syllogism and its formal characteristics. But, if our investigations have been at all properly directed, logic and epistemology have now to move towards one another. Epistemology can divorce itself from psychology and physiology, and logic can divorce itself from pure mathematics: the proper business of both is to study the structures of our arguments in different fields, and to see clearly the nature of the merits and defects characteristic of each type of argument.

In a few fields, where logical self-consciousness can be of practical value, the study of applied logic has already gone a good way—though sometimes under other names. Jurisprudence is one subject which has always embraced a part of logic within its scope, and what we called to begin with 'the jurisprudential analogy' can be seen in retrospect to amount to something more than a mere analogy. If the same as has long been done for legal arguments were done for arguments of other types, logic would make great strides forward.

(2) This joint study—call it 'applied logic' or what you will—must inevitably be a comparative affair. The major distorting factor (we saw) in the development of logical theory hitherto has been the practice of treating arguments in one field as providing a universal standard of merit and validity. Philosophers have set up ideals of 'logical' necessity, 'logical' validity, and 'logical' possibility which can be applied to arguments outside the narrow, analytic field only at the preliminary, consistency-checking stage—or else by an illogical extension. Substantial arguments in natural science, ethics and elsewhere have been severely handled and judged by philosophers, solely on the grounds of not being (what they never pretended to be) analytic; and their quite genuine merits have been accounted negligible as compared with that initial and inevitable sin.

What has to be recognised first is that validity is an intra-field, not an inter-field notion. Arguments within any field can be judged by standards appropriate within that field, and some will fall short; but it must be expected that the standards will be field-dependent, and that the merits to be demanded of an argument in one field will be found to be absent (in the nature of things) from entirely meritorious arguments in another.

We must learn to tolerate in comparative logic a state of affairs long taken for granted in comparative anatomy. A man, a monkey, a pig or a porcupine—to say nothing of a frog, a herring, a thrush and a coelacanth—each will be found to have its own anatomical structure: limbs, bones, organs and tissues arranged in a pattern characteristic of its species. In each species, some individuals will be deformed, either lacking an organ needed for life and survival, or having a part which is prevented by its make-up from serving the creature's life in a fully effective way. Yet what in an individual of one species counts as deformation may represent normality in one of another. A man with a hand the shape of a monkey's would indeed be deformed, and handicapped in living a man's life; but the very features which handicapped the man might be indispensable to the ape—far from being deformities, they could be of positive advantage. In this sense, normality and deformity are 'intra-specific', not 'inter-specific' notions, and the same kind of situation holds for terms of logical assessment. If we ask about the validity, necessity, rigour or impossibility of arguments or conclusions, we must ask these questions within the limits of a given field, and avoid, as it were, condemning an ape for not being a man or a pig for not being a porcupine.

The patterns of argument in geometrical optics, for instance—diagrams in which light rays are traced in their passage from object to image—are distinct from the patterns to be found in other fields: e.g. in a piece of historical speculation, a proof in the infinitesimal calculus, or the case for the plaintiff in a civil suit alleging negligence. Broad similarities there may be between arguments in different fields, both in the major phases of the arguments (which we studied in Essay I) and in their micro-structure (to which we turned in Essay III): it is our business, however, not to insist on finding such resemblances at all costs, but to keep an eye open quite as much for possible differences. Thus, in some fields we should expect to find 'necessary' conclusions as the rule, in others mainly 'presumptive' ones: inferences warranted by 'laws' will have one structure, those depending rather on simple empirical correlations will be somewhat different. Where differences of these kinds are found, we should normally respect them; we are at liberty to try and think up new and better ways of arguing in some field which specially interests us; but we should beware of concluding that there is any field in which all arguments equally must be invalid. The temptation to draw this conclusion should be taken as a danger-sign: it indicates almost certainly that irrelevant canons of judgement have entered into our analysis, and that arguments in the field concerned are being condemned for failing to achieve something which it is no business of theirs to achieve.

(3) Logic conceived in this manner may have to become less of an *a priori* subject than it has recently been; so blurring the distinction between logic itself and the subjects whose arguments the logician scrutinises. (Some philosophers may see in this a reason for confining logic even more determinedly to 'the conditions of intelligible discourse'—namely, consistency and respect for entailments; but we have seen how drastic would be the price of this programme, if carried out completely.) Accepting the need to begin by collecting for study the actual forms of argument current in any field, our starting-point will be confessedly empirical: we shall study ray-tracing techniques because they are used to make optical inferences, presumptive conclusions and 'defeasibility' as an essential feature of many legal arguments, axiomatic systems because they reflect the pattern of our arguments in geometry, dynamics and elsewhere. This will seem a matter for apology only if one is completely wedded to the ideal of logic as a purely formal, *a priori* science.

But not only will logic have to become more empirical; it will inevitably tend to be more historical. To think up new and better methods of arguing in any field is to make a major advance, not just in logic, but in the substantive field itself: great logical innovations are part and parcel of great scientific, moral, political or legal innovations. In the natural sciences, for instance, men such as Kepler, Newton, Lavoisier, Darwin and Freud have transformed not only our beliefs, but also our ways of arguing and our standards of relevance and proof: they have accordingly enriched the logic as well as the content of natural science. Grotius and Bentham, Euclid and Gauss, have performed the same double feat for us in other fields. We must study the ways of arguing which have established themselves in any sphere, accepting them as historical facts; knowing that they may be superseded, but only as the result of a revolutionary advance in our methods of thought. In some cases these methods will not be further justifiable—at any rate by argument: the fact that they have established themselves in practice may have to be enough for us. (In these cases the propriety of our intellectual methods will be what the late R. G. Collingwood called an 'absolute presupposition'.) Even where they can be further justified in terms of more comprehensive conceptions, as the methods of geometrical optics can be justified by being embraced in the wider system of physical optics, the step will not be a formal *a priori* one but a substantial advance at the level of theory; and the conceptions of the wider system itself will in their turn remain something ultimate, whose successful establishment we must for the moment accept as a matter of history. In this way a door is opened out of logic, not only into psychology and sociology, but also into the history of ideas; we can look with new sympathy on Collingwood's vision of philosophy as a study of the methods of argument which at any historical moment have served as the ultimate Court of Appeal in different intellectual disciplines.

Certain ways of thinking about Matter or the State or Conduct exist: others have existed but have been superseded. An indefinitely large number can no doubt be thought up which will be formally self-consistent, but in applied logic we can hardly do anything except start from the point at which we find ourselves. The sciences—natural, moral and practical—are *there*: an applied logician or epistemologist will be kept busy even if he studies only the species of inquiry and argument which have historically existed; and to do this adequately will be a lifetime's work for many men.

The mathematically-minded may, if they please, work out further abstract formal schemata—patterns of possible arguments detached from the actual business of arguing in any known field. But they should beware of fathering the results on to any of the existing sciences unless they are also prepared to do what we have here seen must be done—scrutinise the logical history, structure and *modus operandi* of the sciences using the eye of a naturalist, without preconceptions or prejudices imported from outside. This will mean seeing and describing the arguments in each field as they are, recognising how they work; not setting oneself up to explain why, or to demonstrate that they necessarily must work. What is required, in a phrase, is not epistemological *theory* but epistemological *analysis*.

There is no explanation of the fact that one sort of argument works in physics, for instance, except a deeper argument also within physics. (Practical logic has no escape-route, no bolt-hole into the *a priori*.) To understand the logic of physics is all of a piece with understanding physics. This is not to say that only professional physicists familiar with the latest theories can discuss the principles of that logic, since most of these are the same in elementary as in sophisticated branches of the science, and can be illustrated as well by historical episodes as by present-day ones. But it is to say that here, as also in political philosophy, ethics and even the philosophy of religion, more attention needs to be paid, both to the actual state of the substantive subject at the present time, and to the course of its historical development. Remembering how, in the logic and philosophy of the physical sciences, men such as Duhem, Poincaré and Meyerson were for so long engaged on just this type of inquiry, and pursued it under the very title of *épistémologie*, an Englishman will look back with nostalgia at William Whewell, whose studies of the logic and of the history of the inductive sciences used likewise to illuminate one another. And he may be tempted to murmur under his breath, in parting, the memorable words of Laurence Sterne, 'They order this matter better in France.'

REFERENCES

THE analysis of arguments here presented owes much to Professor Gilbert Ryle, who has thrown out stimulating suggestions about logic both in the course of his book *The Concept of Mind* (London, 1949) and in subsequent papers, such as 'If, So, and Because' (in *Philosophical Analysis*, ed. M. Black, Cornell, 1950) and 'Logic and Professor Anderson' (*Australasian Journal of Philosophy*, 1950, pp. 137 ff.). His ideas about 'inference-licences' were applied to the physical sciences in my own *Philosophy of Science* (London, 1953) where some of the points discussed here in Essay III were treated in greater detail, notably the distinction between statements of scientific law and statements about the range of application of such laws. On the corresponding topic in jurisprudence, see J. L. Montrose, 'Judicial Law Making and Law Applying', in *Butterworth's South African Law Review* (1956), pp. 187 ff.

The discussion of assessment and evaluation in Essay I extends to logical criticism the ideas of J. O. Urmson's paper 'On Grading', which is included in A. G. N. Flew, *Logic and Language: 2nd Series* (Oxford, 1953), pp. 159 ff. The same topic is discussed also in Part II of R. M. Hare's book *The Language of Morals* (Oxford, 1952), where an interesting twist is given to G. E. Moore's famous attack on 'the naturalistic fallacy': cf. *Principia Ethica* (Cambridge, 1903). Hare however makes uncritical use of the sharp distinction between 'descriptive' and 'emotive' utterances, which is criticised in K. E. M. Baier and S. E. Toulmin, 'On Describing', *Mind* (1952), pp. 13 ff. For Essay II, see J. L. Austin's paper 'Other Minds', in *Logic and Language: 2nd Series*, pp. 123 ff., and also J. N. Findlay on 'Probability without Nonsense', *Philosophical Quarterly* (1952), pp. 218 ff. For Essay III, see Ryle's book and papers, and also J. O. Urmson, 'Some Questions Concerning Validity', *Revue Internationale de Philosophie* (1953), pp. 217 ff. (reprinted in Flew, *Essays in Conceptual Analysis* (London, 1956), pp. 120 ff.), D. G. Brown, 'Misconceptions of Inference', *Analysis* (1955), H. L. A. Hart, 'The Ascription of Responsibilities and Rights', in Flew, *Logic and Language: 1st Series* (1951), pp. 145 ff. On the question of 'statement-logic' and 'proposition-logic' touched on in Essay IV, see A. N. Prior, *Time and Modality* (Oxford, 1957), Appendix A. Essay V again owes much to Austin, *loc. cit.*

In conclusion, it is only fair to give precise references to books here criticised, so that a reader can judge for himself how far my strictures are just and where I have misrepresented the views I reject. These include, besides R. M. Hare, *op. cit.*, Rudolf Carnap, *Logical Foundations of Probability* (Chicago & London, 1950), William Kneale, *Probability and Induc-*

tion (Oxford, 1949), A. N. Prior, *Logic and the Basis of Ethics* (Oxford, 1949) and P. F. Strawson, *Introduction to Logical Theory* (London, 1952). The reference to the work of Sir David Ross is to *The Right and the Good* (Oxford, 1930), and that to Professor G. H. von Wright is to his paper on 'Deontic Logic' in *Mind* (1951), pp. 1 ff., and to *An Essay in Modal Logic* (Amsterdam, 1951).

INDEX

1. PROPER NAMES

2. TERMS INTRODUCED OR DISCUSSED